# EMPIRE ANTARCTICA

Gavin Francis was born in 1975 and brought up in Fife, Scotland. After qualifying from medical school in Edinburgh he spent ten years travelling, visiting all seven continents. He has worked in Africa and India, made several trips to the Arctic, and crossed Eurasia and Australasia by motorcycle. His first book, *True North*, was published in 2008. He has lectured widely and his essays have appeared in the *Guardian*, *Granta*, and the *London Review of Books*. He lives in Edinburgh.

www.gavinfrancis.com

ALSO BY GAVIN FRANCIS

*True North: Travels in Arctic Europe*

GAVIN FRANCIS

# Empire Antarctica

## Ice, Silence & Emperor Penguins

VINTAGE BOOKS
London

Published by Vintage 2013

4 6 8 10 9 7 5

Copyright © Gavin Francis 2012

First published in Great Britain in 2012 by
Chatto & Windus

Vintage
Random House, 20 Vauxhall Bridge Road,
London SW1V 2SA

www.vintage-books.co.uk

Addresses for companies within The Random House Group Limited can be found at:
www.randomhouse.co.uk/offices.htm

The Random House Group Limited Reg. No. 954009

A CIP catalogue record for this book
is available from the British Library

ISBN 9780099565963

Typeset in Minion by Palimpsest Book Production Limited,
Falkirk, Stirlingshire

Printed and bound in Great Britain by Clays Ltd, St Ives plc

*In the hope that book dedications,*
*like all the best stories, gain in being shared,*

*to Esa*

*for the space and the silence*

*and also to*

*Allan Thomas, Annette Ryan (née Faux), Ben Norrish,*
*Craig Nicholson, Elaine Cowie, Graeme Barton,*
*Mark Maltby, Mark Stewart, Patrick McGoldrick,*
*Paul Torode, Robert Shortman, Russ Locke & Stuart Colley;*

*the penguins were good company, but so were they.*

# CONTENTS

# LIST OF ILLUSTRATIONS
# AND MAPS

**Plate illustrations**

All photographs, unless otherwise stated, are by the author.

Maps by Paul Torode.

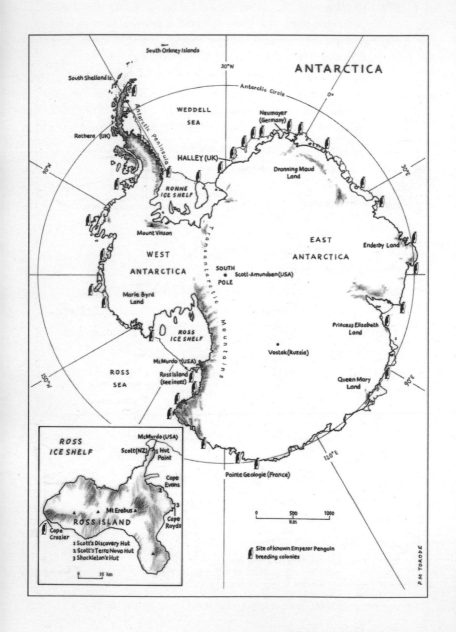

ANTARCTICA

South Orkney Islands

South Shetland Is.

30°W

Antarctic Circle

0°

WEDDELL
SEA

Neumayer
(Germany)

Rothera (UK)

HALLEY (UK)

Dronning Maud
Land

30°E

RONNE
ICE SHELF

Mount Vinson

EAST
ANTARCTICA

Enderby Land

90°W

WEST
ANTARCTICA

SOUTH
POLE

Scott-Amundsen (USA)

Marie Byrd
Land

Princess Elizabeth
Land

ROSS
ICE SHELF

Vostok (Russia)

McMurdo (USA)

Ross Island
(see inset)

ROSS
SEA

Queen Mary
Land

90°E

150°W

Pointe Geologie (France)

120°E

ROSS
ICE SHELF

McMurdo (USA)

Scott (NZ)

1 Hut
Point

Cape
Evans

Mt Erebus

ROSS ISLAND

Cape
Crozier

3

Cape
Royds

1 Scott's Discovery Hut
2 Scott's Terra Nova Hut
3 Shackleton's Hut

0    25 km

0        500      1000
         km

Site of known Emperor Penguin
breeding colonies

P M TORODE

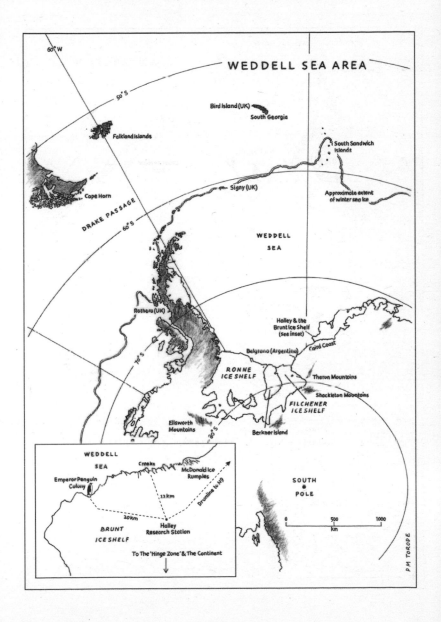

WEDDELL SEA AREA

60° W

50° S

Bird Island (UK)
South Georgia

Falkland Islands

South Sandwich
Islands

Cape Horn

Signy (UK)

Approximate extent
of winter sea ice

DRAKE PASSAGE

60° S

WEDDELL
SEA

Rothera (UK)

70° S

Halley & the
Brunt Ice Shelf
(See inset)

Belgrano (Argentina)    Caird Coast

RONNE
ICE SHELF

Theron Mountains

Shackleton Mountains

FILCHENER
ICE SHELF

Ellsworth
Mountains

80° S

Berkner Island

SOUTH
POLE

WEDDELL
SEA

Creeks

McDonald Ice
Rumples

Emperor Penguin
Colony

12 km

Drumline to N9

20 km

Halley
Research Station

BRUNT
ICE SHELF

0          500          1000
km

To The 'Hinge Zone' & The Continent

P M TORODE

# A Glimpse from the Ice

It is a wonderful place we are in, all new to the world, and yet I feel that I cannot describe it. There is an impression of limitless solitude about it all.

Ernest Shackleton, *The Heart of the Antarctic*

Autumn in Antarctica: sunrise and sunset merge in firestorms of light that seem to warn of the coming darkness. At 75° South the polar night of winter will last three and a half months. Light in Antarctica is refracted and reflected between ice and sky as though through a hall of mirrors; the continent bathes in the colours of flame as the autumn days grow colder. Last year's sea ice has all been broken out by the storms of summer. It is April, soon after the autumnal equinox, and the refreezing of the sea is already well advanced. Emperor penguins are returning from a summer fishing, fat and gleaming, to mate on the new sea ice close to the edges of the continent. They are the only species evolved to survive these coasts through the winter. That they breed through it, carrying eggs on their feet as they shuffle through the darkness, is one of the wonders of the natural world.

It is a twenty-kilometre journey from Halley Research Station to the nearest rookery of emperor penguins. The breeding ground is one of the largest in the world – some 60,000 emperors breed there every autumn. Halley's coast is far across the grinding gyre of the Weddell Sea ice fields, that graveyard of ships, and is accessible for only two months of the year. So remote, it is said to be easier to evacuate a medical casualty from the International Space

Station than it is to bring someone out of Halley in winter. Affectionately or otherwise, some residents call it 'Starbase Halley'. I have come here to live for a year on its empty plains of ice, and today I want to get down to the new sea ice to watch the gathering of the emperors.

Our skidoos are kept covered by tarpaulins to protect them against the blizzards of autumn. It is cold for the season, approaching 40°C below zero. Russ, one of Halley's scientists, has agreed to accompany me; it is considered too dangerous to go alone. Though we leave paraffin heat lamps burning for an hour under the tarps it takes us a further hour to start the skidoos. We take turns pulling on their starter cords until our arms ache, but finally the engines sputter into life.

The ice is roughened by the wind and sculpted into gelid waves, a dead ocean. A gentle rise of ice-covered coast, named the Caird Coast by Ernest Shackleton for one of the sponsors of his *Endurance* expedition, ramps away on our left towards the South Pole. Despite the heated handgrips we have to keep stopping and flailing our arms like windmills, trying to get the feeling back into our thumbs. Each time I stop, Russ pulls up and waits for me. When he stops, I do the same. As we drive we make our own avenue of noise, but when the engines cut it is possible to hear the skittering of the snow against the silence; a muted sound like distant applause.

In high latitudes the sun seems reluctant to set, lingering over its elision with the frozen earth. It glides so gently that its dying colours bleed skywards for hours after it has dipped below the horizon. I realise that I have never seen the sun hover in just this way, flattened and ragged-edged, a tear in the cloth of the sky. Edward Wilson, the doctor, naturalist and visionary who accompanied Captain Scott to the Pole, said of Antarctic sunsets: 'it seems far-fetched to go into chemical details to describe a sky . . . but the light of incandescent potassium does exactly'. For the reds Wilson imagined burning strontium, flaring into the polar night. I have never lived so far from plants and this autumn my mind turns instead to botanical comparisons – the rainbow seep of chlorophylls. The reds are anthocyanins, the oil-rich crimson of autumn maple. The solar penumbra is carotene, the brushed gold of fallen cherry leaves.

We reach a hut on the ice cliffs above the penguin rookery, coated with ice precipitated from the wind. When I reach to unload the skidoos I stop suddenly as if called, noticing the fine grains of snow that swirl in eddies around me. They are 'diamond dust'; tiny, almost weightless fragments of ice that do not sink, but float. Like mirrors they catch the light, animating the air.

Using methylated spirits I prime the stove. Kerosene begins to curdle around minus 40°C, so it is necessary to heat it with meths before it will ignite. With numb fingers I strike seven or eight matches until one sparks. Outside the moon rises in the east, a tangerine moon that springs to a sphere as it escapes from the distorting mirages along the horizon. High above us, noctilucent clouds reflect the last blush of sunset all the way from the Antarctic Peninsula, far into the west. By the time we have set up it is too dark to visit the penguins; they will have to wait until the following morning.

Inside the hut paraffin lamps breathe light and heat into the air. The wind is only fifteen knots but climbing, and comes in gasps and snorts down the stovepipe. The space between the inner skin and the outer shell of the hut has filled with snow that found its way in through small cracks in the roof seals. Blizzarded snow here gets into any recess, packing itself tight as if smoothed into place by tiny hands. As that carapace of snow melts it drips into three buckets that we arrange carefully around the hut. Russ is good company and the only sounds are the hiss of the stove, the sighs of the wind, and the metronomic tap of the melting snow.

The qualities of the emperor penguin are extraordinary. They are the only bird species that breed on sea ice, and the only penguin that may live their whole life without touching land. They are the largest living penguin, weighing in at double their nearest rival, the king penguin of the subantarctic islands. Male emperors incubate their eggs uninterrupted for the longest time of any bird or reptile, two months, all the while shuffling with the egg balanced on their feet (albatrosses incubate longer, but they take turns at the nest). Masters of endurance, they weather the coldest and windiest habitat on earth. They are the only penguin that shows no territorial aggression, having realised that in order to survive personal space is a luxury they cannot afford. They live through storms of hurricane-force winds and temperatures as low as minus 70°C, leading Apsley Cherry-Garrard to observe that in his opinion no creature on earth has a worse time. By the end of their incubation the males have fasted for four months, burning eighty per cent of their fat reserves before beginning to break down their own muscles. The little fat they leave on their bones is just enough to fuel their walk back to open sea at the completion of this fast, a journey of over a hundred miles across rough and broken sea ice. Though they are in some ways closer to reptiles than any other bird alive they produce a milky fat-rich substance to feed their young, as mammals do. The process is astonishing: although starving themselves, the males slough off strips of their own stomach lining, each laden with fat globules, to feed their newly hatched chicks until the females return. The chicks can double their weight on this food.

To survive their appalling environment emperors have evolved the highest density of feathers, the smallest relative size of eggs, and the smallest relative surface area of any bird. They dive deeper, and longer, than any other bird. One tracked emperor plunged over half a kilometre beneath the sea, to a depth that would squeeze it over sixty times atmospheric pressure, and they can stay down for over twenty minutes. Most birds have strong pectorals, bulky muscles that force a downbeat capable of carrying the sky. Emperors have to carry the oceans, and so as well as strong pectorals they have rippling back muscles to force their way down through water columns weighing hundreds of tonnes. Edward Wilson, on the *Discovery* expedition, tried to capture some for their skins. Scott wrote of the attempt, 'It is no easy matter to hold an Emperor; they are extraordinarily strong both in their legs and flippers . . . more than one of the party seem to have been temporarily floored by the wild dashes of the intended victims.' A Dundee whaling crew once tried to capture an emperor by strapping two leather belts around its wings. Like a Victorian strongman the bird simply inhaled, and the belts snapped off.

The Kalevala, an epic of Finnish folklore, describes a 'beauteous duck' who with her eggs becomes the earth and sky. Several Native American creation myths involve *loons*, diving birds like penguins credited with bringing mud from the seabed to create the earth. An indigenous human society has never developed on Antarctica. If it had, the emperor penguin would surely have been worshipped.

Lying in my bunk I listen for the cries of the birds carrying from the rookery. For the last three months the penguins have been out among the monstrous icebergs and reeling floes of the Weddell Sea, where Shackleton's ship *Endurance* was crushed and sank. Emperor penguins do not mate for life. Each autumn they wait to see who has survived the year, making and breaking allegiances anew. The penguins' cries are their songs as each chooses a mate for the year ahead. They have an ethereal polyphonic sound, vaguely metallic, like steel reeds all tuned to different notes. It is as recognisable to the penguins as a barcode is to a computer, or a human face is to us.

There are three iron anchors hammered into the ice near the cliff edge, and in the morning we lace those anchors with rope. After coiling it carefully we throw the rope over the edge and watch it unspool to the bottom of the cliff, forty metres below. I can see the emperors down on the sea ice, their black bodies quivering in the haze like iron filings to a magnet.

Russ clips into his harness, and threads a metal figure-of-eight around the rope's fast end. The wind is getting up, probably reaching twenty knots, and the contrast between the cliff edge and the sea ice below is threatening to dissolve in a thickening pall of spindrift.

'Check?' I ask him.

'Check.'

He jumps backwards off the ice-shelf cliffs and plunges towards the frozen sea surface, trusting himself to gravity and the burning friction of the rope. I begin to clip into my own harness in order to join him. Then, unexpectedly, he stops.

'Everything OK?' I shout down.

The rope is still hanging tight. He hasn't unclipped from it yet.

Minutes seem to pass. 'No, I don't like it,' he yells back up. 'I can't see the penguins any more.'

There is another silence.

'The contrast has gone . . .' His voice is becoming muffled, and then between gusts of wind I catch his words again: '. . . coming back up.'

As I lean out over the edge to hear him, a gust blows light snow from the sea ice up a funnel of the cliffs, gelling my eyelashes in ice. The stubble on my chin is fusing with the ice in my balaclava, stiffening my face to a marble mask. The temperature is milder today, minus 30°C, but the wind is climbing too strongly to think of going down on to the sea ice to watch the emperors. Under high winds sea ice twists and flexes like a living skin, but it can also splinter and crack. We prefer not to take the risk.

And instead of disappointment I can feel *mirth* rising inside me. I begin to smile, my skin tugging against the shell of ice building inside my balaclava. There is a silence beyond the wind, a sudden trusting contentment, my awareness of it heightened by the fact of being in this place and so close to these remarkable creatures. I could be meditating in a silent room for the way I feel my pulse rock in my limbs, my chest, my gums. Awareness spreads like a rising tide: the sucking vacuum of my tongue on my palate; tiny itches appearing and disappearing over my skin; the dry pressure of air in my windpipe. The blizzarding snow around me is so empty of contrast that when I look into it, I can see streams of blood cells coiling through the backs of my own eyes, nourishing me like sap through greenwood, a scarlet surge of blood defying the endless and enveloping whiteness of Antarctica.

# CHAPTER ONE

# Imagining Antarctica

Some deeper quest, or so I think, must lie beneath this pilgrimage to behold the emperor penguin. In my case the quest must have something to do with my lifelong need not to simplify my life – though I need that too – but to 'simplify my self'.

Peter Matthiessen, *End of the Earth*

It is said to be one of our oldest stories, embedded in humanity's DNA, when a young man goes to a far-off land in search of a terrible or wondrous beast. *The Epic of Gilgamesh*, Jason and the Golden Fleece, *Beowulf* – they all fit the template. Bruce Chatwin added his Patagonian journey to the list. For years the idea of Antarctica had murmured in my ambition; a desire to go to the remotest land on our planet, to see one of the most wondrous beasts alive.

I wanted to live alongside emperor penguins in Antarctica. As a boy my most cared-for possession was a copy of Gerald Durrell's *The Amateur Naturalist*. I was a diligent member of the Young Ornithologists Club and had memorised my *Children's Illustrated Book of Birds*. When the thrill of local birdwatching waned I read about birds that never entered the seas or skies of Scotland. On a trip to Edinburgh Zoo I became fascinated by penguins' waddling, boisterous gregariousness. There were glass cutaways in the penguins' tank, it was possible to watch their underwater transformation from ungainly waddlers into lithe muscular hunters. They were so different from any kind of bird I knew that they captured my attention and my imagination.

Later I travelled in the High Arctic and loved the bright true purity I saw in the landscape there. But the Arctic is a ceaselessly roiling frozen ocean where birds and mammals shun mankind (or, in the case of polar bears, hunt us). I learned that penguins, on the other hand, showed no fear of human beings. I was enthralled by the idea of Antarctica, its solidity, silence, enormity, the mythical space it grew to occupy in my imagination, and wanted to meet for myself the birds that lived in it. I saw photographs of ornithologists sitting in rookeries surrounded by thousands of emperor penguins, relief on their faces, as if they felt accepted at last into avian society. I wondered if there at the end of the earth I might learn something from the emperors, of the purity of living in the physical senses, of a life without tangles of motives or the radio-chatter of the mind. They seemed to offer a welcome all too rare in the natural world, perhaps even a kind of forgiveness.

As I learned more about Antarctica I became captivated too by the stories of the early expeditions, particularly those of Scott, Shackleton, and the US Navy admiral, Richard Byrd. In the lush green afternoons of Scottish summers I read of Scott's march to death on the Ross Ice Shelf, of Shackleton's miraculous survival against all the odds, of Byrd's winter alone, manning a meteorological station through months of polar darkness. Edward Wilson, Scott's doctor and chief scientist, held a special fascination for me because of the stories of his tenacity, his kindness, but most of all his love of emperor penguins. I wanted to experience the Antarctic winter that these men had described so vividly, and see for myself that continent that for each had become an obsession.

There was another motive: the silence I imagined there in Antarctica drew me south. My life in Edinburgh often seemed frantic. There were always so many people to meet, things to learn, tasks to complete. At school, medical school and then in work, a succession of well-meaning teachers and mentors steered me towards a high-achieving career. But it felt wrong; I sensed that I needed to take a different path than that of the vertical career ladder and wondered if going to Antarctica might help me decide what to do next. When my life felt filled with obligations and responsibilities I found respite on long cycling and walking trips, periods under canvas or in trekkers' huts where for days I would see no one and feel no need to speak. These trips always felt too short, and I wanted to throw myself into an extended stay somewhere remote, a place where for weeks and months I would have few responsibilities and unlimited mental space. Antarctica seemed the only place that could also offer me that time, space and silence, while still ostensibly working as a doctor. I hoped that having so much time to think might make it clearer to me what path to take in my own future; whether to aim for a life of travel and expeditions, or commit to a profession and put down roots.

While still at medical school I learned that to 'winter' in the Antarctic – spend a full year there – I would have to land a job with the British Antarctic Survey, known as BAS. Of all the stations maintained by the British government only three have resident doctors, and of those three only two are part of continental Antarctica itself. Of those two, Rothera is based on an island off the Antarctic Peninsula, a glaciated serration of peaks that juts across the Antarctic Circle. The Peninsula is the continent's extended finger, whetted by storms and testing the winds off Cape Horn. Only Halley is deep inside the Antarctic Circle, on an ice shelf calving from the body of the continent itself. And of all the BAS stations it is only at Halley that there is a breeding rookery of emperor penguins.

So there were three doctor jobs on offer when, as the leaves in Edinburgh coppered and fell, I took a train to Plymouth to be interviewed by the BAS Medical Unit.

I told them that I liked space and silence. I said I had hitched, hiked and camped alone all over the European Arctic. I said that I wanted to see for myself what it would be like to live through the polar night of an Antarctic winter. I had written to them for advice six years earlier, while still a medical student, and so they already knew that this was no sudden impulse, no escape from a failed love affair or a career's dead end. They asked how I would cope with the claustrophobic pressure cooker of a tiny society where escape was impossible, and I told them that as long as I could safely take a walk outside I would be able to keep my peace. They told me that at Halley, once the ship had departed, there would be no way in and no way out for ten months. The only communication would be by dial-up satellite modem for text emails, and there would be no Internet access. I said that as long as I could take a trunk full of books I would be happy. They noticed that I liked to travel and asked how I would manage to spend a year in the same place, tied to a base that would be my only means of survival. I told them that maybe I had travelled enough and that it was time for me to stop for a while, gather my thoughts and experiences, and unravel them on the widest, blankest canvas on earth.

It was rumoured they only took you if you made it clear you would accept working on any base, as Antarctic logistics often forced a last-minute change of deployment. 'Which would you prefer?' they asked.

'Halley would give me silence and space . . . and the emperor penguins,' I told them, 'but I also love mountains and the sea so I would be happy on South Georgia or Rothera. I would be happy to go wherever you wanted to send me.'

Later that evening my telephone rang. It was Iain Grant, the senior medical officer of the BAS Medical Unit. 'How would you like to spend a winter at Halley?' his voice said in my ear.

My hands shook so much that the telephone drummed against my ear. 'I would be delighted,' I said.

That night I didn't sleep.

What was it, this continent to which I was headed? The Arctic has been written about and imagined for more than 2,000 years, but the imaginative tradition of Antarctica is still young and pliable; its very blankness lends it mutability and a sense of possibility. Antarctica has a younger cultural heritage than either railways or electric lights, both of which were invented long before anyone knew for sure there was a continent in the south at all. Its land-scapes – in terms of geography and in terms of the mind – are still being worked out. When Antarctica was named it was just a blank on the map. Our ideas of it were forged only a century ago during what has been termed the Heroic Age of exploration, when creeping groups of humans, led by men like Robert Scott, Ernest Shackleton, Roald Amundsen and Douglas Mawson, arrived at its edges carrying flags, pemmican and reindeer-fur sleeping bags.

And it was in Antarctica that the Heroic Age fizzled out, the shrill nationalism and empire-building anxiety of the early expeditions lost in the quagmire of two world wars. Its final stages were almost pitiful: Germans flew bombers over the Weddell Sea coasts, spraying thousands of tiny swastikas. By the 1940s Britain, Chile and Argentina had all claimed the Peninsula and thinly disguised 'scientific' bases sprung up along its coasts like mushrooms.

I have always studied a land's history as I travel but Antarctica's paucity of history was paradoxically one of the things that drew me to it. I loved the idea of its *blankness*, the absence of worn paths or cultural memories. Ideas about it are so recent that its interior was probed in the same years that physicists in Europe and North America began to unravel quantum physics. Scott's *Discovery* expedition took place as J. J. Thomson wrote his famous paper 'On the Structure of the Atom', his *Terra Nova* expedition as Ernest Rutherford revealed that the mass of the atom was concentrated in a nucleus. These expeditions involved colossal investment for their time, with few guarantees of return – the rush to claim ownership of the continent was the 'space race' of its day.

The first men who seem to have approached it were the crew of Captain James Cook's second voyage to the Southern Ocean. Cook discovered South Georgia and sailed on past the trailing banner of volcanoes that make up the South Sandwich Islands, searching for the mythical continent Terra Australis Incognita. Cook couldn't get through and, being no stranger to hubris, added that because of the density of the ice no one would ever be able to get further south than he had managed. He did comment that there must certainly be land at some distance to the south, because the immense icebergs he encountered had clearly calved from a hidden continent. Joseph Banks, the acclaimed naturalist on Cook's first voyage, had been replaced for the second journey by a Prussian of Scots descent called Johann Forster. Forster brought back drawings of the king penguin of the subantarctic latitudes, *Aptenodytes patagonicus*, from South Georgia. The name, which had already been given to the penguin in 1768 by the Welsh naturalist Thomas Pennant, means 'the featherless diver of Patagonia', an inaccurate description on two out of three counts:

it no longer lives in Patagonia (though it does live in the Falkland Islands) and does indeed have feathers. It was thought to be the biggest penguin, and was accorded its royal name. No one had yet properly described the closely related and even bigger emperor.

Sealers swarmed over the subantarctic islands from the 1820s. James Weddell, a sealer from Leith, reached further south in 1823 than anyone before him and named the ice-choked sea east of the Peninsula after his sovereign. Perhaps George IV didn't want to be associated with such a forbidding place; the sea later took Weddell's name, along with the fattest and southernmost of the seals he encountered.

In the 1840s the Royal Navy arrived in the indefatigable form of Sir James Clark Ross. Ross, reputedly the most handsome man in the navy, had already spent fourteen winters in the Arctic and located the North Magnetic Pole. Now he wanted to locate its southern counterpart. In wooden ships, strengthened against the ice, and custom-made with a minimum of compass-confounding iron (the *Erebus* and *Terror*, later lost with Sir John Franklin), Ross charted the coastline, discovered a sea, and named an immense mountain chain of land for his snub-nosed Queen back in London. But he still had no idea if those mountains were the tips of islands or part of a great continent.

At the end of his voyage he took emperor skins back to London where they were examined by John Gray, the great taxonomist of the British Museum. Gray thought it was the bird Forster had described on his voyage with Cook sixty years earlier, and gave it the name *Aptenodytes forsteri* – a posthumous honour for a historical mistake. In his book of the voyage Ross describes how difficult it was to kill these birds, 'until we resorted to hydrocyanic acid, of which a tablespoonful effectually accomplished the purpose in less than a minute'. He goes on to discuss how the chasing and capture of them was a great source of entertainment for his men: 'they are remarkably stupid,' he wrote, 'and allow you to approach them so near as to strike them on the head with a bludgeon'. But the bird continued to be confused with the king penguins seen on Cook's voyage. P. L. Sclater, secretary of the London Zoological Society, was still trying to sort out the issue as late as 1888 with his paper *Notes on the Emperor Penguin.\** Describing the mix-up he wrote: 'Several modern authors, however, under the influence of the craze for "priority", have chosen rather to call the Emperor Penguin *Aptenodytes patachonica*, which, as the bird has never been found in or near Patagonia, is not maintainable, even under the most stringent view.'

In 1841 Ross first gazed on the peaks of Victoria Land, Herman Melville embarked as crew on his first whaling ship, and a baby of Scots descent was born in Ontario who would go a long way to unravelling the mystery of Antarctica. John Murray emigrated back to study at Edinburgh, and first sailed in high latitudes as a ship's surgeon on a whaling vessel to Svalbard. Preferring the study of the world's oceans to the practice of medicine in the 1870s, he joined the *Challenger* expedition as assistant scientist. With Charles Wyville Thomson, professor of natural sciences at Edinburgh, he embarked on a four-year tour of the deep oceans of the world. For the work he did on it he is considered the father of oceanography: he discovered the Mid-Atlantic Ridge, the existence of deep ocean trenches, and was the first to observe how wind-blown Saharan sand changes the chemistry of deep ocean sediments. In 1914, knighted, his car spun out of control and he was killed close to Edinburgh. He is buried in his local graveyard, just outside South Queensferry.

In 1893 he addressed the Royal Geographical Society with a lecture entitled 'The Renewal of Antarctic Exploration'. He presented a speculative map of what he proposed might be a continent, derived from soundings and dredgings, and called for the British Empire to lead the way in mapping the blanks. He also proposed that the anglophone world follow the Germans and call this hypothetical continent 'Antarctica'. From simple observations at sea he deduced the polar plateau, its high-pressure weather systems and the volcanic range of mountains down one side. His paper inspired Scott's *Discovery* expedition of 1901–4, which found exactly what Murray had expected it to.

---

\* It was Sclater who recommended Edward Wilson for the *Discovery* expedition. He also arranged for him to meet Joseph Hooker, the naturalist who sailed with Ross on the *Erebus* and *Terror*. Sixty years on, Hooker still kept an emperor skeleton on show in his rooms in London.

A *New York Times* article from 1904 entitled 'Antarctica: The New Continent' reveals how only in the early twentieth century was Terra Australis Incognita being revealed: 'Some day this southern land will be better known. From all that has been seen of it there is little prospect that it will be found to be of any economic importance. But it is quite certain that the ardour for exploration will not subside as long as there remains a land of continental proportions whose extent and shape have not been accurately defined.'

Cartographers call the blank spaces on maps 'sleeping beauties'. There are not many sleeping beauties left, but Antarctica is one of them.

"ANTARCTICA" Larger Than Europe or the United States the New Continent — The South Pole's Vast Frozen Empire, a Half-solved Problem for the Daring Explorers Who Have Braved Its Inhospitable Coasts and Barriers of Icy Mountains.

*

Henry David Thoreau, the great American recluse and prophet of the beauty and value of wilderness, did not believe that we should travel great distances to experience new landscapes. He believed 'the best place for each is where he stands', which for him was the woods of Massachusetts. On hearing of some natural marvel that a speaker had experienced in Canada or distant Arizona, he was likely to sniff: 'I have the seen the same thing here, at Walden Pond.' On 30 August 1856, he wrote in his journal: 'It is in vain to dream of a wildness distant from ourselves . . . A little more manhood or virtue will make the surface of the globe anywhere thrillingly novel or wild.' His vision of the natural world has so deeply influenced modern American literature that the prose poet Annie Dillard in one of her essays merely called him 'the man', imagining that any reader of her own work would immediately know who she meant. His example of travelling deeper into the possibilities of our lives as they are, rather than to exotic countries, has been inspirational for many seekers of a simpler life, as well as a few impressionable and idealistic schoolboys. The following quote has hung on my wall for twenty years:

> I learned this, at least, by my experiment: that if one advances confidently in the direction of his dreams, and endeavors to live the life which he has imagined, he will meet with a success unexpected in common hours. He will put some things behind, will pass an invisible boundary; new, universal and more liberal laws will begin to establish themselves around and within him; or the old laws be expanded, and interpreted in his favour in a more liberal sense, and he will live with the license of a higher order of beings. In proportion as he simplifies his life, the laws of the universe will appear less complex, and solitude will not be solitude, nor poverty poverty, nor weakness weakness. If you have built castles in the air, your work need not be lost; that is where they should be. Now put the foundations under them.

Following Thoreau's advice I should not have been preparing to cross the globe to live on a polar ice shelf and watch penguins. I had an advancing medical career, a close family, a good circle of friends, ample opportunities for personal growth and reflection. I had even (and this story is not uncommon among those destined for long postings overseas) fallen in love just a few months before departure. My new girlfriend Esa thought I was mad to want to live in such a place. Sometimes I agreed with her, not about wanting to reach Antarctica, but what did I think I was doing, leaving just as my life was entering this new phase, and at the beginning of a new relationship? I should have found ways of simplifying my life in Britain, digging foundations in familiar ground. But then in an essay entitled 'Thoreau' by Ralph Waldo Emerson (who knew him well), I found the following statement: 'He seemed a little envious of the Pole, for the coincident sunrise and sunset, or five minutes' day after six months: a splendid fact, which [Massachusetts] had never afforded him.' Although I knew it was ridiculous to seek justification for my choices in life from an American misanthrope dead 150 years, I was pleased that if any landscapes could have tempted Thoreau away from his beloved woods it was the high latitudes beyond the polar circles.

Thoreau might have felt at home in Antarctica. Those polar sunrises were coloured like northern forests in autumn, or spilled animal blood. Nature seems fond of certain colours, certain patterns, and goes on using them. Even the haemoglobin of blood and the chlorophyll of leaves are chemically very similar structures, branched wedding dances of carbon and nitrogen in identical ring arrangements called porphyrins. Only the metal ion in the centre of the ring varies, rust-red iron for haem, and the green glint of magnesium for chlorophyll, as if swapping the bride for the groom had made all the wedding guests change colour.

A year after I was interviewed for Halley another autumn was reddening the leaves. I had passed that year in Edinburgh, Latin America, and then in six idyllic months training with the BAS Medical Unit. With the help of military doctors based at the Derriford Hospital in Plymouth I had learned to give general anaesthetics, analyse my own blood samples, trephine human skulls and drill out rotten teeth. I was relieved to learn that ninety-nine times out of a hundred I would be able to treat appendicitis without laying hold of a scalpel. I had been welcomed into specialist clinics on every subject I might encounter, from audiology to X-rays.

On the day of my departure my parents drove me from Scotland to Immingham in Lincolnshire. None of us spoke much on the way down. Scooped out of the muddy wallow of the river Humber, Immingham is the largest container port in the British Isles and was the place I would join the ship that would take me to the Antarctic, the RRS *Ernest Shackleton*.

It took a while to find her through the dingy sprawl of warehouses and fenced-off lots that spill from every big port. It was a pied ship, red and white, wholesome and shiny with only seven years of salt water to its keels. Its sturdiness settled my mind. But though it would carry me the length of our planet it seemed tiny against the leviathans of globalised trade it was moored amongst: a Norwegian ship with a Croatian crew, registered in the Bahamas, bringing Belgian cars to Britain; two tankers swallowing loaded lorries that did not re-emerge, bound for Newfoundland via Iceland; rusting steel was clawed into the hold of a ship bound for Turkey, to be melted down and returned to Britain as girders. The harbour water was dirty and oil-slicked, loitering between the massive hulls of the vessels. The only green was a solitary patch of grass, about one metre square, and I bent down to thank it for its perseverance.

A crane lifted a snowcat vehicle on to the deck of the *Shackleton*, and I watched it being bolted into place. Piled along the wharf were palettes of food, rolls of piping, a whole laboratory, six skidoos and crates and crates of boxes stamped with 'H' or 'BI' or 'Z', codes for the Antarctic bases they were bound for. I jogged up the gangway and found my way to the bridge. No one could find the captain so the purser showed me to a cabin with bunk beds, a table, my own bathroom and a porthole like a monocle which I imagined framing tropical seas and colossal icebergs. This would be my space, coracle-like, for a two-month passage to the bottom of the world.

# CHAPTER TWO

# The Axis of the Atlantic

At the start of the voyage he had gazed at the new element with the innocent awe of the landsman. He saw boobies. He saw fleets of medusas, ribbons of sea wrack, the prismatic colours on the backs of bonitos and albacores and the pale fire of phosphorescence streaming into the night.

Bruce Chatwin, *The Viceroy of Ouidah*

The chalk cliffs of Kent looked spectral in the fog. The *Shackleton* dodged its way through the straits of Dover by radar, swerving cross-Channel ferries, supertankers and the odd eccentric swimmer. As we moved westwards down the Channel we encountered one of those storms that helped to sink the Spanish Armada. It slew up out of the Bay of Biscay, funnelled between Brittany and Cornwall, and tore the surface of the sea in strips. I could still get a signal on my mobile phone and, gripping the railings of the deck and squinting against the rain, I exchanged a blizzard of text messages with the people I loved. It would be fifteen months before I'd have a chance of seeing any of them again. Esa had just moved to start a new life in Milan, and by rain-lashed text message we wished one another courage for our respective adventures.

When darkness fell the motion of the ship was disorientating. I lay in my bunk feeling my weight plunge and soar as the prow of the *Shackleton* was hoisted and dropped by the rolling swells. The steel hull sobbed through the bulkheads, twisted by the ragged ocean. Seawater swirled around my porthole like suds in a washing machine. The Bay of Biscay hides a gently sloping shelf, a shallow saucer of water easily whipped into ripples by the incoming Atlantic westerlies. The ship was built for the short swells of the North Sea and the long rollers of the Atlantic had plunged it into a pitching motion. The crew called it 'the Polar Roller'.

It took a couple of days to get across the Bay of Biscay. Almost as soon as we rounded Cape Finisterre in Galicia the seas began to calm and I drew breath. As the ship's doctor I had had little to do: stitch a cut finger, give some travel vaccines, check the blood types of all the crew members in case we had to give a transfusion. There would be three weeks of open ocean before we reached our first port of call, Montevideo in Uruguay. The voyage south would become a trial run for me in the skilful use of time. At Halley I would have a whole year with only the sky, the ice and the emperors to keep me busy. I wondered if by gazing out over ice for hour after hour, week after week, month after month, my mind would become like ice: clear, crystalline, uncluttered. And I wondered if all that time moored to one place would allow me to learn a language, become strong and fit, immerse myself in a place in a way that I never managed in my life in Scotland.

Xavier de Maistre, a Frenchman dead 200 years, was my model in this. I had brought his book *Journey Around My Room* along with me. It tells the story of an eighteenth-century Savoir nobleman who was confined to one room under house arrest. Instead of complaining he used his time in exploring the subtle nuances and memories associated with each and every object contained within it. It is a monument to the creativity and versatility of the human spirit. Thinking of the time that I would have to contemplate the ice, I practised by watching the ocean.

The sea rolled so gently now, so sweetly, it was unimaginable that it could have thrown our ship in the air. It was placid, a silken sheen that rose and fell as if all the leviathans in the ocean were breathing in time. I found it hypnotic to move through time and climate zones so slowly, twelve miles per hour, the speed of a leisurely cycle ride. The umbilical cord connecting me to Europe stretched thinner and thinner until finally it dissipated into the seas and skies. To have flown to Antarctica would have jerked it too fast and snapped it too abruptly. I learned to watch the weather approach. The ocean changes all the time, but its changes are subtle. I watched it throughout the day while painting the decks outside, its colours shifting through the transition metals – now like tungsten, now chromium, now iron, now mercury.

We had passed the Straits of Gibraltar and were closing on Madeira. To the Greeks this was Oceanus, the great river that encircled the earth. Dante's Odysseus knew these seas; he 'turned his stern to the morning' and sailed out past Gibraltar, then south into an unknown hemisphere where new stars blazed above the ocean's rim. Each night I watched unfamiliar stars climb into the southern sky. Protected by centuries of exploration and navigation, of charts and GPS, I could still catch a glimpse of that feeling of setting out into the unknown, carrying only blank charts.

An easterly showered the ship in fine red dust, a gift from the Sahara. The wind brought other gifts: West African birds fluttered in the riggings. These little birds were so exhausted that I could stoop and pick them up. The first mate told me he had found an egret on board once, halfway between Côte d'Ivoire and Brazil. He nursed it back to health on fish and bread, but caged it when it started to defecate all over the decks. No matter how well he caged it, how close he made the bars, he would find it in the morning perched on top of the cage. So he called it Houdini and let it wander free, until one morning it was gone. Smells of land must have reached it.

The Cape Verde Islands stood waist-deep in haze. Only their summits, cooled volcanic cones, rose above the tropical fug. Passing Ilha Fogo, which last erupted only a decade before, I tuned into local radio and heard a fusion of African and Latino rhythms gilt with the almost Slavic burr of Portuguese.

We sailed on south, over a kingfisher-blue sea. Despite the heat there was little sign of bird life – warm equatorial water holds less oxygen so less fish live there than in the colder, rougher waters of high latitudes. Occasional schools of flying fish exploded from the surface, sparking and glinting like ball lightning. Sometimes they would land on the steel deck and flop impotently, out of both of their elements. Boobies like creamy gannets trailed the ship, occasionally peeling away from our stern to dive into the sparse and unseen shoals of fish.

A few days later we reached the equator. At the globe's meridian I was out painting the decks and watching the ocean as I had done so many days before, the sweat sliding off me in oily sheets. My shadow had contracted, shrinking to a thin blue puddle around my shoes. We had our ceremony for crossing The Line. In time-honoured navy tradition, the rookies like me who had never sailed over the equator had to hide from the gangs of old hands who prowled the ship armed with buckets of slops to pour over us. I spent the afternoon with the third mate, drinking lager and hiding behind piles of rope in the fo'c'sle. No one found us and in the end we had to jump out on deck, water pistols blazing, and fight our way through to the afterdeck at the stern of the ship.

It was on the afterdeck that the bosun explained to me one day why historically men in the navy so rarely needed to be disciplined. We looked out over the afterwash, the engines ploughing a furrowed white line into the ocean. 'It would only take a second,' he said, 'and you'd be lost.'

I picked a spot in the churning foam and tried to imagine how it would be to be suddenly caught in it, flailing in the waves as the ship receded.

'No one would ever know how you fell. The threat of a shove into that would keep anyone in line.'

We had passed the prison islands of Fernando de Noronha. Brazil lay off the starboard bow. The low green coast came and went from view. Latin American sunsets were fierce, as if by dropping into the Brazilian forests the sun had set the horizon blazing. Stacks of cumulonimbus – anvil-shaped tropical thunderclouds – rolled up along the coastline like galleons with sails of gold foil. Lightning and thunder sparked from them as if cannons were blasting at a naval battle. Instead of birds I found giant moths and butterflies on deck, blown east from the jungle. Humpback whales on migration breached the water near the ship, and through binoculars I watched one floating head down in the water for a full half-hour, tail aloft in a high salute. The ship's community had settled into a routine of drills: Lifeboat Musters, Man Overboard, Casualty in the Engine Room, Piracy. The ship carried no arms – if boarded by pirates we were instructed to turn the fire hoses on them. As we approached the estuary of the Rio de la Plata I prepared a lecture on sexually transmitted diseases for the crew. Many had not been home for four months, and the ship was soon to berth alongside the brothels of Montevideo.

Local pimps mooched around the docks, looking for sailors keen on getting 'ragged, bagged and shagged', code words for alcohol, cocaine and sex. I drank warm Argentinian lager in bars heaving with Korean sailors, and brushed off the advances of undernourished young girls from Paraguay. The following day the crew that had sailed from Immingham flew back to their wives and girlfriends, and a new crew embarked. While in dock the *Shackleton* took on fresh fruit and vegetables, a couple of container-loads of prime frozen beef, and about sixty scientists and support staff bound for the BAS bases.

These were temperate waters now, and out on deck the evening air was cold. The giant moths I had seen off the coast of Brazil were replaced by black-browed albatrosses that skimmed the waves like thrown knives. As we neared Patagonia, magellanic penguins porpoised ahead of the ship's prow, and one magical evening I saw a pair of pilot whales breach beneath the sunset as I leaned out over the gunwale. Nights shortened as we climbed into higher latitudes, deeper into the austral summer. The *Shackleton* was busy with people; games and parties were held each night in the ship's bar. In the dark I would lie out on the helideck looking up into the night sky. Antarctic terns on migration would veer into the ship's lights. The stars of Orion were upside down now, Cassiopeia had slipped away into the ocean to the north. The Pleiades were still with us, a faint smudge of light, and the Milky Way stretched into an infinity of other worlds. My mind felt calmed, eased as it faced the long silence ahead. It is good to see the scale of the universe, to feel tiny and inconsequential before it. Each night I gathered my strength from that.

*    *    *

Low-slung rolling peatland, scoured by winds, the Falkland Islands made me homesick for the Hebrides. Stern hills ran down to empty shores fringed with gold. Beyond them the sea was patched in gun-grey and lapis lazuli, the colours shifting with the motion of the clouds. The clouds themselves were massive, rudder-like, they hurried east as if steering the sky.

I slipped into the frontier drunkenness of Stanley. Beneath gold-framed photographs of Margaret Thatcher I met an Australian who had sailed a yacht from Sydney to Vancouver, built another yacht, then sailed it down the western coast of the Americas and round Cape Horn to the Falkland Islands. He had just returned to the islands after a short visit to Argentina, where he had been fined for 'overstaying his permit' the moment he arrived. He had never visited Argentina before, but as the Argentinians claim ownership of the Falklands his date of entry was calculated from his first arrival in Las Islas Malvinas.

Since the brief conflict in the early 1980s the British military have dominated the archipelago. Their presence doubles the islands' population, maintains the roads, pays the bills, controls the seas and polices the airspace. Most of the soldiers are corralled into the contrarily named Mount Pleasant Facility, known to the squaddies as 'the Death Star'. It is considered a hardship posting. Near the military post office I met a teenage recruit who had been stationed there for six months, living on dried noodles and corn-flakes, and sleeping on a bare mattress. 'How do you pass the day?' I asked her. She pulled back a curtain to show me her floor-to-ceiling collection of DVDs.

In the Ordinance Office a Geordie in a beret gave me maps of the minefields, and a leaflet showing a cow with its leg blown off. During the conflict undernourished Argentinian conscripts whose commanders had fled scattered mines without recording their location. Gas masks and food bags were left booby-trapped on the heather for the incoming Brits. Animals find the mines now, and little remote-controlled vehicles that scour the surface with blowtorches attached to their noses.

Local radio hummed with military jargon and the arrival of the BAS vessels in port was a major item on the news. The *James Clark Ross*, sister vessel to the *Ernest Shackleton*, created a stir when she became the first ship to be searched by the islands' newly acquired sniffer dog. The ship was fresh from Montevideo, and the dog bounded straight for a stash of cocaine. But there is limited jail space in Stanley and it was rumoured that the offender was allowed to pass his sentence pruning the trees and mowing the lawn of the governor's house.

It was a few miles along the shore from Stanley that I first managed to get within an arm's reach of wild penguins, though the emperors still lay hundreds of miles over the southern horizon. I hiked out to a breeding colony of gentoos, a messy and raucous introduction to the penguin family. 'Gentoo' as a name has a bizarre provenance. Pierre Sonnerat, the biologist of an eighteenth-century French expedition to New Guinea, included sketches of three 'manchots' in his ornithological report of the voyage. The French naturalist Buffon had previously objected to the British use of the word 'penguin', already in use for the auks of the northern hemisphere, to a zoologically distinct class of birds in the southern. He suggested the French call penguins manchots, meaning 'one-handed' because of the apparent loss of function in the wings. In Sonnerat's report these newly described penguins are called manchots Papou, or 'Papuan penguins'. The word 'gentoo' is thought to be related to an Indonesian word for 'Hindu'. Sonnerat could not have seen these penguins on his journey to the East Indies, so why was he trying to convince people that he had? Perhaps to make himself seem more intrepid – it now appears that Sonnerat cribbed his drawings from his one-time master, a naturalist called Commerson, who visited Patagonia and the Falklands in the 1760s. This mix-up in naming has, however, carried over into the Linnaean name of the bird, *Pygoscelis papua*, 'the brush-tailed penguin of Papua'.

I enjoyed the happy misunderstanding as I lay on my belly inches from their nests. The gnarly sealers who worked the sub-antarctic called these birds 'Johnny Penguin'. Their manner sometimes suggested hobbling old men, at other times tottering toddlers. They seemed to personify that 'dignified flippancy' that led the publisher Allen Lane to call his sixpence paperback books

Penguins. Penguins often seem comical to us humans, pulling crowds at the world's zoos, drawing tourists on 'penguin tours', selling chocolate biscuits and fluffy toys. A quick search in a bookshop will show you that most books about penguins are aimed at children. Perhaps this is because of the fearless, almost childlike way they have of trusting people when on land. Even seasoned ornithologists have enthused about their uncanny resemblance to humans. But underwater this parody of human movement vanishes, and they move like greased muscles. The parallels that came to mind as I watched them swim were all related to missiles, but there was no violence in it. Think of a peregrine's stoop in a harmless display, the effortless rush through submarine space.

Rays of guano sprayed out from each gentoo nest, and I took care to move if I saw the tell-tale squat and tail-lift that came before each squirt. The tussock grass had all been worn away; the colony seemed built on a hard-packed earthen floor. They were only about two feet tall, and far noisier than the emperors that I was on my way to see. They brawled at one another, jostling between the beach and the colony.

Skuas, the scavenger thugs of high latitudes, flew by watching for unguarded eggs. I brandished driftwood at them, or they would have gone for me too. Sometimes they simply dropped from the air and crashed into an incubating penguin, attempting to knock it from its nest. At other times they would work in pairs, one pulling on a penguin's tail feathers while another jumped in to break the eggs. I had read that skuas each defend a 'territory' of about 2,000 penguins. This number was reported to be so accurate that to count penguin colonies it is enough to count the skuas and multiply by 2,000. Their genus is *Stercorarius, sterco* being Latin for 'shit'. I wondered if the name came from the colouring of their feathers, or their habits. After gorging themselves they often defecate in order to be able to take off, earning them the unforgettable epithet 'shite-hawks'.

Behind me a school of Commerson's dolphins played in the shallows. Piebald and miniature, the dolphins' striped backs glistened like ice smeared with tar. The yellow sand of the sea floor refracted through the water, as if they splashed through liquid amber. After a while they sauntered away, surging and rolling in leaps. Standing on a Falklands beach it felt as if the environment around me was pouring with abundance and diversity. It all still felt a long way from the frozen world that lay to the south.

Only a day's sail south of the Falkland Islands I noticed that the blade-like black-browed albatrosses had been replaced by solitary and occasional wandering albatrosses. I never saw majesty and nobility so sure of itself, so embodied in grace of motion as in the flight of the wandering albatross. We had entered the latitudes of the Furious Fifties, a belt of gales that blow ceaseless westerlies clockwise around Antarctica. Each line of latitude we raised was like climbing rungs of a ladder, up into a higher, freer, windier place. It was intoxicating to stand out on the stern watching the albatrosses harness the air. Another day further south and we crossed the Antarctic Convergence, that line where the relatively warm waters of the Atlantic hit an impassive wall of polar sea. I watched the shift in temperature on the ship's instruments as we passed over the fault line, the two seas abutting like tectonic plates. We were sailing through waters measuring up to 7–8°C, then suddenly the isotherms narrowed to a zebra crossing. We were awash in seas measuring between only 1–2°C. The two bodies of water seemed stunned by one another, immiscible, facing up like two heavyweights reluctant to give way. The meeting of the waters forced a compromise: cold dense water went down, warm light water came up, and the resultant churning and upwelling brought fish and krill to the surface. There was a visible line on the surface, and it frothed with life. Fin whales and southern right whales rolled their island bulk along the convergence. Albatrosses flensed the air, angling their bodies to the swell as if they were suspended on wires. Petrels danced on the wave crests, 'little Peters', tiptoeing with a tentative hesitancy the way St Peter walked on Galilee. A little way further south we passed a pod of orcas sailing north to join the party.

To mark our entrance into Antarctic seas, a viscous fog settled in and blinkered us. Giant icebergs appeared on the radar, one measuring forty miles in length. These icy seas have a long history in the Western imagination. Pliny wrote of the 'Cronian Sea', and

Milton too: 'As when two Polar Winds blowing adverse upon the Cronian Sea, together drive mountains of Ice'. I saw my first iceberg off the port side, ghostly in the fog, its tabular perfection sloped towards one corner and its sides folded and crenellated like a Leonardo tablecloth. My first impression was of purity and immensity. The waves burst and the swell rolled but the berg was immovable, an anchor pin of the oceans. It looked as if it would last for centuries, but in reality I knew it could be gone next week. Another giant berg came up on the starboard side and we passed between the two as if through a gateway.

The wind dropped and the sea fell like a wet silk shroud. It felt dead in the mist, a *mare mortium*, the petrels swirling at the cliffs of ice could be bats at the gates of hell. When speaking of the Dead Sea, the Book of Joshua described a *mare solitudinis*: a lonely, desolate place. But then I would catch a glimpse of those albatrosses and feel as if we were being escorted by angels.

Samuel Taylor Coleridge was a West Country boy, a vicar's son from Devon, one of thirteen children. He grew up into a soldier, reluctant husband, university dropout, opium abuser and one of England's most cherished poets. He famously formed an alliance with William and Dorothy Wordsworth, travelling and living with them both in England and on the Continent. Just before the turn of the nineteenth century he was living in Somerset and writing his most famous narrative poems, 'Kubla Khan' and 'The Rime of the Ancient Mariner'. The latter was inspired by the furious storms of the South Atlantic, which Coleridge had never seen. In it he manages to evoke the experience so skilfully that he has given the English language some memorable expressions ('water water everywhere nor any drop to drink') and iconic images (the wearing of an albatross around your neck).

The thought of anyone managing to live with an albatross around their neck is ridiculous, but Coleridge knew his audience would not be able to imagine the great size of these birds. In the poem the living albatross seems to represent the Christian soul, or the promise of Redemption, as it tries to lead the mariners out of the cursed Antarctic seas. The mariner shoots the albatross but is criticised for it by the crew, who then force him to wear it around his neck: 'Instead of the cross, the albatross/About my neck was hung'.

How did he portray the South Atlantic so accurately while walking the hills of Somerset? According to Wordsworth, the two men had both been reading a book by George Shelvocke, a pirate who went on plundering missions to the Spanish ports of what are now Argentina and Chile. To get there he had been blown deep into Antarctic waters, and in a book called *A Voyage Round the World by way of the Great South Sea* he described the experience. First published in 1726, I had found a reprint in a second-hand bookshop not far from Coleridge's alma mater, Jesus College, Cambridge.

Shelvocke was one of the first to enter these seas; James Cook's great second voyage would not come for another half century. He begins with a description of the subantarctic latitudes, even accurate three centuries later: 'Though we were pretty much advanced in the summer season and had the days very long, we were nevertheless subject to continuous squalls of sleet, snow and rain, and the heavens were perpetually hidden from us by gloomy, dismal clouds.' The ship was being trailed by a solitary 'disconsolate black albatross', perhaps a sooty albatross. Shelvocke's second mate Hatley decided that the bird was an ill omen because of its dark colour, bringing the 'contrary tempestuous winds' that prevented them reaching their pillaging grounds on coastal Latin America. Hatley shot the albatross, leaving the crew 'without a companion which would have somewhat diverted our thoughts from the reflection of being in such a remote part of the world'.

I envied Shelvocke and the Ancient Mariner's sense of sailing deep into unknown seas. From the Rime I suspect that Coleridge did too:

> The fair breeze blew, the white foam flew,
> The furrow followed free;
> We were the first that ever burst
> Into that silent sea.

*

At 60° latitude we crossed another line, this time an imaginary one laid down at the negotiating tables of the north. Beyond it the Antarctic Treaty came into force, active since 1961. This time there was no line visible on the sea. It is a convenient dividing line, the lands further south were not well explored or even claimed by any country until the twentieth century. The treaty signatories have all agreed to hold territorial claims 'in abeyance' – at least for the moment. In that warring century it was perhaps wise to leave one continent out of the scrimmage.

I woke at 5 a.m. to see icebergs at my porthole, and rushed outside to watch them pass. There was something architectural about them; fairy-tale castles sculpted into turrets and spires. One looked like the Gothic cathedral of Milan, lolling lopsided into a gleaming piazza of sea ice. Snow petrels – porcelain-white birds like little doves – whirled between the ship and the walls of ice. Chinstrap and adélie penguins crowded like cruise passengers at the prow and stern of each berg. They are both smaller species than the gentoos I had met on the Falklands, and their Linnaean names have none of the latter's intrigue. *Pygoscelis adeliae* was named for a French explorer's wife, and *Pygoscelis antarcticus* shows a contemptible lack of imagination.

The sky looked as if the topmost layer of the sea had been peeled off and hung up in it to dry. The tips of the South Orkney Islands rose over the southern horizon. The ship was cutting through the sea ice, riding over the thicker plates and hanging for moments before crashing through. The effect was like Napoleon's cannons at Austerlitz, the penguins ran in disarray across the plains of cracking ice. We could see them falling into the gaps and porpoising away unhurt. Fat crabeater seals lay snoozing in the cold wind unfazed, looking up at the ship through frosty eyelashes.

The bay beneath the base at Signy Island was ice-free, and a small boat known as a tender was lowered over the side by crane. We were to leave staff and provisions at the BAS station, and as medical officer I was allowed ashore to check the base medical supplies. With the third mate piloting the tender we crossed the bay, skirting bergs. We passed so closely to one that I leaned over and picked a rock from it. The only rocks within hundreds of miles of Halley would be those on the seabed deep beneath the ice.

Signy is a field station for biologists and environmental chemists, as well as a marker point at the furthest limit of truly Antarctic territory once claimed by the British as a Falklands Island Dependency. A hydrologist told me about her work, then in spite of the best intentions of the Antarctic Treaty stamped my passport with the unambiguous statement 'Signy: British Antarctic Territory'.

The South Orkneys are a magnificent place to live; if they had staffed the place with a doctor year-round I would have been tempted to stay on. Lying in the heaving seas around the Antarctic Convergence, flung from the tip of the Peninsula, it thrummed with life. I tiptoed up to elephant and crabeater seals, chinstrap and adélie penguins and their chicks, sheathbills and skuas, only to find that as on the Falklands, they were oblivious to my presence. I bounced, hopped and danced along the shores between boulders and whalebones covered in algae. Around one corner I came upon a wonder that stopped me suddenly, afraid to breathe in case I disturbed the scene.

A leopard seal, coiled like an eel, was lying in the shallow water waiting for chinstrap penguins. *Hydrurga leptonyx*, 'the slender, dark, water-worker', is the alpha-predator of the Antarctic food chain. As every Antarctic cruise guide will tell you, polar bears have never made it to the south. Like albatrosses they could never pass the hot windless section around the equator. In the Antarctic the bear's ecological niche is filled by the leopard seal.

The seal lay to the side of a small bay where the chinstraps scrabbled ashore. Denied both the freedom of the open water and the rough terrain of the land, they were vulnerable there in the shallows. I watched the leopard spring for them, jaws agape, more like a shark than a mammal. Each time it lunged the water thrashed, and through the spray I caught a glimpse of teeth curved like talons. Finally it caught a penguin and uncoiled, mouth bloodied, sinking beneath the surface with its victim held firm.

I stayed on Signy only a few hours. The *Shackleton* left that evening, splintering through the ice in the dusky light. Iron-grey patches of water-sky smudged the underbellies of the clouds to the east, reflecting open water ahead. Captains of polar vessels use these patches on the clouds to pick their way through the ice. The converse of water-sky is known as 'ice-blink', luminous white patches on the clouds mirroring fields of sea ice to be avoided. 'Water-sky', 'ice-blink' – the Antarctic seemed to blur distinctions between water and air. Even the horizon could not be relied upon to separate the ocean from the sky. The sun set behind the stern, a golden seam like a hinge shone along the western rim of the sea. It narrowed as I watched, as if a door from some other place was being edged to a close.

Mist clung to the peaks of Coronation Island and the fading sun glistened over a glacier called Sunshine. The cliffs were black against the ice and mist, but light bounced around me as if the sky was mirrored in silver. For me the South Orkneys had been a magnificent gateway to the Antarctic but despite their great beauty I was glad to be heading on. I had seen this landscape before, in Svalbard and Greenland. Having come so far I wanted to see something new.

To avoid the worst of the Weddell Sea ice the *Shackleton* would have to approach Halley from the east, and we still had two more bases to visit before we reached it. They were 900 kilometres away to the north-east and so, feeling as if we were turning our backs on Antarctica, we climbed back down the rungs of latitude in the direction of South Georgia.

Off the eastern tip of the South Orkneys, the Argentinians maintain a research station called Orcades, the word Tacitus used for the boreal Orkney archipelago. They consider it part of Argentina, under the jurisdiction of Tierra del Fuego, but the base itself was established by the Scots. The Scottish National Antarctic Expedition of 1902–4 was the first to establish a scientific presence on the islands; before them there had been only sealers and whalers (many of them Orcadians). Its leader, William Spiers Bruce, was a medical-school dropout who had first sailed south as scientific assistant on the *Balæna*, a Dundee whaling vessel. He fell in love with the glaciated world that he saw there and over the following years made a few trips to the High Arctic. But the Antarctic had him hooked. He was put forward for Scott's *Discovery* expedition but was turned down (though some maintain that it was *he* who turned Scott down). In the end he made his own way to Antarctica.

With massive sponsorship he refitted a Norwegian whaling vessel and renamed it the *Scotia*. With it he explored the Weddell Sea more carefully than anyone had managed before him and did oceanographic work that revealed the Scotia Arc, a submarine mountain chain looping from the Peninsula out towards the South Sandwich Islands and tucking back into the Andes at Cape Horn. It is Bruce who called the sector of Antarctica at the southernmost end of the Weddell 'Coats Land' in honour of the Paisley textile magnates who paid for two-thirds of his expedition. He reached the furthest south in the region since the English sealer James Weddell in 1823, deep into emperor penguin territory, where he facilitated the first known meeting between an emperor penguin and a kilted bagpiper.

But Bruce fell foul of the British geographical establishment who preferred to bolster Scott's achievements. Despite all that he achieved he was never offered a Polar Medal. Perhaps his misdemeanour was to get too friendly with the Argentinians. They hosted him in Buenos Aires and offered him a good price for his base, where they promised to keep his meteorological station running. He accepted and the comments of his colleagues give an idea why; the Scots clearly felt mistreated by the British authorities back home. In the official account of the expedition they sniffed 'it is significant to note how the Argentine Government willingly spent money on a scientific object such as this while nearer home we have had the deplorable occurrence of an ignorant Government closing one of the most important meteorological observatories in its country'. Orcades has been staffed ever since, a continuous presence reaching back to the earliest days of Antarctic exploration.

The captain knew I liked to watch the albatrosses trailing the ship. 'Make sure you get up early tomorrow,' he told me, 'you'll be in for a treat.'

'What sort of time?' I asked him.

'We'll be reaching Bird Island at about 5 a.m.'

By 3.30 I was out on deck watching the mountains of South Georgia climb over a spreading eastern horizon. The shins of the cliffs were lapped by mist. The sea was unruly, boisterous, pushing and slapping against the ship's hull. Wandering albatrosses followed us in the half-light, stripping a seam between the wave-crest spray and the broadening sky. They rose and fell as if held in the breath of the sea, their wings so sensitive that they can follow minute changes in air pressure over the waves. I imagined how it would be to have such bones, lofted within, the air inside them tugging to be reunited with the great oceans of sky above. Then, as we neared the island, fur seals appeared around the prow of the vessel, pirouetting through the spume. They led us on to the beaches where they breed in their thousands.

The sun was rising over the cordillera of South Georgia, alpine summits sunk in an iron sea. Bird Island is a stumpy rock splintered from its western cape. A procession of stately icebergs were grounded on the shallow seabed between them, lined up like stanchions for a bridge across the strait.

The *Shackleton* lay at anchor beneath the grey hulk of the island. The base itself was hidden in the fog. I jumped into the tender with a bag of medical supplies and the first mate steered us into the mist. Kelp mats threatened to tangle our propeller, and we had to reverse a few times to find a way through. We did not need to use our eyes, it was enough to follow the clamorous din of the seals on the beach. Paying attention to our ears and noses we moved between banks of mist. Around the boat the water was a soup of kelp gulls, giant petrels and macaroni penguins. It was like crossing the Styx; the corpse of something dead floated past, a giant petrel's head buried deep in its flank. Its bat-like wings were stained with blood, flailing for balance as it tore into the carcass. An isolated landing stage appeared – I couldn't see the base at the other end of it. The smells were of matted fur, fetid breath, rotting meat, faeces, urine, blood. There was a ceaseless yelping and barking, a low pitiful moaning. We tied up at the pier and I began to make out individual seals on the beach ahead. The rumbles coming from the throats of even the small females were startling. I saw that each had its pup, a mewling bundle of greasy fur with wide, obsidian eyes.

We were met on the pier by two biologists who handed us each a long pole. At the beach they led us in a walk up the riverbed – it was the least claimed part of the shoreline – but even there we quickly found a use for the poles. 'Aim for the noses,' we were told, 'they're most sensitive there.' The ground was littered with bones and fallen canines sharp as meathooks. Fur-seal saliva contains special enzymes to prevent wounds from healing. Wielding my stick I was reminded that *Homo sapiens* can be a prey species too.

At Bird Island we slurped tea and ate cake beneath a signed photograph of the Queen, 'Elizabeth R'. The hut was raised on stilts above the shingle, and the groans and shrieks of the fur seals reverberated through the floorboards. Only three biologists live on Bird Island, one to study the albatrosses, one for the seals, and one for the macaroni penguins. A fourth winter member is usually a plumber or an electrician, it being assumed that none of the scientists will know what to do if the generator breaks down. They all know how lucky they are.

Chris, one of the biologists, was just starting out on a two-and-a-half-year contract to study the macaroni penguin colony, one of the world's largest at 600,000 penguins. He took me to see it: a tight squawking mass of bodies crammed into a stubby little valley. The colony was so huge it even had a 'motorway', a path through to the centre that the penguins left clear of nest sites by seeming mutual consent. They competed in noise and ungainly belligerence with the fur seals on the far side of the island. I watched them a while but my time on the island was limited, and on my way to the colony I had seen the wandering albatross nests. I was fidgeting to get back up and sit with them again; they seemed to have the silence and the dignity I imagined for the emperors.

Wingspans of these birds can approach twelve feet, a reach so wide they cannot flap to take off. Instead they nest on the highest, most exposed ridges so that it is enough to merely stretch their wings into the wind and be vaulted skywards. After take-off they can watch the ocean heave beneath them for two years straight without touching earth or rock. Human beings seem so marginal to their lives that I had the sense that they could barely see me, as if their gaze passed right through me. I sat within inches of one nest, and though the bird sat stiffly and was clearly uncomfortable on land it breathed an air of impassive serenity. Its feathers trembled like dusted snow, a dazzling, laundered whiteness. The plumage of albatross wings becomes whiter as they get older, and an albatross can live for more than sixty years. It was odd to see the soul of flight so grounded. *Diomedea exulans* – they were named by Linnaeus for exiled Diomedes, the 'God-counselled' (*Dio-medea*), a warrior who fought at Troy. According to Ovid's *Metamorphoses*, he was shipwrecked on the way from Troy to Italy, and Venus turned all his companions into birds. I like the idea that the wanderers, being named for Diomedes who was spared avian transformation, cannot be considered true birds but something purer, higher, and more heroic. Given their exiled wanderings around the Southern Ocean it would perhaps have been more appropriate to name them for Odysseus.

A wandering albatross taking off from Bird Island was tracked by a satellite; in one year it circumnavigated the globe flying to Brazil, across the Pacific, past the southern coasts of New Zealand and Australia, and back across the Indian and Atlantic oceans *twice* without touching land. The wind sustains and animates them, their lives are one with it. Darwin said that of all the world's creatures the albatross is the one most at ease in the tempestuous weather of the Southern Ocean, 'as if the storm were their proper sphere'.

They mate for life, and with increasing numbers lost to long-line fishing hooks more of them are standing lonely vigils on the ridges of Bird Island, waiting for mates that never return. Populations are falling as a result. Ornithologists tell us that albatrosses are not clever birds. Developmentally they are quite primitive, and the stereotyped patterns of their behaviour are sluggish and slow to adapt. But as I sat and watched them I thought not of illegal fishing or their reported simplicity but of Herman Melville's awe on an encounter with them: 'At intervals it arched forth its vast archangel wings, as if to embrace some holy ark. Wondrous flutterings and throbbings shook it . . . Through its inexpressible, strange eyes, methought I peeped to secrets which took hold of God. As Abraham before the angels, I bowed myself.'

# CHAPTER THREE

# Of Kings and Emperors

A penguin finds no difficulty in being a penguin, it simply is.
This also is possible for you.

A. L. Kennedy, 'On Having More Sense'

The *Shackleton* steamed along the northern coast of South Georgia, passing abandoned whaling stations: Leith, Husvik, Stromness, their names betraying the origins of their founders – whaling men accustomed to a hard life in high latitudes. Scanning Stromness with binoculars I found the station manager's house. Ernest Shackleton had dragged himself here out of the hell that his *Endurance* expedition became. Above Husvik harbour I saw the coiled folds of rock strata that had helped to guide him to this bay, and his salvation.

The story has been retold many times, but has not lost the power to astonish. In 1914, as Europe tore itself apart, Shackleton embarked on his Imperial Trans-Antarctic Expedition. In December of that year, he sailed from South Georgia and into the grinding pack ice of the Weddell. He was headed for the Coats Land named and described by Bruce on his Scottish National Antarctic Expedition.

Shackleton sailed with the *Endurance* while the other half of his expedition were on the *Aurora* in the Ross Sea with orders to lay depots of supplies across the Ross Barrier, the great plain of ice on which Scott had died only two years earlier. The depots were to feed Shackleton and his men as they completed the first ever crossing of the continent from the Weddell to the Ross Sea via the South Pole. The *Aurora* crew succeeded in their mission despite the loss of three lives, but because of the Weddell ice Shackleton failed even to reach continental Antarctica.

By December 1914 they had drifted past the ice shelf where Halley would later be built and named the coast behind it for Sir James Caird, the main sponsor of their expedition. By mid-January 1915, at 76° 34′ South and only a hundred miles from their destination, the *Endurance* was beset in sea ice. They were helpless, recording their ship's location as the ice wheeled them a little further south, and then north and west away from the coast they needed to reach. By late February temperatures were plummeting and Shackleton knew his plans for the expedition were over. The *Aurora* party would continue to risk their lives to lay depots that would never be reached, but for Shackleton it would be enough to get his men out alive.

It is difficult to imagine now how they must have felt through those months of darkness, trapped on board a ship built for motion, but moored fast to a limitless plain of ice. The grinding Weddell pulled them north through the polar night, the ship riding the ice like a grain on a millstone. By July it was clear that the ice around the ship was on the move again and giant floes began to raft over one another, pinching the hull. Three months later the *Endurance* became so distorted by the ice that it had to be abandoned. Pitching tents on the ice nearby they continued to edge northwards, salvaging whatever they could from the ship. Another month, late November, and the *Endurance* finally split and sank. As a second Christmas truce broke over the trenches near Calais, Shackleton marched his men north-west, towards the Antarctic Peninsula.

The *Endurance* carried three lifeboats named for generous sponsors of the expedition: the *Dudley Docker*, the *Stancomb-Wills* and the *James Caird*. For nearly four months the men heaved those lifeboats across pressure-ridged floes and paddled across open leads in the ice, finally making Elephant Island in the South Shetlands on 15 April 1916. They had not stepped on land for sixteen months but quickly built huts of stone and roofed them with two of the three lifeboats. Winter was narrowing down their options – there would be no passing whaling ships this late in the season. It was decided that six men, including Shackleton and the *Endurance* captain Frank Worsley, would use the *James Caird* to cross 800 miles of the Furious Fifties to reach South Georgia and raise the alarm.

They worked fast, but even so it took over a week from their arrival on Elephant Island until the *James Caird* was ready for the voyage. It was to be across one of the stormiest stretches of ocean in the world, a sea ribbed by the colossal swells that roll around Cape Horn. The gunwales of the boat were raised by eighteen inches, boulders were piled in for ballast, a makeshift mast was bolted to its keel, and in the absence of spare wood canvas was stretched across bow and stern. An Irishman called Frank Wild was left in charge of the men and Shackleton left instructions that if they heard nothing by the spring they were to assume the worst and try to make their own way to safety. On 24 April, just before the sea ice closed in again, the *James Caird* sailed.

At this point the achievements of the *Endurance* crew begin to take on a mythical dimension. Their clothes and sleeping bags were soaked, they lost their sea anchor, they were constantly moving ballast boulders around to balance the boat through the storm-blown waves. The sky was overcast so much of the time that on only four occasions did Frank Worsley catch a glimpse of the sun to calculate their bearings; the rest of the time he steered by dead reckoning. Despite all these difficulties only two weeks out of Elephant Island they raised South Georgia.

What then? Shackleton hoped to steer the lifeboat around to the sheltered northern coast of the island and into the bays of the whalers. Instead the wind beat them on to the cliffs of the southern coast, where for two days they were blown on to sheer rocks or again out to sea. They even lost sight of South Georgia and were almost blown on towards Australia. As night fell on 10 May, Worsley finally managed to slip the *James Caird* into one of the few sheltered bays on the south coast. They were on the wrong side of the island, twenty-two miles from Stromness whaling station, and two of the six men were ill. But they had solid ground underfoot, and they were alive. After feasting on albatross chicks, Shackleton and Worsley, together with the Irish second mate Tom

Crean, decided to hazard a crossing of the island.

No one had ever crossed South Georgia, and the maps Shackleton had seen showed only blank spaces. He knew that there would be icefalls and glaciers to traverse and so he removed screws from the planking of the *James Caird* and embedded them in the soles of his boots. He also took a stove, a carpenter's adze to cut ice steps, and a length of rope, but no camping equipment.

If their journey to reach South Georgia astonishes, that they survived the crossing of the island is miraculous. It took them thirty-six hours of climbs, sheer descents, dead ends and ice traverses to reach the other side. Worsley and Crean slept for only five minutes during this time, Shackleton not at all. In the final hours they had to lower themselves down a waterfall leaving the rope behind, throwing away everything except the adze and Worsley's log which they knew they would need to tell the tale of their expedition. Shackleton's description of this moment hints at an almost mystical transformation in perspective effected by his journey: 'that was all we brought, except our wet clothes, from the Antarctic, which a year and a half before we had entered with a well-found ship, full equipment and high hopes. That was all of tangible things; but in memories we were rich. We had pierced the veneer of outside things. We had seen God in His splendours, we had heard the text that Nature renders. We had reached the naked soul of man.'

The clothes of the men were filthy and their hair and beards matted, but in Stromness Shackleton's status as a British gentleman reasserted itself. They tried to make themselves look more presentable: 'the thought that there might be women at the station made us painfully conscious of our uncivilized appearance', he wrote. And when he was finally introduced to the station manager his first thought was of Europe:

'"Tell me, when was the war over?" I asked.

'"The war is not over," he answered. "Millions are being killed. Europe is mad. The world is mad."'

It took four attempts to rescue the men he left on Elephant Island, thanks in large part to the generosity of the British community in Chilean Punta Arenas. All of the crew of the *Endurance*, including a stowaway called Blackborow, made it back to Europe. They survived the Weddell ice, but not all were to survive the trenches of France.

South Georgia lies at only 54° South, the same latitude as Yorkshire, but despite its temperate latitude its mountains are meshed together in a dense matrix of glacial ice. I looked up at those glaciers imagining Shackleton, Worsley and Crean crossing them nearly a century before. The chilling effect of the immense Antarctic continent, still 2,000 miles away, was so profound that here they spilled in their ponderous enormity directly into the sea while Yorkshire's glaciers shrivelled away 10,000 years ago. Light glanced from ice pockets in the mountains high above me, and spindrift streamed from the peaks in banners that misted into rainbows.

The *Shackleton* was to drop supplies and more staff at the BAS research station at King Edward Point, close to the abandoned whaling station of Grytviken. Six years after his return to civilisation, Shackleton had died there. He and Frank Worsley had arrived in South Georgia as part of their crazed *Quest* expedition, Shackleton's sponsors having indulged his mania to reach Antarctica one last time. After he died, his body was crated up and shipped to Montevideo before his wife, Emily, intervened. 'His spirit has no place in England' it was said, and the body was returned to Grytviken.

From the ship that bore his name I walked up to his grave, weighing a small whale rib in my hand as a defence against the elephant seals. The great explorer proved to have a weak heart after all. The little graveyard was fenced off against the seals – they had flattened grave markers in the past. A rough-hewn slab of British granite was inscribed 'Ernest Henry Shackleton: Explorer'. Around it shallow depressions in the grass betrayed the graves of the whalers who lay beside him. Shackleton would have appreciated the view, and approved of the company.

Climbing on over the hill I came upon a broad vale cut by the 'Penguin River'. It was a turquoise and grey torrent of glacial meltwater, lined by king penguins. Though king and emperor penguins are thought to have diverged 40 million years ago they are each other's closest living relatives, and share a genus, *Aptenodytes*. King penguins are rarely found higher than 60° of latitude, and emperors are rarely found lower than 60°, though the two cousins must occasionally meet.

There are about 2 million king penguins worldwide, of which hundreds of thousands breed on South Georgia. Perhaps populations were once much larger; the early whalers and sealers used their bodies as fuel for blubber rending, burning penguins like faggots beneath their colossal whale-oil cauldrons. When Grytviken was founded in 1904 by the legendary Norwegian whaler Carl Larsen he found those pots scattered along the shoreline – they gave rise to its name: *gryt* is Norwegian for 'pot' and *vik* means 'bay'.* Later, when whale and seal blubber grew scarce, penguins themselves were rendered down into a lower grade of oil. Penguins like these were herded in their thousands up planks, only to fall alive into cauldrons of already-boiling oil. Apsley Cherry-Garrard campaigned vocally against the practice, publishing angry calculations in *The Times* that each penguin's death gained its hunters less than a farthing.

They were as fearless as I had hoped, and I crept up to one close enough to see my reflection in its beetle-black eye. It blinked slowly, sheening its cornea. Like the others standing along the banks of the river it was statuesque, seemingly deep in meditation. They are much slimmer than emperors – about half the weight – but almost as tall, and like emperor penguins have fiery auricular patches on each side towards the back of the head. Without these patches they become unrecognisable to other penguins, and are unable to find a mate. The king penguin's patches are a lurid orange with black margins. They looked like foam-rubber headphones slung on each side of its head. The emperor's corresponding patches are a soft gold like spilled yolk, fading into white the way a buttercup glows on pale skin.

I had seen king penguins plenty of times. My nursery school took us to see them at Edinburgh Zoo where one of them, christened 'Nils Olav', has been bizarrely claimed by the Norwegian

---

* Larsen still holds the record for catching the largest creature yet found on earth, a female blue whale measuring over 110 feet in length.

military, paraded in uniform with the soldiers on special occasions (surely the most extreme example of *Aptenodytes* anthropomorphism). They appeared nightly on British TV through the 1980s selling chocolate biscuits. They even popped up in one of the Batman movies. But seeing them on South Georgia was different. Their freedom lent them an unexpected dignity.

The seminal studies on the king penguin of South Georgia were carried out by Bernard Stonehouse in the early 1950s. After wartime flying training in the Royal Navy, Stonehouse had first become fascinated by penguins further south in Antarctica. In 1947 he had been serving as a meteorologist and pilot at a British base on Stonington Island off the Antarctic Peninsula. Flying with another pilot and a surveyor his plane was forced into an emergency landing on sea ice in poor conditions. The plane's skis hit a lump of ice which flipped it over and wrecked it. Surprised to find themselves uninjured the men made a sledge out of a petrol tank and started hauling their few possessions back towards base. They managed only three or four miles a day, sharing a single sleeping bag in turn by night, and rationing themselves to 500 calories every twenty-four hours. After a week's walking they were spotted by an American plane flying overhead, and rescued.

Dr Stonehouse, now long retired from university teaching, lives just outside Cambridge, where he is still active with the Scott Polar Research Institute. A mutual friend gave me his phone number, and after my return to Europe from Antarctica I met him for lunch.

He wore a blue blazer with a paisley cravat and walked erect, without a stick. His voice was warm and crisp, kind and educated. A lifetime in Oxbridge colleges had stripped it of his native Humberside. 'How did you end up studying penguins?' I asked him.

'Well, when our plane crashed – it was too flimsy for the Antarctic anyway – I had nothing left to do you see,' he explained. 'Only the odd bit of meteorology, and so I started casting around for something to keep me busy.'

Leading a sledging party in a survey of northern Marguerite Bay, he had unexpectedly encountered a small colony of emperor penguins on the Dion Islets, just off the Peninsula and accessible from Stonington. He noted the colony with interest, but it was only when his relief ship failed to arrive that he thought about studying them in earnest. He had already spent two winters in Antarctica and now faced a third. He decided to spend it under canvas at the Dion Islets, about fifty miles from base. 'As far as I'm concerned any kind of hut is better than any kind of tent,' he told me, which illustrates just how desperate he must have been to get away from base. Vivian Fuchs, his base commander at Stonington (and later director of BAS), radioed back to the Falklands to ask permission. 'Permission was not forthcoming,' Bernard said.

'So how did you manage it?' I asked him.

'I think that was one of those occasions when we conveniently had "radio interference". . . and didn't quite hear the orders', he said, his eyes twinkling. 'That was one of the advantages of the poor communications of those days, you could still do your own thing. Fuchs knew that the last thing you want through a winter is a man who doesn't want to be there.'

'How was it to be so cut off from everyone, to have so little contact for three years?' I asked him.

'Oh . . . I suppose it made us all feel terribly heroic,' he said, laughing at the memory.

Knowing the appalling lengths to which Edward Wilson, Apsley Cherry-Garrard and Birdie Bowers had gone to obtain emperor eggs nearly forty years earlier, he proposed to make a timed series of embryos at the Dion Islets rookery. He arrived just too late to witness mating, but in plenty of time to watch the resultant egg-laying. Through his winter under canvas he collected emperor eggs timed with approximate gestational ages. His specimens went a long way to outlining the embryology of the emperor penguin, which had been Edward Wilson's holy grail.

'How did you know what to do with the embryos,' I asked him, 'if you had been trained as a navy pilot?'

'If I were a religious man, which I'm not, I would say it was divine providence.' He explained: before his naval service he had spent a few months reading zoology at Hull University College, during which – rather unusually – he learned the practical skills of opening eggs to remove and preserve early embryos. 'I had no particular interest in birds, it's just the way it happened,' he said, 'our principal lecturer was a bird embryologist.' Then at Stonington the base was visited by a Chilean ship with a German zoologist on board. 'This was before I'd seen the rookery at Dion Islets,' he told me. 'I told the zoologist that I had thought of collecting adélie penguin embryos, but did not have any of the special fixative, Bouin's solution, to preserve embryonic tissue. When the Chileans invited us all on board for a party the German presented me with a great big bottle of . . . Bouin's solution!' By a series of remarkable coincidences he had been taught how to remove embryos, had a bottle of fixative in hand, and then discovered the first known accessible emperor rookery.

On returning to England he entered University College London to complete his degree in zoology. He published a note on his emperor penguin observations in the world-class scientific journal *Nature*, then a fuller account of their behaviour and breeding cycle in a series of reports for the Falkland Islands Dependencies Survey (FIDS). With a degree under his belt, and two prestigious publications, he was accepted for a doctorate at Oxford. With the Stonington Island base closed there was no way he could get back to his beloved emperor penguins. But the government of the Falkland Islands offered to provide facilities for him to study king penguins, their nearest relatives, on South Georgia.

His report on the breeding, behaviour and development of the king penguin, the product of twenty months living and working on South Georgia, is peppered with references to and anecdotes about the birds' southern cousins. It devotes a whole section to comparisons of the king and emperor penguins, and radiates admiration for the way only emperors can survive a deep Antarctic winter. He is not so much fascinated by the way the two *Aptenodytes* species are so similar, but by the way they are so different: 'presumably as a result of unusually strong and divergent evolutionary pressures,' he wrote, 'the two differ more in their breeding behaviour than any other congeneric species of penguins, or indeed than of any other two closely related species of birds'. It would not be long now until I saw the emperors for myself.

*    *    *

Listing against Grytviken pier was one of the last South Georgia steel-hulled whalers, the *Petrel*. Its stern had sunk beneath the water and its harpoon pointed harmlessly into the hillside. Tied up alongside it was a century-old Cornish wooden sailing cutter, *Curlew*. The story of how it came to be there reads like an escapist fantasy, or a drama of pioneer living. Tim and Pauline Carr had found it derelict in Malta in 1967 and restored it from the keel up. They had been living in the boat more or less ever since, sailing around the world several times over without the benefits of radar, GPS or even an engine.

A decade earlier they had blown into King Edward Cove for a brief stint at the newly established museum and stayed on as curators. Despite the asbestos and fuel oil, old dynamite and military waste, it had seemed like a paradise to them. Their book *Antarctic Oasis* drew attention to the unique ecosystems they found, the life pouring from the seas around South Georgia, and blared a clarion call about the urgency of protecting the archipelago. In those days Grytviken was still occupied by the British military. Tim and Pauline were the first to question the environmental practices that had become commonplace among the residents.

Grytviken feels close to the edge of the world, but now with a museum shop and a cruise-ship season it has become a place of passing strangers as well as frontier living. The museum had grown from just a small specialist venture to a guardian of the heritage of the islands, a living demonstration that there is more to South Georgia than just Shackleton, whaling or the army. For the first few years they had had to sleep in *Curlew* as the old station manager's offices that housed the museum were too dilapidated. In the decade Tim and Pauline had lived at Grytviken they had completely refurbished the museum, and brought to shelter many artefacts at risk of looting from the other whaling stations along the coast.

I strolled through the exhibits. A stuffed albatross trembled at the ceiling joists, as if yearning to be free. A series of friezes showed the conditions for explorers like Shackleton a century ago. Hundreds of objects drawn from the lives of the whalers were displayed along glass cabinets and reconstructed rooms. But what fascinated me most about the museum were the curators themselves. They welcomed me into their kitchen and brought mugs of tea and plates of toast while I quizzed them about their sailing adventures. Their gaze at rest was distant, as if set for ocean horizons. Their gentle and generous modesty was inspirational.

'When are you leaving for Halley?' Tim asked me.

'Tomorrow.'

'Well there's a few of us going ski-mountaineering tonight,' he said. 'The sunrise from the top of the pass is out of this world. You'd be welcome to join us.'

I set my alarm for 1 a.m., and ate breakfast at the edge of the *Shackleton* bar with a late-night party still in full swing. With Penny, the ship-bound dentist, I stumbled along to the museum, taking care to step around the elephant seals that lay burping and sneezing on the beach. Tim made us strong coffee and found skis that would fit my boots.

For the first half-hour it was a hike through rubble and scree, skis balanced on our shoulders as we stepped into the pools of light that jerked from our headtorches. At the edge of the snow line we strapped 'skins' to our skis, thin strips of cloth that grip the snow and allowed us to walk up the mountainside. It was 3 a.m. when we made it to the pass, just as the first tide of lilac lapped into the east.

It was soul-quietening to sit at the pass, curled in the lee of the wind, munching chocolate and drinking hot blackcurrant. I watched lenticular clouds phosphoresce gently before igniting into crimson. They slid on through the fiery colours of the spectrum before washing into a morning blue, the silhouetted peaks filling out into three dimensions as the air gathered light. Snow petrels swung through the air around us, whirling down the valley and out towards the ocean. I felt as if I was saying goodbye to rock and sea, to life's abundance, preparing myself ahead of our departure for Halley.

By 4 a.m. we decided that we should be getting back as it would be unforgivable to delay the ship. Tim slid off down the mountainside in gentle arcs, making neat Telemark turns. I made my way down less gracefully, my bruises spreading before I even reached the bottom.

In Grytviken a soft rain was falling. I said goodbye to Tim among the rusting sheds and rotting boards of the whaling station, a melancholy place at five in the morning. King penguins were spaced out along the shore like marker posts guiding me back towards the *Shackleton*. None even lifted their heads to watch me go.

At 7.30 a.m. the voice of the first mate boomed from loudspeakers into every cabin on the *Shackleton*: 'Anyone not wishing to go to Halley please get off the ship.' By afternoon South Georgia was gone. I watched it recede, a sublime backdrop to the whales that breached from the sea and slapped their tails goodbye.

The ship steamed south and east, skirting the edge of the great dial of Weddell Sea ice and edging past the South Sandwich Islands in heavy fog. I stood out on deck sniffing the breeze for hints of the sulphurous fumes that pour from the volcanic cone of Zavodovski, straining my eyes to catch the outline of Southern Thule. These are some of the remotest islands in the world. A few hundred miles beyond them lay Bouvet Island, often described as *the* most remote island in the world.

On the world map that hangs on my wall at home Bouvet does not even appear. Roughly equidistant from Argentina, South Africa and Dronning Maud Land in Antarctica, its position is hidden beneath the 'L' of 'WORLD'. Nominally Norwegian since the 1920s, Bouvet is so inhospitable that it supports only unmanned weather stations, and even these are periodically destroyed by landslides. But in 1979 a double flash was noticed by the American satellite *Vela Hotel* – someone had set off a nuclear explosion on or close to Bouvet. The French, Israelis and South Africans have all been under suspicion for the nuclear test, but so far no one has owned up.

It thrilled me that to reach Halley we had to traverse these remote seas, where even a nuclear bomb could slip by almost unnoticed. Halley is the end of the line, the furthest flung and most inaccessible of the British research stations in Antarctica. Each of the bases has a code letter used in official communications, often the first letter of the base's name. Halley, though, has been assigned 'Z'. In the early days of its history it was even given the romantic dignity of the name Ice Station Zebra. The furthest base has been strung out to the end of the alphabet, given the last and least used consonant in English. One night in the *Shackleton* bar I was pleased to discover my new title, 'Zdoc', earned me sixteen points at Scrabble.

On 21 December the *Shackleton* crossed the Antarctic Circle, and we began the long slide towards winter. We had been smashing through vast floes of plated sea ice for a couple of days, shoving them aside like pieces of a mixed-up jigsaw. Finally we broke into a polynya about the size of Lebanon. Polynyas are broad stretches of open water that perforate the mantle of sea ice like drill-holes in a wooden board. Following satellite imagery the ship would try to steer for them, cutting a line through the ice like a saw blade following a stencil. In places the ice beyond the polynya became so tortured that the *Shackleton* had to drive itself high on to it, hanging suspended for a few moments before crashing through. During these seismic shudders the hull groaned in distress.

One morning, as I watched the floes, I heard a cry from the conning tower at the top of the ship: 'It's the ice shelf!' I swung my binoculars to the south but saw only broken shards of sea ice to the horizon. When I reached the conning tower I tried again.

The Riiser-Larsen Ice Shelf. It was a wall of alabastered ice, perhaps a hundred feet high, rippling along the horizon, fissured with an intricacy which caught the eye and forced an appreciation of its immensity, the quality of its soft blue light. Western explorers like Scott and Shackleton often talk of the stern grandeur of the ice shelves, their hostility and unapproachability, but there are alternative perspectives. I enjoy the description given in the book of the often forgotten National Japanese expedition of 1911. The Ross Ice Barrier was creased, it reports, 'like white folding screens'. The convolutions of the coastline were a 'gigantic white snake at rest'.

'At last,' I wrote in my diary that evening, 'Antarctica!'

# SUMMER

# CHAPTER FOUR

# *Antarctica at Last!*

Snow rolled on forever to meet the sky in a round of unbroken horizon. Here was the spaciousness of the desert; the spaciousness, you might say, of the raw materials of creation.

Richard Byrd, *Alone*

Cruising alongside the plains of ice, the relentless eternity of stretched and unravelling ice, I wondered at the colossal weight of its silence, at the extraordinary fact of its emptiness. The spread heart of Antarctica was staked out beneath a merciless sky. The ice seemed to bear up that sky, cradling its weight with the broadest of palms. Comparative theologians tell us that most human societies start out with a masculine sky-god, a stern patriarch who glowers from on high, holding humanity at his pleasure. The Greeks castrated theirs, Ouranos, and threw in their lot with Apollo and Aphrodite. But gods of the earth and the seasons make little sense at 75° South. Beneath an Antarctic sky I felt the need to restore Ouranos, to beg for his protection.

The air here was a lens, a dense layer along the horizon transformed and folded the light into mirages. Icebergs glimpsed in the distance yawned and stretched skywards, their brittle granular structures rendered malleable by the light and moulded by thermal layers. Their sheer blank faces peeped around the curvature of the earth. Above my head the sun was centred within a great halo of light. The area inside the halo was darker than its surroundings, shaded like an iris glancing from heaven. That eye swivelled a circuit of the horizon through the twenty-four-hour clock, as if policing the sky. At each cardinal point of the halo, a shard of brighter light could often be seen splintered from the sun itself: a parhelion or 'sun-dog', a phenomenon of such miraculous and beautiful generosity that the earliest Arctic explorers took it as a gift from God.

From the Riiser-Larsen Ice Shelf to Halley there are few places at which a ship can stop and moor. At one point the seabed rises beneath the shelf, a nose of the earth tents up the shroud of ice into the Lydden Ice Rise. The shelf bulges to the south of it as an ice stream pours out to sea, the Stancomb-Wills Glacier, then narrows in again and gathers a new name, the Brunt. Within the Brunt another rise in the seabed noses up the McDonald Ice Rumples. The ripples and cracks in the ice shelf caused by this rise are the reason why ships can moor by the Brunt, and the reason why it was chosen as the site for Halley Base. Sea ice fills the cracks, allowing relatively sheltered harbours for 4,000-tonne vessels like the *Shackleton*, as well as a stable platform for emperor penguins to breed on. The cracks fill with drifted snow that compacts to ramps. These ramps are the means by which vehicles can pull cargo between the sea ice and the base, which lies twelve kilometres inland on the shelf ice that pours off the continent. And so it is that the cracks caused by the Rumples have brought penguins and humans to the same stretch of coast.

Surgeon Commodore David Dalgliesh chose the position for Halley Base in 1956. He was its first base commander, but his curriculum vitae also included deputy medical director of the Royal Navy, stevedore, dog-handler, cook, Queen's physician, horti-culturalist and chorister. When I met him he was seated among the rose beds of his Devonshire garden. 'It was just a shell when we bought this,' he said, waving a hand towards the cottage behind him. 'The gable end was built by some Danish Viking. I think it's in the Domesday Book.' His face was tired and lined, but a spark of irony still gleamed at the corner of his eye.

I had gone to see him to ask advice about living at Halley. Dalgliesh had founded the base as the commander of the Royal Society's Antarctic contribution to the International Geophysical Year of 1957–8. Governments all over the world were pouring money into supporting observation stations. It was hoped that simultaneous meteorological, geological and astronomical data from sites all over the planet could give humanity a unique snapshot of its workings.

'Best advice I can give you is to choose your own men,' he told me. 'I wasn't allowed to, and ended up with a couple of real troublemakers.' I stammered that I too would be unlikely to get the chance to choose my own men. 'Too bad,' he said. 'Once the bad apples are in there it's jolly difficult to get them out.'

Dalgliesh had orders to put his base along the Caird Coast south of 75°, towards Vahsel Bay on the Filchner Ice Shelf.

'We got as far as 76½° but couldn't go on through heavy ice,' he told me. 'The place where you are going was the only bit where we could actually drive the tractors up on to the ice shelf . . . I believe they found out later that it was one of the best places in the world to observe the aurora.' He sniffed, with just a hint of pride. 'But of course I had no idea of that at the time.'

His wife Cally hovered in the background; Dalgliesh was elderly now and she was careful of his rest. She, on the other hand, had energy to spare and bounced back and forth between the house and the garden. 'I must show you something,' she called out from the doorway. 'And would you like a cup of tea?' Together with their daughter the couple had not long returned from a nostalgic trip to Greenland. Dalgliesh had gone there in the 1950s to select the huskies to take to Halley. He had loved Greenland, had relished the chance to see it again. A tenth the size of Antarctica, visiting Greenland is the next best thing to visiting the southern continent itself – and for Europeans at least a great deal more accessible. She brought out a photograph album thick with ice caps, mountains, icebergs. Descendants of the dogs Dalgliesh had chosen had gone on living and working at Halley until 1980. 'Just with milk in a mug, I take it?' she asked. 'A mug of builder's tea?'

Dalgliesh had been to the Antarctic before, as medical officer at Stonington Island in the late 1940s. He had wintered under canvas with Bernard Stonehouse at the Dion Islets emperor rookery. In a memoir he wrote on his return in 1950, later published in a hospital journal, he describes how he was drafted into the expedition. 'At the Admiralty, I asked somewhat idly, whether any expeditions went anywhere nowadays, and was told, to my eternal surprise, "Yes, an expedition want a doctor to go to the Antarctic in 14 days' time – would you like to go?"'

He was supposed to be back the following year, but the relief ship couldn't get through the ice. They were all trapped for another winter. Dalgliesh knew the importance of personal space – before leaving for the Dion Islets he prescribed a separate room for the men who faced their third consecutive winter, and honed his carpentry skills in order to build it. 'We dubbed it the first-class compartment,' wrote Stonehouse later, 'where anyone who felt the strain of our crowded quarters could retire and just be quiet for a time.' Of the emperors at Dion Islets Dalgliesh wrote 'how strange it was to find such colourful birds among the snow. They are rightly named Emperors, possessing a natural grace and dignity.'

'Did you manage to spend much time with the emperors at Halley?' I asked him. Cally had arrived with the tea, and set it down steaming on the bench beside me.

'Oh yes,' he said, 'we were only a mile back from the sea ice then. Make sure you try Emperor Egg Omelette.' He chuckled at the memory, 'One egg will feed three hungry men!'

By his retirement Dalgliesh had had a medical career that spanned the globe, and he told me a potted summary: medical officer on the Royal Yacht *Britannia*, then posted to Hong Kong, later promoted to fleet medical officer in Singapore.

'How does Antarctica compare with all those exotic postings?' I asked him.

'Compare? Well . . .' he said, pausing for a moment. 'Let me put it this way, if I was feeling a bit fitter I wouldn't mind going down there with you.'

It was Christmas Eve when we cruised up to the 'creeks' of the Brunt, the cracks at which Dalgliesh had unloaded his tractors. A crowd of us stood out on the fo'c'sle singing Christmas carols in the evening sunlight, complete with Santa hats and reindeer antlers. The sky was a depthless blue cupola, the ice threw off a lacquered white sheen. I was belting out 'Hark the Herald Angels Sing' when, looking over the gunwale, I saw my first emperor penguin.

There are many ways in which we can make first encounters

in the natural world. Keen ornithologists, desperate to see an emperor, had told me they had been alerted to the moment by tannoy: 'Penguin alert! Penguin alert!' as they and their fellow passengers rush to the rails to see an indistinct black shape in the water race away from them. I have taken such cruises in the Arctic, where tannoys blare out polar bear alerts. But fortunately this time there was no fanfare, no race to the rails. A couple of my fellow carol singers leaned over and smiled. 'Look,' said one, 'an emperor penguin.' 'Looks a bit like a fat king penguin,' said another. A boisterous gaggle of adélie penguins were fussing in and out of the gelid soup at the edge of the sea ice. Behind them stood the emperor, chin held aloft in a suitably regal pose, as if watching the *Shackleton* pass by was just another boring but necessary inspection of the guard. I was captivated, as if in its own way it had turned out to welcome me to the Caird Coast.

Four able-bodied seamen were craned by cargo net down on to the ice, spadework saw four holes dug down to the toughest sea ice and a drill finished the job. Posts called 'dead men' were sunk about three metres deep; Immense ropes were pulled out by skidoos, then the ropes looped around the dead men. The *Shackleton* was fast to the ice, and we were just in time for Christmas.

The sea ice has been known to be four metres deep; we could have sunk the post-holes with high explosives instead of drills without damaging it. It had to be strong: over the next few days the *Shackleton* would unload 2,000 forty-five-gallon drums of aviation-grade kerosene on to the trailers of waiting snowcats. The ice would need to bear the weight of the snowcats, trailers and fuel without cracking.

In 1940, worried about being dragged into a European winter war, an American called N. Ernest Dorsey was asked to look into the logistics of taking an army out on ice. Dorsey worked for the American government's Bureau of Standards and Measures in Maryland, though he seems to have spent his days imagining tanks rolling over a frozen Danube. His book on the subject is considered a classic, and is often referred to by geochemists today.

Ice only two inches thick could, he reports, support 'a man or properly spaced infantry'. Doubling the thickness meant the ice could manage 'a horse and rider, and light guns'. At ten inches he felt more secure, it might support 'an army, an innumerable multitude', and at fifteen inches 'railroad trains and tracks'. Greater weights than this Dorsey did not contemplate, but he did comment on a report he had found, that at two-feet thick ice could withstand a train carriage full of passengers falling on to it from sixty feet, 'but not the engine'.

Normally on reaching Halley both ship and base swing into a frenetic period of unloading cargo, with every available hand working twelve-hour shifts through the twenty-four-hour sunlight until the ship is emptied and then reloaded with a year's worth of base waste. The captain had been in communication with the Halley Base commander up on the Brunt by VHF radio. Together they decided that Halley Relief could wait another day; Christmas Day would be a holiday.

Out on deck the carol singing continued, attended by an audience of adélies. The solitary emperor penguin strutted between them like a Shogun inspecting his infantry. Far across the sea ice, from the bottom of one of the ramps up on to the shelf, a few tiny figures dressed in orange padded boilersuits could be seen making their way towards the *Shackleton*. Twin-propeller aeroplanes from the Peninsula had already broken the winterers' isolation, but the planes had not brought any alcohol with them. The outgoing winterers were picking their way across the ice to meet their replacements, sit in the sauna (the *Shackleton* was built by Scandinavians, after all), and drink some fresh beer.

Up on the shelf, Christmas morning, and the wind was literally freezing. Gusts of it blew in from the South Pole, and ice began to form on my hair. The outgoing Zdoc, Lindsey Bone, came down to meet me on her skidoo. We had trained in the same class at medical school, but had not seen each other for years. She looked strong and fit, with sunburned cheeks and a rangy stride as she walked across the ice towards me. As she took off her hat I noticed that she'd shaved off her tawny hair. 'It's less itchy this way,' she said, rubbing her head by way of explanation, 'you know, under the hats.' I tried to divine something from her manner, something about the experience that awaited me and how best to meet the winter ahead. Though her movements were quick and energetic I saw that her eyes glazed over easily and at times she didn't finish her sentences. 'This place is amazing,' she said after a while, 'just amazing.'

'Any advice?' I asked.

'I've spent days deciding whether to give you loads of advice or none at all. I think I've decided for none at all, you've just got to live it yourself.'

I jumped nervously on to the back of her skidoo for a white-knuckle tour. It was my first trip up on the ice shelf and within minutes my cheek muscles locked solid, freezing my nervous smile to a rictus grin. I hoped everyone else felt like this when they first arrived in Antarctica. I wondered how I was going to survive a year in this place.

First impressions were of space, silence, cold, ice, flatness. The ice had a smell, like the purest, subtlest and most easily lost scent you might pick up from a cool mountain stream. A 360-degree horizon of whiteness, a polar desert, surrounded our skidoo. Lindsey called the plain of ice the 'bondoo', and looking more carefully I realised it was not entirely flat, but rolled with a gentle, marine undulation.

This year would offer me space and time in quantities that I could not yet fully imagine. A Mahabharata and Ramayana of time, I could read the epic stories of every great culture on earth if I chose. The year stood ahead of me like an abacus with 365 beads. There would be no locked doors, no keys to remember, no bills, no money. There was even a chef to prepare my meals. There would be no professional or intellectual challenges that I did not freely choose, only the social and emotional pressures of sardine-can living at the bottom of the world. And environmental challenges, I reminded myself – humans are tropical mammals. This environment will kill you if you're not careful.

We approached the base. Buildings at Halley face an unusual problem: the same snow accumulation that allowed the shelf to exist at all would bury any permanent structure within a year or two. As the explorer Richard Byrd observed, even the Empire State Building would be quickly buried by snowdrifts in the Antarctic. Architects had solved the paradox in two ways: by jacking buildings on legs, and by putting them on runners so that they could be periodically dragged up on to the surface of the steadily accumulating ice. This was the fifth Halley station on the Brunt. The previous four had all been left to get buried so that access into base was through hatches and tunnels, the entrances of which had to be extended to the new, and higher, snow surface every year. It worked fine for a decade or so, but the buckling weight of ice and the length of the access tunnels eventually made living conditions deplorable.

The main Laws building was of the kind that is jacked up annually. From a distance it resembled a box of Swan Vestas matches on stilts. I had seen the building in hundreds of photographs, ever since I first heard of the possibility of a job there. Now I climbed up to its front door, Royal Mail red, emblazoned with a 'Post Office' sign and the treaty-defying statement 'British Antarctic Territory'. A foot bar meant it could be opened with both hands full. I kicked it aside and walked in, marvelling at the width of the central corridor that ran the length of the platform, so spacious after the narrow warrens of the *Shackleton*. Stretching my arms out I could not reach the walls. Rooms were arranged to the left and right of this corridor. As I entered, a boot room for outdoor clothing and footwear was to the right, and the room housing the generators to the left. Further inside there were storerooms, kit rooms, a washing machine and tumble-dryer room, then a living room/bar area opposite a kitchen and dining room. Past the living and dining areas there was a library, photographic darkroom, minuscule gym, radio room, male and female toilets, then the doctor's surgery. Past all these (it was a long corridor) and separate from the rest of the base, was the sleeping area of 'pit-rooms', each with blackout blinds against the relentless glare outside. The rooms themselves were 3 m long by 1.8 m wide, no more than small cubicles, entirely filled by bunk beds and a wardrobe.

I had seen enough of the other bases now to know the format: greying institutional panelling, faded photographs of bearded men of decades past, walls shelved with videos and DVDs and the mandatory signed photograph of the Queen. We sat down to Christmas lunch under Her Majesty's gaze. Carol music wafted through from the bar. There were about thirty of us in the dining hall, the others were all still down at the ship. We had frozen turkey with reconstituted cranberry jelly, pulled crackers, groaned at the bad jokes that fell from them, and donned our party hats. Everyone tried hard not to think about our loved ones back home.

Later, from the radio room, I called Esa over the impossibly expensive US-maintained satellite phone. The line kept dropping, and I could barely hear her over the crackle and whine of interference. 'Describe it for me!' she said, her voice bouncing tens of thousands of miles through a matrix of satellites. I stuttered and hesitated, the line fell, and I couldn't make contact again. I was alone in the radio room with a hissing telephone handset, looking out of the window.

How to describe it? An empire of ice and of isolation, a limitless plain of brilliant white, a binary world of ice and sky. I could not yet fathom that it was a scene I would watch every day for a year. It was the earth as in Genesis, at the moment of 'Let there be light.' The line between ice and sky was so distinct that I saw it suddenly as if the thin skin of our atmosphere had been peeled away. Outer space began at the ice surface, and I felt as if Starbase Halley, hanging suspended off the bottom of our world, was orbiting through it. I might as well be an astronaut, I thought to myself, though an astronaut would have found it easier to get back home.

Boxing Day, and Halley Relief was underway. Eight snowcat vehicles, equivalent to 1,500 horses in terms of power, were pulling sledges loaded with fuel drums back and forwards between the base and the sea-ice beside the *Shackleton*. There were four 'sea-ice cats' and four 'shelf cats', the former pulling sledges across the sea ice and up the snow ramp to the shelf before uncoupling, the latter pulling sledges the twelve kilometres from the cliff edge to the base itself. Sea-ice cats were chosen for their escapability. They had sunroofs as escape hatches in case the vehicle broke through the ice and the driver had to make a quick exit. Two teams of mechanics worked shifts, welding broken chassis and coaxing tired engines. Most of the year the snowcats were stored on the ice under tarpaulins, but every Relief their Cummins diesel engines ran around the clock. For a week they were never allowed to get cold.

Radiating from the base were a series of lines of empty forty-five-gallon drums, routes that had been certified crevasse-free. They allowed safe travel and were guiding paths back to base in case of a blizzard. The snowcats and their sledges followed one drum line to the north, strung between the ship's mooring and the base. Another line went out west towards a headland over the sea ice where the emperors gather for winter. Another went out east to a tall four-kilometre marker, used by the base meteorologists to estimate visibility. A more broadly spaced line went east to a part of the ice shelf known as N9, where the shelf was low enough for the *Shackleton* to crane goods directly on to the Brunt. N9 was used only when there was no sea ice to work on, because of the distances the cargo would have to be hauled. In addition to these route markers a circular drum line lay at a one-kilometre radius from the Laws platform – all the buildings on base lay within its boundary.

At Halley the doctor is always allocated the pit-room through the wall from the surgery in an attempt to safeguard patient confidentiality. As long as Lindsey was still on base she would keep that room, so I shared another with a monosyllabic scientist who merely grunted 'I'll take the bottom bunk.' In the frantic buzz of the two-month Halley summer season, where everyone worked long hours by day and shared these tiny spaces by night, I knew I had to find a place outside to be silent.

I felt like a newly caged animal exploring the limits of its enclosure. My first evening at Halley I set off on foot to examine more closely the places that Lindsey, on her white-knuckle tour, had named in passing. The garage and the summer accommodation building lay to the north. Busy with vehicles and temporary staff, I realised both of them were best avoided. A service hut for the aeroplane landing ski-way lay beyond them, and was also busy. To the east and south were the Simpson and Piggott platforms, miniature versions of the main Laws platform, which dealt with meteorology and atmospheric science respectively. Scientists and support staff came and went from them day and night, and I left them well alone. To the south-east a new laboratory was being built, for air sampling. Visiting the sector was discouraged in case of contaminating some of the cleanest air on earth as it blew in from the Pole. I tramped out to the south-west, towards a promising little red and white striped hut at the furthest limit of the perimeter. 'What's that called?' I had asked one of the previous year's winterers.

'The Optical Caboose,' I was told.

'And what does it do?'

'In the winter it takes pictures of the auroras, and snapshots of the upper atmosphere.'

'Is it doing anything now?' I asked.

'Don't think so,' she said.

No ongoing science, no vehicles in the area, no machines to disrupt, the Optical Caboose was perfect for my needs. Most of the huts at Halley were known as cabooses, a North American word once intended for the last carriage of a freight train, where a crew might sleep and prepare meals. Brought into Antarctic vocabulary a caboose was usually a small mobile hut, a place to get away from base, from noise and clatter, from the pressures and demands of close-knit communal living. The chatter of base was constant, both indoors and outdoors. Like all the others I wore a VHF radio harnessed to my chest, tuned to channel 6, and the banter between snowcats, mechanics, ship and base formed a constant background murmur to the day.

It was 11 p.m. when I reached the Optical Caboose, longitudinal midnight. Skiing out to it I had been circled by a Wilson's storm petrel, a tiny brown and white bird with wing-beats like a butterfly's, more used to the waves and gales of the Southern Ocean than an endless desert of ice. Maybe it had had enough of storms, and I was glad of its company. The sun hung over the South Pole, still high enough that there was no blush on the clouds. I climbed up the metal steps of the caboose and sat outside the door, facing towards the sun. From the Laws no one could see me. The petrel fluttered back towards the coast. A sigh of wind blew against my face, the breath of a continent. I switched off my radio and let the silence close in.

\*   \*   \*

Of all the outgoing personnel on base, the doctor had the least time to hand over. As soon as Relief was over, less than a week away, the ship would leave for the Falklands and Lindsey would leave with it. It would return in about six weeks to bring the last pieces of cargo before winter, and take all the summer personnel away again. There were sixty of us on base now – when the ship left for the second time it would leave only fourteen. The sea would freeze over and we would be isolated for about ten months. No one would be getting in or out until the planes and the ship came back the following summer.

Among the forty or so who came for the summer there were scientists, steel erectors, plumbers, aeroplane mechanics, mast engineers, crane drivers, even an extra couple of chefs. Most of them stayed over on a separate summer accommodation building called The Drewry. The steel erectors were good company – a gang of Geordies, many had given up well-paid work to come here just to have the chance to see Antarctica, albeit from the top of a scaffold or a crane. I spent an afternoon with one of them – nicknamed 'Dad' in honour of his four kids – up a ladder. As we jacked the legs of the Laws he told me about how each of them was doing at school, and how proud he was of his wife, back home holding the fort. It was the first Christmas he'd missed, but gesturing out towards the South Pole he said, 'But my wife knew I just had to see this.' Many of the others had a similar perspective, a deep gratitude to have had the chance to see a place that no amount of money could have arranged for them to visit. Another was a sculptor in steel in his spare time back home. 'I never thought I'd have the chance,' he said to me one day as he gazed out over the ice towards the Pole. 'I honestly never thought I'd manage to make it down here.'

Outside the medical-room window the depot lines lengthened as the snowcats switched from bringing cargo to sledges of fuel drums. Lindsey and I picked up medical supplies as they arrived on the depot line and prepared field medical boxes for the staff who would spend the six-week summer out on the ice, 'deep field', doing research. She showed me the emergency supplies secreted around base, contingencies in case the main platform burned down. We pulled out and assembled every type of stretcher, splint and machine hidden in the medical-room cupboards. There was a guide to penguin taxidermy and a neurosurgical drill pack. There was an antediluvian X-ray machine which, with a high-pitched whine, turned megawatts of electricity into radiation. We took experimental films of one another's hands and developed them in the custom-built darkroom (on the *Shackleton* I had had to develop X-rays in the bath). One of my most regular tasks would be to perform dental checks, and, considering the amount of chocolate consumed at Halley, I knew it wouldn't be long until I had the chance to try out the drilling and filling equipment.

Some of the material in Halley's medical room had been there since the base's inception and I found the confidential medical reports, one for every year since the base was founded. Picking two reports at random I read an opening line: 'Something is rotten in the state of Denmark.' The next was no better, describing plummeting morale on base over the course of the winter, the formation of factions, the breakdown of social cohesion, the dwindling mental health of individual base members. Another described how a wintering team had become so disenfranchised and irritated by orders from HQ that when the relief ship arrived, they refused to go down to the coast to meet it. I closed the report and decided not to look at any more until my year was complete. I realised now why some Antarctic programmes do not allow new staff to meet any of the outgoing winterers.

Glancing at these reports reinforced to me how doctors in Antarctica have an unusual mixture of responsibilities. They monitor the physical and mental health of personnel, the safety of the base environment itself, train individuals in first aid, plan for medical emergencies and major incidents, and are available at short notice to deal with injury or illness. Perhaps most importantly they should stay out of cliques, be accessible to all, and maintain absolute confidentiality within the tiny community. His or her role might be pharmacist, counsellor, dentist, anaesthetist, neurosurgeon, radiologist, and in my case, bin man and aeroplane assistant. The doctor has a direct line to HQ so that even the health of the base commander can be discussed in confidence. German bases avoid this potential conflict by making their doctors double as base commanders, but the British, whose Antarctic programmes originated as naval expeditions, have always preferred to keep the two roles separate. To be both might prove too much responsibility for one individual, or that individual might turn out to be untrustworthy.

By New Year's Eve we were all back on to twelve-hour day shifts. Relief was almost over. For our party we lit a barbecue on the Laws platform. Midnight came and went but the sun wheeled through the sky regardless. Concepts of day or night, one year or the next, had no meaning in this place.

Lindsey would be leaving the following day, and had already moved her luggage down to the ship. I asked her for some last nuggets of advice, and she relented a little from her original line. 'Just enjoy yourself,' she said, 'sometimes it will be hard, and seem long, but before you know it you'll be sitting where I am and handing it all over to some other doc.'

'Anything else?'

'This place is like a gift,' she said, 'a unique gift that hardly anyone has been given. The feel of the ice under your feet when you walk out into the stillness, there's nothing else like it. Try not to forget that.'

That night I moved my bags into the doctor's pit-room, glad to have a space of my own again. The year stretched ahead but it felt a relief to be into the next stage, to become Zdoc at last. And soon I'd get the chance to see the emperors.

For the humans in Antarctica, as well as for the penguins, summer is a time of preparation. Penguins too spend their time laying up stores and on the all-important job of maintenance – feather maintenance. While moulting they cannot swim or hunt, and so for over a month they fast until the process is complete. A gregarious species who feed, travel, breed and incubate in gangs, the summer moult is their annual solitary retreat, their forty days in the desert. It is not known whether they feel their conscious state alter, whether they feel themselves closer to their penguin god after the ordeal.

The moult seems to be triggered by a drop in activity in the 'third eye', the pineal gland that lies between the two hemispheres of the brain. The pineal still carries traces of sensitivity to light; in some very primitive species it may respond to light that filters on to it through the head. But in penguins, as in humans, it senses ambient light via neurons derailed from the retina. Antarctic summers do not offer much darkness, and over-exposure of the pineal gland must be involved in some way with triggering the summer moult.

Other factors must be thrown into the mix. They are not able to find food for their chicks, and so the chicks must be fledged and fending for themselves. As well as the pineal, the thyroid gland too is important. Once the bird is ready to moult, the thyroid glands (there are two in birds) start to swell, taking in iodine and pumping out thyroxine hormone. Body metabolic rate starts to rise. A transformation turns fish meal to feathers, the energy required supplied by burning off newly laid reserves of fat. At the peak of the moult a 30 kg penguin can lose a kilogram of fat a day. The emperor penguin has the highest density of feathers of any species, one hundred per square inch. In order to maximise insulation against the cold the new feathers are formed while the old are still attached. It is an annual transformation that we humans, with our naked, continually renewing skin, cannot imagine.

Not all emperor penguins choose a lonely retreat. At Halley, a solitary emperor chose to moult behind the garage. It must have climbed a ramp from the sea ice and followed a drum line to the base. Every day I skied over to sit with it, watching it pick out the old feathers that clung to it like lint on a jumper, preening the new ones to a slick gleam with oil from a gland at the base of its tail. A glorious lustre came over it. The grey-blue-black of its back and flippers developed a glossy vinyl sheen. A saffron tint edged into the feathers of its breast. It was oblivious to the snowcats, skidoos, mobile cranes and bulldozers that threatened its tranquillity. Standing its ground outside the garage it got on with the business of making new feathers.

# CHAPTER FIVE

# High Days and Holidays

> The majority of fieldwork is also restricted to the summer
> months of comparative warmth and long daylength . . . blizzards
> still have to be endured and the weather often limits what can
> be accomplished.
>
> BAS Staff Handbook

There was much work to do. Each of the marker drums on the
lines radiating from base had to be raised on to the new snow
level. Waste had to be collected and packaged ready to go on to
the ship at its final call. Old depots of fuel drums buried in the
ice had to be shattered out by sledgehammer and crane. Vehicles
had to be maintained. Tunnels for plumbing and wiring, now
buried twenty metres beneath the surface, had to be serviced and
access shafts raised. Buildings and masts had to be jacked, new
guiding hand lines had to be set, and every day vast amounts of
snow had to be shovelled down a chute into the 'melt tank', from
which we took all our drinking and washing water. And science
projects of course, the reason why we were all supposed to be
there in the first place, had to be worked on. 'Recreation' time was
brief, and events were strictly timetabled – lubricated by a
maximum of two beers per individual per evening – a rule enforced
for the whole of the summer period. Every night a pool champi-
onship progressed in the bar, which came to be dominated by the
steel erectors and a couple of mast engineers from the RAF. One
weekend a football pitch was bulldozed out on the ice west of the
Laws, and on another a stunt skidoo track, complete with ramps

and skid-ways, was thrashed out. It was after the stunt-track weekend that someone wrote 'Danger Doc' on my skidoo. I had been allocated one of the fastest and newest models, but after my stunt-track accidents a limiter was placed on the accelerator.

The doctor is the only base member who officially has nothing to do; I had only to be available in case of an accident. Having nothing to do meant I could get involved in all of the above, and more. But being 'available' at short notice meant I was often called down to the ski-way to work with the aircraft. Two twin-propeller Twin Otter aircraft were based at Halley for the two-month summer period. Their wheels were covered by landing skis, meaning that they could take off and land anywhere on the continent if the ice was smooth enough. They supported scientists on deep-field projects, took maintenance staff out to automated weather stations, and restocked remote fuel depots. Each time a plane took off or landed I had to be present at the ski-way, a fire extinguisher trailer hitched to my skidoo, then handle all the cargo and refuelling.

Two of the air mechanics seconded from the RAF were my guides. Like the many other military and ex-military people working for BAS they were glad to be sent to the Antarctic instead of to a war zone. BAS had just enough of a hierarchical, institutional air about it to appeal to them, without the discipline and danger of a military deployment. In the bar they were glad to show off the pool skills they'd honed in the likes of Mount Pleasant, Bagram and Basra.

Both of them told me to make sure I got up in one of the planes. The pilots flew single-handed but always wanted a 'co-pilot' to help them with loading fuel and unloading cargo when they reached their destination. Often they had to refuel from old depots deep into the heart of the continent. An extra pair of hands to dig out fuel drums, which were often encased in ice, was always appreciated. Air safety rules meant they were supposed to fly with someone else who could shut off the fuel supply should the pilot collapse or become incapacitated. How you were supposed to land the plane on your own was never mentioned.

Only the rich, the dedicated or the lucky have the pleasure of taking off into flight from their own backyard, of seeing the familiar landmarks of home dwindle in size and be absorbed into a landscape whose immensity and continuity can only be appreciated from the air. A co-pilot trip to our nearest neighbour to the east, the German base of Neumayer 1,200 kilometres away, was awarded to one of the meteorologists who had already been on base for a year. A much rarer trip to the American station at the South Pole was given to one of the permanent scientists, a man who had been coming to Antarctica every summer for decades. I had befriended Lez, the pilot, and indicated to him how keen I was to get up in the air. Lez was a taciturn, easy-going giant with a bear-paw grip and a scar like an apostrophe at the edge of his lip. He spent his austral summers flying in the Antarctic and his northern summers crop-spraying from the air in Holland. As a life, it seemed to suit him. Pilots in Antarctica, no matter their views or their manners, are always very popular members of base – it's up to them who flies as co-pilot.

The next flight was to pick up samples at the deep-field ice-core drilling station on Berkner Island, 650 kilometres to the west. When a couple of the scientists there mentioned on the radio that they were developing a skin rash I had my chance; all the way to Berkner Island for a couple of five-minute consultations.

We took off towards the east, looping over the base in a lazy skyward spiral. I watched the Laws platform shrink to a tiny brick of Lego, tossed out on the ice rink of the Brunt. We followed the cliffs of the ice shelf as they cut away south. An indentation in the coast formed the bight known as Precious Bay. The shelf looked so fragile, precariously thin as it crept out into the great vortex of the Weddell at a speed of two metres a day. It looked as if the mildest of winds could snap it off and send it floating northwards. The icebergs that stood grounded in the bay shone an iridescent blue beneath the surface, as if lit from below. Antarctic petrels whirled around the peaks of the bergs. We wore headphones, and a voice-activated microphone was positioned over my lips. 'Push this button if you want to speak to me,' Lez had said, 'but if you push the other one you're speaking to the world. It transmits on short-wave radio.'

We flew in silence over the icebergs and followed the coastline of Coats Land, south-west towards the Filchner Ice Shelf. The whiteness below us was streaked in a wash, like a poorly-applied emulsion slapped on blue glass. After a couple of hours' flying he asked me to look down. There, lost in a turmoil of ridged and fissured ice, were some smudges of black. 'Solid rock,' he said. 'Nunataks coming up through the ice sheet.'

'And there's something red down there.'

'Belgrano, the Argentinian base,' he said. 'They're your closest neighbours. Why don't we go down and see if there is anyone home.' He swooped lower to take a closer look. No calls came up on the radio, and there were no tracks in the snow outside the base. A couple of red huts with black roofs were clustered round a collection of masts and dish antennae. There was no landing strip. It did not look like an easy place to reach, perched on a frozen rock and surrounded by crevasses.

'It's only soldiers that they put there,' Lez told me, 'and they relieve it by helicopter. An Argentine ice-breaker gets as close as it can and then they fly people and food in and people and waste out. I saw them relieve it once in late February as we were getting the hell out, sea ice forming all around them. Brave lads.'

'So why do you think no one is at home?' I asked him.

'Big economic problems in Argentina right now,' he said. 'Last year I heard that the Argentinians asked the British to come down and take out their men. Must have hurt them, coming asking the Brits for help after all their squabbles in this part of the world. Logistics department said they'd do it, for a price, but we never heard any more. Price must have been too steep. I wonder how they got them out in the end.'

I looked down at the base. It was nestled in below a curved ridge, and must have stood in shadow much of the time. It was a couple of degrees further south than Halley, nearly 78° South, and being up on a nunatak must be colder too. It did not seem like a good place to get trapped for an extra year.

'So we've got no neighbours this year?' I asked him.

'Doesn't look like it. But then you never know, they may fly them in at the last minute.'

Lez told me a story of just how difficult life in Belgrano could become. Like the mad Persian Cambyses marching his troops into oblivion, one of the Argentinian commanders once announced

his intention to march south from Belgrano. They would fill a
snowcat with provisions, hitch a sledge full of fuel, and drive to
the South Pole. The journey was breathtakingly dangerous, the
base itself is surrounded by crevasses and they would have to travel
over 1,000 miles with no support or backup. 'Did they make it?'
I asked Lez.

'They made it all right,' he said, 'but I'm not sure whether they
managed to get back.'

The project at Berkner we were flying to meet was a joint French–
British expedition to drill a core deep into the mantle of ice that
rolls over the submerged island. The ice was a kilometre thick.
The cores would be packaged up and flown out to Halley, then
dragged to the *Shackleton*'s freezers and taken back to Cambridge
for analysis. Tiny bubbles trapped in the ice would be analysed
for evidence of the earth's atmospheric make-up centuries ago.
Layers of ice patterns would give hints of previous fluctuations in
global climate.

My guide around the base was Genviève, one of the laboratory
scientists who worked handling the ice. Her work had given her
an exaggerated sense of attention to detail, and she was fanatical
about avoiding contamination of the ice. She had very delicate
hands, and wore a patterned woolly hat with a pompom more
suited to the pistes of Val d'Isère than this frozen world. I pointed
at one of the ice cores, stored in a long grey plastic tube. 'So the
ice in that tube there,' I asked, 'when did it fall as snow?'

'Oh that one?' she sniffed, 'That one is pretty shallow. Maybe
about the time of the Hundred Years War.'

Berkner Island had been gradually buried in the ice that flows
from the hub of the continent out towards the Weddell. It divides
a colossal ice shelf, a 'barrier', into two: the Ronne to the west,
and the Filchner to the east. The 'island' itself was a 200-mile
double hump that pushed up the ice of these shelves in a smooth
undulation. Drilling camps had been established on both the North
Dome and the South Dome in the past. Different climate models
could not agree on whether the island had even been covered in
ice before the last ice age. Whether it was or was not covered had
implications for models of past sea level worldwide, and so it was

decided that, despite the logistical difficulties involved, drilling to the bottom of Berkner would give the answers to a few important questions. The South Dome, at 79° 32′ South, was agreed to be the best one to drill into and these scientists, led by Rob Mulvaney of BAS, were going to try to drill right to the bedrock.

A French tricolour flapped alongside a Union Jack. Around the flags were arrayed a series of pyramid tents, basic accommodation for a long summer whose design has not changed in a century of Antarctic exploration. Off to one side stood the 'drilling tent', a plastic half-moon like a gardener's polytunnel that we entered through a passageway burrowed down beneath the ice surface.

Inside was a grotto of transcendent blue. The low roof of the tent now stood high above us like an arched ceiling. A wooden trapdoor in the floor pulled aside to reveal ice-cut steps descending even further into a sanctum, a holy of holies. A hushed reverence came over the drilling team as we approached the core itself. At the bottom was a hole, not much wider than a drainpipe, and the drill that would reach down a kilometre suspended within it.

They would spend three more summer seasons here, flying in each December from Rothera, on the Peninsula. 'How old do you think the ice is at the bottom?' I asked Genviève.

'Current models put it at about 30,000 years old,' she said. 'We'll just have to see when we get there.'*

For our 'tour' there was not much else to see. The overcast sky gave no contrast to the ice, and there were no markers to give it depth. There was no horizon. An oil drum left out on the bondoo could have been a tin can, it was impossible to gauge distance. Being on the South Dome of Berkner Island was like being inside a cloud, or in some dream-like realm where the rules of perspective were suspended. There was a palpable sense of unreality. I asked how she managed to fill the long evenings and light nights when she was not at work. 'Well we eat a lot of chocolate,' she said, 'and play a lot of cards.'

If ice and silence were what I was looking for, a *tabula rasa* to play out all my thoughts, memories, ideas and ambitions, then

---

* They did reach the bottom, two years later, and estimated the ice there at 140,000 years old.

there could be no better place in which to do it. A year on Berkner South Dome would certainly offer little in the way of distraction. I wondered if Halley was really so different, a flat ice shelf with only the hint of a continent rising to the south, mirages of icebergs occasionally in the north. But then Halley has the emperors, I reminded myself. Without the companionship of at least one other species I might become completely unmoored.

It was a three-hour flight back to the Brunt, cruising at 150 miles per hour. We flew at 7,000 feet, the wings of the aircraft like knives being honed on the undersides of the clouds. There were breaks in its canopy which dappled the light as it shone through on to the plains of ice below. I had the sensation that we were flying underwater; in the cloud canopy were the waves, and light was mottling the seabed beneath us. The Twin Otter cast a rainbow-haloed Glory on to the ice, the aviation equivalent of the Spectre of Brocken. It was a landscape without reference points: we could have been flying at 30,000 feet or skimming the surface for all there was a scale to it. The patterns of ice repeat themselves endlessly whether in the form of a snowflake or in an ice stream as wide as an ocean.

We approached the Brunt across Precious Bay. The folds and wrinkles of the Hinge Zone, the crease along which the Brunt joins the continent, looked close enough to touch though they were over fifty kilometres away. Lez swooped in low over the emperor rookery. Thousands of emperors! A lichen of black adults and grey fledglings stippled the ice. Over their heads I could see Halley in the distance, black angular shapes like letters on an empty page. I had a flash of horror, imagining the worst of the year ahead. The base was so fragile, so impossibly distant from the world that I knew, from safety. Dark wings of dread fluttered, threatening to unfold inside me. I wondered if in time the atmosphere on base would turn bitter and sour, and what I would do if I were to fall seriously ill – there was no one on base trained to look after me.

But then the shapes reformed themselves, gathered into the garage and the Laws platform, the mast array and the Optical Caboose. And I realised it was not just a blot on the whiteness, that it was part of a landscape that had contours and edges. The base was not just a collection of buildings on stilts but my home, a personalised space. Looking down I saw the hollow in the ice where I had spent an afternoon digging out a fuel depot, on the other side I saw the spot where I had helped the meteorologists release weather balloons. There were memories associated with the landscape already.

J. D. Salinger has one of his characters say that wherever we go in the course of our lives we move between different pieces of holy ground. It was an appealing philosophy, and following Salinger's logic I told myself that the Brunt Ice Shelf too must be holy ground. As we came in towards the landing strip the dread folded away and I thought that if I cannot bear the silence of this place, its emptiness and its distance from the people that I love, then I will have been unable to open myself to that vision.

The chicks of most penguin species hatch on the frozen graves of their predecessors. The dead carcasses of each generation are trampled into gravel, encased in ice through the winter, then a new layer is added the following year. Some chinstrap and adélie rookeries on the Peninsula are metres-thick with tarry strata of corpses and guano.

Emperors are the only species that hatch eggs on sea ice. Each summer that ice breaks out and floats north, where it will melt and merge with the enormity of the Southern Ocean. The summer storms wipe clean their memories; every year could be the colony's first. It was as if the further south I had travelled life had become increasingly forgetful, and became easier to renew.

Soon after the first relief a crowd of us prepared for our first holiday from work – a trip to visit the penguins. We wrapped up warm and climbed on to the sledge of a snowcat to be pulled down to the ice cliffs at the rookery. There was a penumbra around the sun, rainbows sparked from its edges like flint struck on steel. At the end of the drum line a caboose marked the abseil point from the cliffs down on to the sea ice. It was lipstick red, a welcome daub of colour against the relentless white. One by one we climbed off the sledge, laughing and joking together, convivial and excited. It could have been the Cairngorm Plateau in Scotland, not an ice shelf off the bottom of the world. In turn we roped up and approached the cliff edge. The ice of the cornice was curled and ornate, as if the Brunt was edged with Corinthian capitals. There was a tungsten brilliance about them, a splendid contrast against the iron sea and the dull water-sky to the north.

Towards the bottom of the cliffs massive ballasts of ice were crumpling with gentle dignity into the 'tide crack'. In places the crack seemed like solid ice, in others, open water. It was the hinge along which the relentless heave of the tide had pulled the sea ice away from cliffs. Ice caves at the cliff foot glowed ultramarine blue – they looked inviting but I knew them to be deadly. Fathom-long icicles hung from their mouths like fangs.

There was very little sea ice left. I abseiled down to a snow bridge over the crack, and unhitched from the rope. Scarlet guano like spat blood stained the snow, a sign that the emperors had been gorging on shoals of krill. Concentrated patches of it had melted the surface so that I walked not on flat ice but on a knee-high three-dimensional landscape of plateaux, valleys and sanguinary deltas. One pink-tinged area was melting down like gently deflating lungs. Further away from the cliffs there were bulbous pillars of yellowing ice, smooth as salt licks, vertical shards that had been broken by storms long past and refrozen into a new position. Sea ice that is fast to land is tapered, a subtle wedge at the shore, but here, moored only to ice shelf, the sea was wild and deep below me. I felt the water arching its back with the tide, straining against the thin glaze beneath my feet.

I had to watch my step; my clumsy boots were insulated with two-inch soles and a double foil and foam lining, but they gave no support to my ankles. They were 'mukluks', like 'caboose' a Canadian word transposed on to this continent without a history. The Canadian Inuit who first made mukluks used sealskin lined with duck down. They must have crept over the ice feeling every crack and ridge, while I felt as if I walked on stilts.

I stumbled on towards the colony. Chicks were crowded in gangs, unsure of themselves, but some of the 'crèches' no longer had a supervisory adult and soon their hunger would pull them out to sea. Embedded within the ice like nuts in toffee were the frozen bodies of those that had died of starvation and exposure.

Emperor penguin chicks make a high-pitched skirling cry, the timbre of which is unique for each chick. Its frequency climbs, falls and climbs again before petering out, a wolf whistle of desperation, of lust for food. I saw a lone chick, smaller than the rest, hunkered down in the snow. Its cry had shrunk to a tonal gasp, and spin-drifting snow had already begun to gather on it. I tried to see in its death a necessity, that the species could never have adapted so well to this environment without a selection pressure that allows only the fittest to survive. Antarctica first began to freeze over 30–40 million years ago, and one by one all the other species had left. Only the emperors, through their extraordinary adaptations, had managed to hold on through all those changes in climate.

I tried not to think too much about climate change at Halley. Perhaps some part of me didn't want to acknowledge that Antarctica was connected to the rest of the world, was in communion with it, or was in any way a victim of it. Perhaps I was in guilty denial over my small part in the tonnes of ship's fuel and generator kerosene we had burned to reach the continent and live there. One of the main purposes of Halley's research is to contribute to global climate models – we were there to study the very process that we might be contributing to. I tried to reassure myself that if I hadn't gone the fuel would have been burned anyway – a common enough excuse.

I walked past the dying chick, and left it to its fate. In only two epochs of the last 570 million years has there been a south polar ice cap. If current trends continue we seem to be losing ours again, and whether climate change is man-made or is part of a natural cycle will be irrelevant to the penguins. If Antarctica melts again sea levels worldwide will rise by sixty metres, inundating floodplains and swamping most of humanity's coastal cities (if any are left by then). While other Antarctic birds adapted to the chilling of the continent by leaving for the winter, only the emperor managed to survive this most recent period of glaciation. It would be bitter irony for the emperors, but nature has no favourites, if the very adaptations that allowed them to hold on are the same ones that might now lead to their extinction in a newer, rewarming Antarctic.

Almost a century before I arrived in Antarctica Ernest Shackleton's ship, the *Endurance*, had drifted helplessly past this same stretch of ice. The coastline would have been different then, the ice cliffs that now loomed over our penguin rookery would have been part of the shelf seventy or so kilometres inland. Emperors have a mean survival of about twenty years, though many are thought to live and breed up to the age of forty. It has been estimated that one per cent even reach the age of fifty. So it is conceivable that the grandparents and great-grandparents of at least some of the emperors around me saw the *Endurance* wheel past, or might once have been chased over the ice by Shackleton's men.

The biologist on the *Endurance* was a man called Clark, a humourless Aberdonian icthyologist who, as his ship was crushed, spent his time drilling holes and fishing for specimens. He had little interest in penguins, preferring them on his plate to the dissecting table. Of penguins, nothing he recorded has been preserved.

The captain, Frank Worsley, was more interested in penguins – perhaps they reminded him of his childhood in New Zealand. He marked penguin sightings in his notes on their route, the ones that survived the journey by sea ice, open boat, and foot across South Georgia. Devotees of the Shackleton cult can pay homage to copies of them at the Scott Polar Research Institute in Cambridge. But there are clues other than Worsley's notes of how close to the Brunt the *Endurance* came. Charlie Green, the expedition's cook, told Bernard Stonehouse that as the expedition wheeled south and west, caught in the Weddell ice, the men gorged themselves on emperor chicks in down. 'They have a better flavour,' he told Stonehouse, 'and more tender meat.' Charlie always weighed the chicks before putting them in the pot, and in that was a better ornithologist than Clark.

When I spoke with Bernard Stonehouse about the Brunt Ice Shelf he told me that not only Worsley's charts, but Charlie's stories told him just how close to the Brunt Shackleton's expedition must have come. The chicks in down that Charlie skinned for the pot could not have been more than a few kilometres from the rookery. Stonehouse had only met Charlie Green by chance – on his first return from the ice in 1950 his local newspaper in Hull had run a story about his adventure: his plane crash, walking to safety, his long winter with the emperors. Shortly afterwards he received a phone call: 'I was in the Antarctic . . . do you want to meet for a pint?' Charlie Green was living in Hull, and more than thirty years after the *Endurance* sank was still working as a ship's cook.

Frank Worsley had said of Charlie Green 'our sooty-faced cook was a marvel . . . his cheerful grin never deserted him'. Worsley also described how Charlie was one of Shackleton's favourites: 'Sir Ernest was the cook's protector,' he wrote, going on to discuss how Shackleton knew how closely his men's health and morale was related to the happiness of their stomachs.

'Don't just rely on official records when you're doing research,' Stonehouse told me, 'you'll miss valuable data.' Meeting Charlie himself allowed him to gather a new perspective on the *Endurance* expedition, and on Shackleton. 'He was really a rogue, a kind of pirate,' Stonehouse said, 'two or three generations earlier he would have been a pirate too.' By the 1940s the *Endurance* story had already been sanctified into a great British legend. 'Load of rubbish,' Charlie Green had said in that pub in Hull. 'It's just as well they never made it on to the continent, Shackleton would have had them all killed.' He explained that none of the leaders had any experience with sledge dogs, and that they spent the whole time arguing amongst themselves. 'Get one of them gentleman adventurers into the galley and you could still get some work done,' Charlie had said, 'but get two or three of them in there and they'd start arguing about the best way to chop an onion.'

The pilots were preparing for their long flight west across the Ronne and Filchner ice barriers, up the Peninsula to Rothera base, and then the job-of-a-lifetime 'ferry-flight' back up the long spine of the Americas. Like Antarctic terns the aeroplanes would summer all over again in the Arctic.

Lez asked if I would co-pilot for him on one last flight before he left. He wanted to leave fuel at a dump out on the ice in the deep south, fuel that could be located by pilots the following season. We would leave it next to an AGO, an automated geophysical observatory that would record climatic data through the winter.

From Halley we climbed over boisterous, pillow-fighting clouds that tumbled over one another as they rolled in from the sea. Once we had left them behind I looked down on the whorl of the north-flowing continental ice. The sky above was vast, curved, elemental, as if its light reflected from a polished axe.

The nose of the Twin Otter pointed south, the midday sun right behind us as if it was chasing us down to the Pole. I felt the enormity of the continent beneath us, how easily it could swallow me up. After three and a half hours flying over an immensity of nothing, Lez began studying the radar. The ice stretched on just as smoothly but on the screen appeared a little green spot, an aphid of light that began to swell. 'That's the AGO,' Lez said, 'right on target.' The wings spilled wind and we dropped closer to the bondoo. Lez had extraordinarily acute eyesight. 'See it yet?' he asked me.

And then I saw it with my own eyes, a solitary pixel of black on a white-out screen. He swooped lower, the skis hit the ice and the whole plane began to shudder. The rotors swivelled into a reverse corkscrew pulling us to a halt. Swivelling them back and pulling on the throttle Lez began to drive us bumpily towards the fuel dump and AGO. Its presence there seemed to defy the laws of logic, perspective and nature. It was absurd that a pile of fuel drums and electronic circuitry could exist out here, could be part of this great emptiness.

81° South, this was likely as close as I would get to the South Pole. The Pole itself still lay 600 miles over the southern horizon. I pulled off my headphones, waited for the nod from Lez, pushed open the aeroplane door and jumped out.

The ice beneath my boots was brittle and hard, like ceramic. It was not flat, it climbed towards the Pole on a gentle incline. The ridges and pits in it were deep and curved like giants' finger-prints. At my first inhalation I felt a tightening high in my nose. The purity, aridity and coldness of the air was freeze-drying my sinuses, and I switched to mouth breathing. Immediately the sensation moved to my lips, a bristling sensation as if the air was attaching itself there. I mentioned it to Lez. 'It happens at about minus 20°C,' he said. 'That feeling is going to get more and more familiar to you.' It is an old Renaissance idea that the soul of the body is most firmly attached at the lips, that on our death we might feel it pull away from us there. The air tugged at the moistness in my mouth and I wondered if this is how a detaching soul would feel.

I began to take great gulps of the air, trying to pull the cleanliness and purity down into me. But it caught at my throat, triggering spasms of coughing. 'Careful with that,' Lez laughed, 'some folks have been known to cough up blood if ice forms in their lungs.'

With snow shovels we started to dig out the fuel drums that had sunk into the ice. Spindrift and the melting of snow on their black metal surfaces meant that many were encased in thawed then refrozen ice, embedded as if set deep in a casket of glass. A sledgehammer was often more useful than the shovel, and as each drum shivered free of its shell of ice we rolled them up on to wooden planks to prevent them melting their way back under the surface. Finally there were the new drums to be rolled out of the Twin Otter and piled up by the old ones, and more fuel to be put into the plane.

As we sat on the drums Lez produced a flask of tea and opened a packet of chocolate biscuits. There was no other sound. The naturalist W. H. Hudson spent years in the nineteenth century exploring Patagonia, seeking untouched landscapes, for it was only in those that he felt he could find peace: 'To my mind there is nothing in life so delightful as that feeling of relief, of escape, and absolute freedom which one experiences in a vast solitude.' If he could feel it in Patagonia, I thought, how much more intensely would he have felt it here.

A breeze brushed my face, the lightest of winds yet it pricked my skin. When I breathed the air I felt it crackling in my chest, electric and alive. Our breath binds us to air, and through it I felt bound to everything that lives, though we were the only beings for hundreds of miles in any direction that drew breath.

\*    \*    \*

It was late February, and the planes had gone. We had been due one more plane visit from Rothera, but at the last minute it had been cancelled. It would be ten months before our next delivery of post.

At midnight the sun now dipped below the southern horizon. It was a relief to have a dusk, to see a warmth in the light, to have the ice flooded in lilac and crimson instead of that blasting relentless white. It was as if the furnace of summer, banking down for winter, was being reduced to an ember glow. The moon became clearer, a chalky moon of crisp, blue-grey craters and arid Latin seas. I had thrown a bag of mail into the back of the last plane to leave. The letters I had written would be flown via fuelling depots on the Ronne and Filchner shelves to Rothera, transferred to a Dash-7 plane for the Falklands, and then be flown to RAF Brize Norton via Ascension Island in the tropical Atlantic. If the mailbag was lucky it could be in Europe within four days.

I had received a phone call from my boss, crackling and stuttering over the satellite phone. 'You know, Gavin,' he said, 'we are always here on email. But now the planes have left we're not able to come and get you or anyone else out of there until next year. Any second thoughts?' But there were no second thoughts, just the gathering awareness that there might be a hard road ahead, a steeling of my nerve for whatever would come.

During an unexpected cold snap the sea began to freeze over. The crew of the *Shackleton* had returned from the Falklands, had loaded a year's worth of base waste, and were keen to head north before their ship became as trapped as its namesake's had been. Like the adélie penguins they were leaving for the sunnier north. On the back of a snowcat the fourteen of us who would stay for the winter went down to the edge of the Brunt to say goodbye.

Approaching the ice edge, I saw that all of the sea ice had blown out. The shelf ice ended abruptly, the frozen sea surface had snapped off entirely along the line where the rise and fall of the tide had cracked a hinge. The *Shackleton*'s thrusters, designed to hold it close to a North Sea oil rig in a storm, held it snug to the bottom of the amputated snow ramp. The last of the summerers were craned on to the deck by cargo net. Graeme, the ship's third engineer, had been persuaded to stay on as our generator mechanic. The other engineers stood on the afterdeck jeering at him.

The hum of the thrusters changed key and the *Shackleton* began to creep northwards through an archipelago of icebergs. We stood at the edge of the continent lighting old distress flares and waving them in broad arcs at arm's length. They billowed purple smoke, burnishing our faces and the ice around us in flame-bursts of lilac and magenta. As the ship dwindled in size we could hear the shouts of the summerers on deck fading until, finally, we stood alone on the ice.

People have asked me how it felt to watch the only means of escape disappear over the horizon. For me there was a great sense of relief, that the isolation so long anticipated had begun. There was wonder in it, at the scale of the distances that would separate us from other humans, and from society. My perspective took flight, lifting above our huddled group at the brink of the ice and up into the atmosphere, astonished at the height it would reach before it could see another mark made by humans. There was an eagerness about the space and silence that would flood my life, the unbounded gift of time. But there was also an element of anxiety, a tense, dry feeling that fluttered in my gut like a trapped moth.

There was trepidation that all would not go well with our little community; that anger, irritation and claustrophobia would creep in and make a prison of this ice.

Ben, the vehicle mechanic, drove us back to the base. We sat side by side on a snowcat sledge, bumping over sastrugi, a nervous cheerfulness in our voices. I climbed the steps to the Laws platform and once inside felt a new atmosphere in the place that I did not recognise. It was silent. For two months there had been projects and logistics, work parties signing in and out day and night as they came and went from the platform. Now there was no one else and our voices echoed from the panelled walls. A few of us went into the dining room and rearranged the tables. It was BAS policy or tradition, no one was sure which, that the wintering party must always eat together in a circle. I took my place there thinking of the 300 breakfasts, lunches, dinners that were ahead of me. Out of the window opposite I could see two tones of white split by the eastern horizon, the expanse of ice mirrored in the cloud-sheeted sky. The terrestrial and the celestial were, on that day, a perfect reflection of one another. It was a world of the infinite, the extreme, and in many ways the very simple. And between these two vastnesses of ice and sky I felt the smallness of our base, the complexity of it, its irrelevance to this silent continent.

# AUTUMN

# CHAPTER SIX

# The Hinge of the Continent

There is, I feel sure, no region in the world more grand in
its scenery than the Antarctic, and no place more transcendent
in its beauty. It is a vast wonderland laid out on a giant scale.

R. N. Rudmose Brown, *The Voyage of the Scotia*

The first evening alone on the continent, we heated up the water
in the melt tank of the Drewry building to a luxuriant 40°, and
climbed in. It would be our last bath for over a year, the tank
wouldn't be needed until the following summer. Sweating in the
hot tub while a blizzard whipped up outside, our group struggled
towards a new dynamic. We began to reveal more about our pasts,
our personalities, our families, our reasons for being in this place.
But we did so warily – ten months is a long time to share a small
plywood box and no one wanted to leave themselves too vulnerable. We shared ourselves in careful and calculated ways, like
members at an Alcoholics Anonymous meeting where no one
wants to stand up first.

Of course we were not alone on the continent, but by midwinter
there would be only a few hundred other *Homo sapiens* on the
broad face of Antarctica. Many of these would be based at
McMurdo, the American super-station on the New Zealand side
of the continent which has over 1,000 residents in summer (with
ATMs, a bowling alley and the remains of a decommissioned
nuclear reactor). Many others would dwell in the constellation of
small bases scattered up the Peninsula. The landscape of the
Peninsula is dramatic, the winters are short, and some bases are

so close together that Antarcticans of different nationalities can visit one another. With Halley's plains of ice, our long winter and no possible visitors, we consoled ourselves that of the British, only we were experiencing 'the real Antarctic'. The others, we said privately and with just a hint of envy, were holidaymakers up in 'the banana belt'.

It is a well-documented paradox that people who apply to work in the Antarctic are often self-reliant independent-minded loners. They are attracted to the continent for the lure of extreme experiences, the appeal for which men supposedly responded to Shackleton's (sadly apocryphal) advertisement in *The Times*: 'Men wanted for hazardous journey. Small wages. Bitter cold. Long months of complete darkness. Constant danger. Safe return doubtful. Honour and recognition in case of success.' These individualists choose to place themselves in a situation of absolute interdependency on a team of others, of close-knit living in a place from which it is often impossible to leave. Being the leader, or manager, of a group like this carries particular challenges.

Shackleton's men, trapped off the Caird Coast, were in a double bind with regard to their leader. His timing was poor, perhaps the ice was worse the year they sailed south, but their incarceration could be blamed only on the one man who had the drive and energy to get them out – Shackleton himself. But he seems to have been a master manager of both difficult situations and of people. After the loss of the *Endurance*, group cohesion must have been under tremendous strain. Similar shipwrecks in the Arctic have seen the crew rapidly factionalise and turn against one another, but in account after account, the crew of the *Endurance* stuck behind their man. Even after all they had been through Shackleton was referred to as simply 'The Boss', and his word was final.

Several books have been written, and careers made, discussing Shackleton's style of leadership and the lessons that it may have for the rest of us. Other careers have been made trying to narrow down the qualities that make a good Antarctic winterer in today's modern, relatively safe and comfortable bases. American psychologists working for the US Navy calculated that industriousness, emotional stability and sociability are the ideal triumvirate of personality factors to see you through a winter. Until recently BAS were the only major national programme that used no psychological screening in their selection procedures, applications being based, as they were in Shackleton's day, on a medical examination and performance in an interview with a panel of 'old Antarctic hands'. Panellists have told me that their decision is made on a gut feeling – 'could I winter with this man?' They argue that this approach has served them well, but a recent study suggested that had they used psychological assessment questionnaires they would have a better chance of finding those who turn out to be rated 'exceptionally well adapted' to the Antarctic, and weeding out those who wouldn't cope. The study also found women cope better than men in the Antarctic, but are less likely to be selected.

Commanders of modern Antarctic bases do not face the challenges that men like Shackleton and Scott faced, but for all that seem more plagued with low morale. Maybe the relative safety is part of the problem – other studies have found that the more 'stressful' events a remote team endures, the lower the overall anxiety levels. Luckily for most commanders not every winterer expects a Shackleton to lead them, or anticipates a major life-threatening crisis. But to be a successful leader, to manage a team through the long months of a polar night, base commanders do well to take some hints from The Boss: be optimistic but realistic, help the struggling members of the team without singling them out, be friendly and available to everyone, allow complainers a voice but don't let them take over. And in the context of Halley, always, no matter the weather, take your turn to shovel snow into the melt tank.

There would be fourteen of us for this polar night, just short of a rugby team, but too many for football. We were a mixed bunch.

Ben, our vehicle mechanic, was an ex-paratrooper from the West Country with shoulders like a blacksmith's anvil. His training to jump out of aeroplanes in the dark holding a gun had given him an air of immense and unassailable calm. Nothing he could be asked to do in the Antarctic could be as difficult. He worked hard and drank harder than anyone else on base when the summer drinking rules were relaxed. When I arrived at Halley he was starting his second year without a break. In addition to his responsibilities as 'Zmech' he was also 'Zporn', meaning that the vast library of pornography accrued over decades as a male-only base was stored in his pit-room.

Stuart, one of the meteorologists, was an astronomer from London. He had worked at observatories in North America, Britain and Australia, and wanted to visit Antarctica though all Halley had was a broken old tripod telescope. He was the world authority on a revolving star that had no name, the peculiarities of which could be discussed only through the language of mathematics. I asked him why planets don't twinkle and he said, 'It's turbulence in the interstellar medium that causes twinkling.' After Halley he worked on satellite surveillance in Afghanistan.

Russ was the engineer who looked after the Advanced Ionospheric Sounder, or as he called it, 'The Beast'. This was a box of fragile and temperamental 1980s electronics designed to gather images of the state of the polar ionosphere. When it broke, which was often, an alarm would sound in the Laws platform and Russ would have to go over to an unheated caboose, whatever the time or weather, and fix it. He spoke with a deep Oxfordshire brogue, and was liked and respected by everyone. After two years at Halley he moved back to a house called World's End near Oxford and made parts for superconductors destined for the International Space Station.

Graeme was a marine engineer from Anstruther. He signed up for a six-week tour on the *Shackleton* and ended up in Halley for over two years as a generator mechanic, though he did any job that needed doing. He was open, guileless, loyal, versatile, and like Ben he worked very hard. He had spent years on tankers under flags of convenience, most of which he had hated, and had accumulated a vast knowledge of obscure Icelandic pop groups. Though he preferred life ashore he always called his room his 'cabin' and the kitchen 'the galley'. When Craig, the chef, made him a birthday meal he had deep-fried Mars bars.

Craig was a Yorkshireman on the move. He had been offered hotels and restaurants to run all over the world, but his restlessness dragged him on to increasingly bizarre catering opportunities. Halley was his oddest yet. Used to running hotel kitchens cooking for 200, he found preparing meals for fourteen laughably easy. His preparation for the day was always finished by 9 a.m., and he spent the rest of the day in the library, reading a book a day. Early on he had decided that Antarctica was too cold for him, and after arranging a complex swap for his melt-tank duty went for three months without stepping outside.

Mark Maltby was a physicist from Lincolnshire. Like Russ he maintained an experiment that studied the ionosphere, but looked at auroral activity. The Southern Hemisphere Auroral Radar Experiment sprayed high frequency radio waves across 4 million square kilometres of the Antarctic sky every two minutes, and broke down much less often than the AIS. After two and a half years at Halley, and another winter at Rothera, Mark felt the burden of being ice-bound beneath his radar array. On his final return from the Antarctic he sat his pilot's licence, and took to the skies.

Elaine, a meteorologist, had a Salty Aberdonian accent straight from Deeside fish market, and was into her second year at Halley. A glossary to her dialect was fixed to the wall of the bar ('Fa's dae'in Fit? = Who is doing What?') Weighing in at about forty kilos she struggled with the daily weather balloons and laboured more than most to get to the Simpson platform in a blizzard. She had got together with Ben the year before, effectively shielding herself from unwanted male attention.

Paul Torode, or as he preferred it, 'Toddy', was our resident mountaineer and a Channel Islander who spent his life trying to get higher, and colder. He moved in a blur of agitated energy, and harboured a useful mania for fixing and repairing things. He spent hours tinkering with the kit room's treadle sewing machine, or the cine-reel projector. About halfway through the year he also revealed he had two university degrees. As the man on whom we all depended for our safety when out on the ice he showed an obsessive tendency for gauging the weather and mapping crevasses. After Halley he went straight to a winter at Rothera, and on his return from the Antarctic he bought himself a chainsaw and disappeared into the Scottish mountains for long weeks of free-lance forestry. I could understand his yearning for trees.

Rob the plumber, the man on whom our vital heating system depended, had been parachuted in at the final call of the *Shackleton*.

Plumbers were earning such good money in Britain that no one had applied for the first round of interviews. On the question of why *he* had applied he was strangely silent, and it was rumoured (falsely, it turned out) that he was on the run from the law. As the only smoker on base Rob was condemned to stand outside several times a day in temperatures approaching 50° below zero just to have a cigarette. This probably meant he saw more auroras than the rest of us.

Pat the carpenter/builder had wintered before – he had been one of the team to build the Laws platform twelve or thirteen years earlier. His wintering team then were all tradesmen, and he told stories of drunken rages, chair-throwing fights, and multiple heating and lighting failures. It was astonishing that he had come back. It is a BAS tradition that one of the second-year winterers takes responsibility for being 'winter base commander', sworn in as a magistrate, opening the post office if visitors from other bases fly in, and responsible for communicating with HQ. None of them were keen to do it, and so Pat, having lived at Halley before, was promoted.

Annette, the third meteorologist, had arrived in the Antarctic fresh from Leicester where she had studied space science. She was an expert in astrophysics and had written a thesis on the spectacular subject of space weather. Halley is one of the world centres for measuring space weather, but she had somehow ended up getting a job measuring real weather instead. She was a voracious reader of science fiction and fantasy novels, and when I was looking for someone to come down to the penguins with me she would usually volunteer. She was on her second year of a two-year contract and her boyfriend, having done three winters at Halley, had left with the *Shackleton*'s second call. That both of the women on base were resolutely unavailable is likely to have neutralised a great many conflicts before they began.

Mark Stewart was the data manager and communications officer, which meant he was the only person on base capable of battling with the computer system, its tenuous satellite connection, and the gigabytes of data that flowed out of the science platforms every day. This would be his third winter at Halley. The American psychologists who insisted on sociability as an essential Antarctic survival skill would have thrown up their hands in despair at Mark, but on industriousness and emotional stability he would have had full marks. He was the only other winterer who went out every day, no matter the weather, and it was several months before we had a conversation.

Allan Thomas, or 'Tommo', was our ventripotent electrician, from Redcar near Middlesbrough. When I first met him, I said 'I'm Gavin, the doctor.' He said 'I'm Tommo, the hypochondriac.' The only way to tell when he was drunk was to count how many times he pushed his spectacles up his nose. Soon after his arrival he put up a poster of fluffy kittens in the pit-room corridor with the legend: 'Every time you masturbate God kills a kitten.' He stayed on in Halley two years, then wintered at two more bases before going home. Of the fourteen of us, the American psychologists would have been happiest with him.

When I got home from Halley the vogue for reality television, where a group of conflicting characters is forced into a house and recorded night and day, was gathering pace. Having lived it, I saw little entertainment in watching it second-hand.

The prophet Jeremiah knew that birds come and go with the seasons. In Chapter 8, Verse 7, he wrote 'the stork in the heaven knoweth her appointed times; and the turtle and the crane and the swallow observe the time of their coming'. Pliny the Elder, who was ten years old when Jesus of Nazareth died, was not so observant. He believed that most birds hid in the ground for the winter. Wheatears, he said, wait for 'the rising of Sirius' before finding a suitable hole and creeping into it. He probably lifted this idea directly from Aristotle, who knew of migration but believed that as well as flying to another country and hiding in holes many birds changed form between summer and winter. The robin and the redstart, for example, he believed to be one and the same species in alternate forms. Pliny and Aristotle were not alone: the annual appearance and disappearance of certain species of birds has, until recent decades, been one of life's great mysteries for those who observe and think about the world around us.

Gilbert White, a clergyman and one of the most sensitive

naturalists of the European Enlightenment, loved birds over all other creatures. A scientist with a flair for the poetic, he wrote of birds' calls: 'the language of birds is very ancient, and, like other ancient modes of speech, very elliptical: little is said, but much is meant and understood'. He took a keen interest in all birds though he rarely strayed more than a few miles from his native Selborne in Hampshire. In 1767 he wrote to Thomas Pennant (the man who would a year later have the king penguin named *Aptenodytes patagonicus*) that he had had a revolutionary idea: perhaps swallows flew away to some other land in the autumn. Later he recanted and went back to the prevailing orthodoxy, but for a while it seemed that the mystery was being unravelled. Even Johann Forster, the man in whose honour the emperor penguin was named *forsteri*, believed that swallows hid in riverbeds for winter. In a note to his translation of Pehr Kalm's *Travels into North America* (1773) Forster claimed to have personally seen swallows pulled from the Vistula in a state of winter torpor. Intellectual heavyweights of the period like Carl Linnaeus and Samuel Johnson agreed. Johnson turned his literary flair to an account of how, after flying round and round in a swarm swallows 'conglobulate' together and fall into riverbeds to sleep.

The restlessness that drives their migration, their lust to *move*, was first recognised by the German ornithologist Johann Andreas Naumann, another of the towering intellects of the European Enlightenment. Studying orioles and flycatchers he observed how, if caged around the time of their migrations, the birds would become restless in their cages, hopping repeatedly towards the direction they were drawn to migrate. He called it *zugunruhe*, from *zug*, to pull or tug, and *unruhe*, unrest or disquiet.

Emperors, I learned, do not exhibit classical *zugunruhe*, they are much too self-contained for that. After his studies on the emperor rookery, Bernard Stonehouse had brought three adults and two chicks back to base to continue measuring the chicks' growth. The birds settled in a wire-netting enclosure, where they soon learnt to accept food from their captors. They did not batter the walls of their enclosure, but gathered always at the end nearest the sea and the colony. Clearly they knew in which direction lay freedom and their normal life.

Agitation in the penguins has been recorded in only one condition – starvation. In a gruelling and some would say unnecessary experiment J.-P. Robin caged emperor penguins and enforced a fast beyond what they would ordinarily tolerate. At about 24 kg in weight, representing a weight loss of about forty per cent, he remarked dryly that emperor penguins showed a marked increase in 'locomotor activity', suggesting an increased motivation to feed. This is the weight at which a male emperor, if not relieved by his mate, will abandon the chick he has carried for two months through the worst conditions on earth.

Birds appear to find their way by sun, stars and the magnetic field of the earth – in other words, by any means available to them. Penguin biologists have told me that adélie penguins on migration are more sluggish and appear more purposeless in cloudy conditions, accelerating towards their goal when the position of the sun becomes clear to them. Perhaps they use magnetism too, but more weakly. Traces of iron in the Atlantic seabed show that the polarity of the earth's magnetic field has switched thirty times in last 5 million years. For that reason birds that use magnetism have to follow the *pitch* of the magnetic field rather than its polarity. Near the magnetic poles lines of magnetism are angled steeply, streaming perpendicularly up from the earth's crust into the sky. Closer to the equator those lines are flattened, curving into an earth-following trajectory. Emperor penguins live in a triptych world of sea, ice and sky, devoid of bearings and recognisable landmarks. Patterns in the ice coastline change every year. Their internal landscape must be mapped with constellations, solar angulations and magnetic contours that give Antarctica a depth and texture invisible to us.

Autumn now, and the adélie penguins of Halley had gone. They would travel from the ice edge of the continent up into the Southern Ocean as the first of the winter storms arrived. A gaggle of them had strutted round the garage for much of the summer, welcoming visitors, clucking and tutting at the heavy vehicles that came and went. They were grudgingly tolerated, despite their affection for shitting on the pile of snow destined for our drinking water.

Of all the penguin species adélies seem most possessed of a mania for migration, of an unusual wanderlust. I heard a report from Fossil Bluff, a field refuelling station at 71° South, of a solitary adélie found wandering up the mountainside. It had walked more than sixty miles uphill from the sea. The men of the station chased it, bundled it into a bag, and handed it over to a Twin Otter pilot heading north. The pilot released it at the shore only to watch it turn round and start waddling away from the water, back into the heart of the continent.

In his film about Antarctica, *Encounters at the End of the World*, Werner Herzog stated that he did not want to make 'a film about penguins'. That said, he did manage to question an ornithologist on the incidence of penguin homosexuality, and capture one of these wanderlustful adélies at the moment of striking out for the South Pole. I wondered if adélie penguins are hard-wired into unusual migrations, if a proportion of them will always doggedly break new trails in unexpected directions. Some research suggests that a proportion of the population always migrate in the opposite direction to the one they *should* take. To a Darwinist this theory might explain a great deal: that there is a survival advantage in having a few members of each community that are willing to try to find new feeding and breeding grounds, pulling away from the herd in potentially suicidal directions. But I prefer the alternative: that some adélies really are wanderers at heart, that like Richard Bach's Jonathan Livingston Seagull, or certain dead British explorers, some of them prefer a solitary and dangerous life at the extremes of experience to a humdrum life of ice floes, breeding and fish.

Emperors wander in this way too. Back in 1973 a wayfaring emperor, in adult plumage, was found walking the beaches of southern New Zealand. In 2011 a juvenile washed up on a beach not too far away, newly fledged and with a belly full of sand (some thought it had mistaken the sand for snow). It is likely that others have reached Tasmania, the Falkland Islands, South Georgia and Patagonia, but have gone unrecorded because of the sparseness of human populations there. I had crossed oceans and ice fields to have the chance of living in the habitat of the emperor. It pleased me that at least some of the emperors had made the reciprocal journey, and after unknowable trials had managed to reach the habitat of the human.

Antarctic opinion is that recreational trips are expensive to equip, disruptive to base routine, and of all the activities in Antarctica are the most likely to get you killed. Luckily for us, the British allowed them anyway. Many other Antarctic programmes are not so obliging.

Soon after the ship left, 26 February, Toddy began to split us up into groups of three. With him as a fourth each group would set out in turn to explore the Hinge Zone, the area of broken and tortured ice where the Brunt was hinged to the Caird Coast. I was already keen to get away from the base. These 'winter trips', which for safety's sake at Halley could never take place during the actual winter, were considered a chance to blow away the cramped, restless stiffness of base routine, to sleep under canvas far from walled rooms, to get a chance to experience Antarctica unfiltered by the conveniences and demands of base life.

We had looked through old cine-reels of trips out of Halley back in the 1960s and 1970s. The bearded men, sometimes two to a skidoo, could be seen buzzing un-roped over the rolled and crevassed ice, exploring the changing icescape of the most glacially active, and treacherous, region for hundreds of miles around. In those days they traversed the Hinge Zone to strike out for the Theron and Shackleton mountain ranges, hundreds of miles over our horizon to the south-west. That was in the days when BAS, in the words of the Deputy Director John Dudeney, 'was killing a man a year'.

It is different now. We would drive the fifty kilometres to the Zone on separate skidoos each hitched to a Nansen sledge provisioned with enough food for a month. Each pair of skidoos would be roped together in case one fell into a crevasse, and there were two tents for each pair just in case one blew away in a storm.

There was a fog the morning we were due to leave. It had come up through the night, and there was no more contrast on the ice than you'd find inside a frosted light bulb. The slumps in the snow surface that hint at crevasses would be invisible, and so we could go nowhere. With our minds grinding in frustration we waited. When the fog rolled back a couple of days later it did so quickly, like an eyelid opening from sleep.

The clouds were high and dappled, shaped like ripples in the sand at low tide. As they moved across the sky they morphed and merged in herringbone patterns of silver, grey and opaline blue. Great fields of glistering light played over the surface of the snow as it shone though the breaks in the canopy. It was a day of Manley Hopkins grandeur, with shook-foil sunshine on the clouds, and dappled light on the ice. The skidoo skimmed over the crests of sastrugi, spume-white like waves frozen in motion. I realised that for almost a year I would not hear the sounds of the waves.

The Inuit, who are the only people who really know how to survive polar environments unsupported, know the importance of a good tent. In their culture the leader of a household was known in old Greenlandic as an *igtuat*, which may be related to words meaning 'tent-owner'. After the death of an *igtuat*, his son would inherit the tent and automatically take responsibility for his father's widows, slaves and foster-children. A good tent, endlessly repaired, was the best insurance policy a family could have.

On our sledge we carried a four-pole pyramid tent, its colour bleached to a blotchy carrot by accumulated years of twenty-four-hour sunlight. Ash-framed, the Nansen sledges were built to a specification that had not changed since the Norwegian polymath designed them over a century ago. The continent to the south was a white shield glancing sunlight; the base was invisible over the northern horizon. As I exhaled my breath hung in the air as it froze, a gelid mist, refracting the sunlight into evanescent blooms of colour. It was a novel experience to breathe in air and breathe out rainbows. Under Toddy's instruction, Annette and I began to dig out a tray of snow to bed the tent in beneath the ice surface. Without doing this the risk was that the wind could find its way underneath our tent. We did not want to lose ours the way Cherry-Garrard, Wilson and Bowers lost theirs on the Worst Journey in the World. Though human activity in the Antarctic was only a little more than a century old our predecessors had given us a keen sense of the dangers that are inherent in the landscape. The materials we used for our clothes, our sleeping bags, our cooking and lighting, were not very different from those available to Scott or Amundsen, but what we were rich in was the knowledge of past failures, the wisdom of what *not* to do.

Our tent would sleep two of us, and once it was up Annette began to hand in the layers we would put between us and the ice: groundsheet, plywood board (or our bodies would melt hummocks into the ice surface) foam karrimat, thermarest, two sheepskins, canvas bag and in it a four-season polar-rated duck-down sleeping bag. As long as we stayed dry we would not be getting cold. Into the sleeping bags every evening, along with ourselves, would go tubes of sunblock (or it would freeze to the consistency of tar sand), cameras, water bottles, clothes for the next day, and pee-bottles. Being in an Antarctic sleeping bag was a bit like lying in a Bronze Age grave – I felt as if had to share space with all of my most important possessions, just in case they were needed for the afterlife.

Between the two bed-rolls we placed a series of sledging boxes – field medical box, cooking box and 'man-food' box (though the need to distinguish from 'dog-food boxes' was long since irrelevant). Beneath the dehydrated pemmican and the army-issue 'Biscuits – Brown' I found a bag of Iraqi dates, packed over twenty years earlier. In all that time they had never had a chance to thaw. Our Primus stove had instructions inscribed in a flourishing Arabic script, intended for journeys in warmer deserts.

The man-food boxes were packed with the modern equivalent of 'hoosh', that pre-packed dehydrated pemmican mix that kept the old-time explorers going. The word 'hoosh' apparently comes from the North American 'hooch', but the reference to alcohol is misleading. Frank Worsley, captain of the *Endurance*, the *James Caird* and the *Quest*, wrote of how much he came to look forward to it: 'Made up in half-pound bricks for one man's meal, it had the consistency of new cheese and a yellow-brown colour, but looked, when boiled with water, like thick pea-soup. In cooking, the aroma of this ambrosia rose like an incense to the gods. Any one of us would have cheerfully murdered a Chinaman for a pound of it.' I can't say I shared his enthusiasm, but then I never got as hungry as he did.

Both the inner skin and the outer shell of the tent had circular doors like truncated wind socks that could be tied off with a shoe lace against storms. Toddy told us to keep our fuel outside on the left, ice blocks to melt for water on the right. We would need to pour our cooking waste away between the inner and outer skins of the tent. It would melt its own downpipe as it funnelled into the ice. Our toilet would have to do the same – it was at an area marked by a flag known as 'the pee flag'. 'Just don't pee ON the flag,' Toddy said, 'or we'll never get it out again.'

Crevasses lay around our camp like sleeping giants whose wrath could be awakened with one false step. The surface of the shelf had been buckled by the pressure of the flow of continental ice. In places it was folded like caramel, rolled and twisted, riven with deep cracks forced by unimaginable pressures. I saw seawater welling into the deepest of them – the shelf was so thin – and wondered at the wisdom at camping near such a place. Boulders of ice lay where they had rolled down in avalanches. 'Winter is coming,' Toddy said, trying to reassure us. 'There shouldn't be too much more movement this year.'

Blaise Pascal, the seventeenth-century French mathematical genius, found encounters with sublime landscapes frightening. He felt diminished by enormity, elemental powers, the infinity of space, and wrote that he felt 'swallowed up in the eternity before and after, the little space which I fill . . . the eternal silence of these infinite spaces terrifies me!' Pascal was tormented by pains, by a 'nervous affliction', and by his belief in a stern and judgemental God. His experience of the sublime was heavily influenced by his vision of mankind as fallen and corrupt. He perceived these numinous encounters as an assault on the self, rather than having the potential to snap us out of the quotidian realities of our lives. Pascal would have hated Antarctica, and been intimidated and overwhelmed by his irrelevance to it.

Vladimir Nabokov, a man very much of the twentieth century, who shifted languages and nationalities as easily as he changed his tweed jacket and tie, had a different experience. For him the nature of the sublime was less important than the pleasure of experiencing it: 'It is like a momentary vacuum into which rushes all that I love. A sense of oneness with sun and stone. A thrill of gratitude to whom it may concern – to the contrapuntal genius of human fate or to tender ghosts humouring a lucky mortal.' I like to think that, despite its lack of his beloved butterflies, he would have enjoyed the Antarctic. He would have felt something expansive and splendid in it.

In the West we are heir to both of these traditions, and are in the fortunate position of being able to dip in and out of both as well as forge our own. The common ground between them seems to be that sublime landscapes can teach us a lesson that we might otherwise only learn through hardships: that the universe is unimaginably vast, that we are relatively small and fragile, that we must accept our limitations, and get on with enjoying the magnificent aspects of being alive. It's a valuable perspective to remind oneself of.

Just before leaving Scotland, an old friend had posted me a book by the philosopher Jonathan Glover. It was a weighty tome, a doorstopper, the kind of book that she thought I would only get around to reading if given the sort of isolation she imagined Antarctica would provide. Its title was formidable: *Humanity: A Moral History of the Twentieth Century*. It glanced a philosopher's eye over some of the most appalling episodes of that fractious century: the imbroglio of the Balkan Wars, the genocide in Rwanda, the Holocaust, the decision to drop the atom bomb on Japan. Initially I was reluctant to open it – I did not want to bring the darkest underbelly of humanity into that bright pure landscape – but at the Hinge Zone, during days trapped in the tent by winds and poor contrast, I began to read. There, in a landscape empty of the human, off the bottom of all the maps I had known as a child, I found the perfect place to read such a book. It was as if the landscape itself was neutral enough to allow the space in which to examine a world heaving with catastrophes and misery. I contemplated refugee crises, suicide bombers, nuclear missile détentes, the sorrow of destroyed cultures, unconscionable cruelty. I recalled the faces of people I had met in the past blunted and distorted by suffering. Each chapter was punctuated by visits outside for blocks of ice to melt for tea, or trips to the pee flag. I realised that for me the tracks worn by human relationships, by the burdens they carry, can make towns and cities feel so *tired*. Antarctica could never be tired; it was simultaneously new, ancient and ageless, and gave the impression of being able to stand outside human history.

But this, I realised, was an illusion. Human history has caught up with Antarctica, it is just that it lies so lightly there. Frozen bodies are sunk beneath the pristine ice, and names of ship's captains and sovereigns have been sprinkled over the map. And it *has* been mapped now, the blank spaces are shrinking, and the signs of human habitation are growing. The language of those explorers – duty, endeavour, sacrifice – has given a nobility to our vision of the continent that is only part of the story.

I lay in my tent, warm in layers of duck down, and waited for the contrast to improve. I envied those early explorers their vision of the continent, uncluttered by the stories of others, even as I was grateful to learn from their mistakes.

One morning I looked out through the tent hatch on to a transformed world. Soft snow, like cotton wool pulled from medicine bottles, piled on our sledges and lay thick on the guy ropes of the tent. The flakes fell gently in the chill stillness of minus 25°C. Each was a perfect hexagonal crystal, intricate and filigreed, a rococo masterpiece in miniature. Some were up to a centimetre wide, and landed unbroken. But they were only microns thick, disappeared side-on, and collapsed on contact with my outstretched hand. Ice can evaporate directly into air without assuming the properties of water. The verb for the process is 'to sublime'.

Contrast was poor, a thin band of ambrosial gold was suspended in the crack between ice and sky. There was a pastel-blue wash of water-sky on the clouds to the west – the newly formed sea ice there must have moved out in the night. Toddy said he had been out exploring the crevasses in the area and had driven some snow anchors into the surface near one of them. I put on my thermal underwear, fleece dungarees, fleece sweater, a suit of the fine cotton twill clothing known as Ventile, a balaclava, heavy ski gloves and a rock-climbing helmet, and climbed out. We strapped on our climbing harnesses and crampons then Annette and I roped up.

'Careful now,' said Toddy, 'you've a pair of lethal weapons attached to your feet.'

Roped together we tramped to the crevasse he had chosen. The metal teeth of the crampons scraped over the hard ice beneath the snow. The only other sounds were the heavy pant of our breaths and the muffled swish of the rope.

Eventually we arrived at the crevasse mouth, a jagged blue crack in the surface, just before a fog came over. We wondered if we should get straight back to camp, but Toddy already had a fix on our direction home. 'Now we've made it here we can stay,' he said. The sky and ice both softened to the same milky opacity and the crack became almost invisible. I tied into the rope that Toddy had fixed to the snow anchors, lay down on my belly, and edged backwards towards the crevasse. He reached across with a small folding spade. 'Dig it out a bit,' he said, 'cut it back to some stronger ice before you go in.' I reached out with the spade in one hand, dunking it up and down through the loose granular ice. Great lumps fell away, and then suddenly, the spade had slipped out of my hand and was falling with them. 'Don't worry,' Toddy said, 'just see if you can reach it once you get in.'

My legs found the space and my hips swung them down, kicking into the void. It took a great effort of mind, struggling against all my body's instincts, to ease off on the rope and slip in staccato jerks into the hole. For the second time that day my world transformed.

Lilac and azure flooded my eyes; I had dropped into a cathedral of light. When I looked up I saw ice latticeworks of geometric perfection growing down from a vaulted cupola. I lowered myself on the spindle-thin rope, beneath immense arches that gathered towards the ceiling. I could feel myself becoming frigid, still, part of this subglacial world. The membranes high in my nose began to freeze with each breath. Ice bridges had collapsed as the crevasse had yawned apart, their broken ends curled under themselves like acanthus leaves on temple columns. Stalagmites jutted from the walls like arms raised in praise.

I lowered myself all the way to the end of the rope, forty metres. Looking across I could see the handle of the spade; it had bounced a few metres to one side. The light at the bottom was deeper in tone, crystalline as if refracted through amethyst. To the side of me tapering walls of ice, fissured and veined like cracked glass, sheered away into an endlessly changing labyrinth that would never, could never, be explored. I thought of the great beauty beneath the ice all around this continent, a beauty that is almost never enjoyed by human eyes. I lay back against the wall for a while, breathing hard, enjoying the quilted quality of the silence.

Scrabbling against the glassy walls that narrowed to a wedge I reached for the spade, and my boots jammed. For a few seconds I was locked in place, squeezed between the walls of glowing ice. I pictured myself trapped and embedded here, emerging frozen at the shelf face in centuries' time like the Iceman mummy of Ötztal. BAS has lost several men this way. I thought I heard something, a low seismic reverberation almost below the threshold of hearing. It trembled in my bones as much as in my ears. Suddenly it did not feel so peaceful to be there in the belly of the glacier. Then I heard a definite sound, a lighter, tinkling noise, splintering like gin poured over ice cubes. Something had fallen, this crevasse was on the move. Pebbles of fear lumped up under my skin, a glissade of it prickled down my spine. I need to get out of here, I thought. My legs had frozen, but I managed to get a foot out and into the loop of the jumar ascenders that would let me climb the rope. I forgot about the spade.

Panting, I pulled myself the forty metres to the top of the rope and grabbed the ice axe from my harness belt. Lunging over the edge, I threw the pick of the axe into the ice surface as far away from the crack as I could reach, and hauled myself to safety.

It was a weary tramp back to base camp. But already I wanted to go back down to breathe that air, absorb that silence, and be suffused with that light.

I had one other book with me in the tent for that trip, Vivian Fuchs' and Sir Edmund Hillary's *The Crossing of Antarctica*. It was published in 1958, and describes their motorised journey across the continent as part of the International Geophysical Year (IGY) in 1956–7. It's a stodgy read, dutifully listing the stores and personnel for every aspect of the expedition, and turns up suspiciously often in second-hand bookshops. Despite the book's style it seemed important to read, describing as it does the juncture between the small and highly risky operations of the Heroic Age and the settled base-led Antarctica that expedition members often experience now. Understanding their journey would, I thought, give me insights into BAS and the Antarctic traditions that had lived on since the beginning. I'd taken it to the Hinge Zone thinking that if the tent was snowbound I'd have no option but to read it. I was right – after exhausting the tome on moral philosophy, two of Annette's sci-fi blockbusters, and the first-aid manual in the medical box, I had run out of excuses.

If there was any heroism left in the idea of a Heroic Age of exploration, Fuchs' Trans-Antarctic journey was its swansong. He had his route scouted out by aeroplane before risking his vehicles, and many among the public found it difficult to get excited about the idea of sitting in the cab of a tractor while it trundled across an empty desert of snow. Scott had hauled there after all, and even Amundsen had stood on a sledge pulled by dogs. Neither had a crowd of Americans cheering them on from aeroplanes flying overhead, or waiting for them with bottles of champagne at 90° South as Fuchs did. There were many who questioned whether the whole idea were not a little outdated, though others argued that it was the only part of the IGY that *did* capture the imagination. The expedition discovered the Theron and Shackleton Mountain Ranges, but these were spotted by the aeroplanes on reconnaissance flights prior to any attempt to cross the continent on the ground.

Sir Edmund Hillary, buoyant with his recent conquest of Everest, was drafted in to play the part of Shackleton's *Aurora*, commanding the depot-laying from the Ross Sea side of the continent. While Fuchs used dog-teams to find routes for his snowcat vehicles, Hillary carried out his work with converted Ferguson farm tractors. His instructions were to lay depots onto the Polar Plateau and survey the ground for a descent through the mountains to the Ross Sea side. But once Hillary got up there, and realised he was closer to the South Pole than he was to his own base on Ross Island, he decided to make a run for it. He arrived at the South Pole at midday on 4 January 1958, two weeks before Fuchs' party limped in, slowed as they were by their dogs and the seismic work for the IGY they carried out on the way. While relaxing at the Pole Hillary had even radioed over to Fuchs that he was being so slow he might as well give up on the idea of completing the crossing, and allow the Americans to fly him and his men out. Fuchs, spluttering with barely contained fury, refused, though he did let the Americans fly his beloved dogs north to the Ross Sea.

Later commentators, including Fuchs himself, were keen to silence any suggestion that Hillary exceeded his orders and decided to make a race for the Pole. Fuchs was the director of FIDS and remained in charge through the transition to BAS up until 1973. Thirty years after he retired his impact on BAS was still profound. He was a stern figure, a commander of the old school, who inspired respect and admiration, as well as some jokes at his expense. In the BAS cafeteria discussion of the Trans-Antarctic Expedition alternated between tones of hushed reverence and schoolboy smirking.

'There was to be no doubt that it was to be Fuchs' show,' one of the old-timers who knew him told me. 'He must have been hopping mad when he found out Hillary beat him to it with a couple of old Ferguson tractors.'

We spent days of sunshine walking in the Hinge Zone. Roped together we explored gentle valleys, angled gorges, fluted scoops of ice, learning the rudiments of ice climbing in a place where there could be no other sort. Some of the peaks and gulleys of the Hinge Zone have been constant for many years now, and successive years of BAS personnel have given them names. There was Whale Meat Sausage Berg, a wide glen called Superbowl and an inverted lump of ice that had dragged up stones from the submerged Caird Coast beneath us, imaginatively christened Stony Berg. We basked on it in the sunshine, examining the rocks. To the south we watched the light play over the Brunt Icefalls, glacial plains that climbed towards the Pole, their contours revealing the continent beneath. After a full day out on the ice our eyes would begin to smart with the pinprick stabs of snowblindness, even though we wore maximum-strength sunglasses against the glare. It was a relief to close your eyes for a while and shut the whiteness out.

In the evenings we would come back to our base camp and radio in to Halley. We used old military field radios, antenna wires strung between two ski poles, dialling up the bandwidth and listening through the ionospheric interference for Pat's voice calling us, 'Sledge Alpha, Sledge Alpha, this is Halley, do you read me, over.' Often we had to try different bandwidths according to a prearranged sequence, the one we had initially chosen being blitzed by solar wind, or lost to space, or even on one occasion taken over by the yammering din of a Latin American taxi company. Unimaginable now that Shackleton's or Scott's expeditions did not have this luxury of calling base from the field.

It is one of the most poignant aspects of those explorers' failures in the Antarctic that had those expeditions waited only a few years, revolutionary technology with the power to keep them safe would have become available. Radios were already available by the time of Scott's *Terra Nova* expedition but were not yet portable. Shackleton carried one on the *Endurance*, but its range was pitiful. Only a few years later, the military started experimenting with the use of field radios, but shortly afterwards air travel made the idea of man-hauling to the Pole almost irrelevant. Only thirteen years after Shackleton pulled himself over South Georgia towards the sound of a whaling station's whistle, Richard Byrd flew an *aeroplane* over the South Pole. The new technology, and the ease with which the next generation used it, made the deaths of the early explorers and the imperial impatience that brought them there seem an absurd and tragic waste.

By day the light was relentless, but at night the sky was beginning to darken, the sun dropping far enough below the southern horizon at midnight for me to see the stars. The darkness was welcome, my eyes eased and I luxuriated in the softness of the sky. With my rabbit-fur hat, padded in down, and clutching a paper star chart that froze stiff as a board, I would climb out around midnight to lie on my back on the ice. Off the bottom of the world, protected by radio, stuck down to our planet by a force I did not understand, I tried to familiarise myself with a new heaven.

# CHAPTER SEVEN

# Waiting for Winter

HORIZON *n*. an explication. The first range of hills that encircles the scanty vale of human life is the HORIZON for the majority of its inhabitants. Coleridge: *Biographia Literaria*
Ian Hamilton Finlay, *Six Definitions*

When I returned to base the air was still, as if trapped inside a cold frame. Nothing moved, neither air, water or ice. I skied outside in a deep quiet, listening only to the cochlear hum of a polar silence. Then the halyard on the flagpole began to whisper, then to rattle and thrum, and then gusts from the east built themselves up over a few hours into a great gale. Apsley Cherry-Garrard described these Antarctic gales best: 'as if the world was having a fit of hysterics', and ever since reading his book I had wanted to experience one. As the storm swelled in intensity it became difficult to get down the steps from the main platform, but I had resolved to take a walk outside every day of the long winter ahead.

A friend in Britain had sent me an email about the 'sport' of extreme ironing – men and women who mocked the machismo of extreme sports by combining them with the most domestic of activities. Enthusiasts had tried to do their ironing in scuba outfits, on mountaintops, even hanging suspended over gorges by high-tension wires. 'You should try that,' she had written, and I thought that maybe this was my chance.

I gathered up an ironing board, duvet cover, iron and a two

kilowatt generator, then geared up against the wind in the boot room. Tommo agreed to come with me, to document the event for my friend back home. Groping my way outside I was blinded by a rasping wind that scrubbed ice granules across my face like sandpaper. My ski goggles filled quickly with fine frozen dust that blew up through the sponge lattice of the goggles' air vent, powdered like the drill tailings of plaster. The silence of a few days earlier had been replaced by a great rush reverberating through the sky like the roar of a forest fire. Tommo and I bent our heads into the wind, gripping the hand-lines that were strung between platforms for just this situation. Once I'd finished the duvet cover was more dishevelled than ever.

Afterwards, back in the safety of my pit-room I heard the wind whistling and moaning through the rigging of the antennae, shaking the Laws platform the way the sea heaves the hull of a ship. There is an Inuit song created by two individuals blowing alternately down one another's vocal cords, an echoing reverberation similar to the one that now moaned through the ceiling. My windows became encased in ice. I heard scurrying, skittering noises as ice broke from the masts and shattered above my pit-room ceiling. At about a hundred miles per hour, the anemometer on the Simpson platform snapped off and we lost our record of the wind speed.

Ever since the first Portuguese seafarers, those interested in predicting the weather have constructed 'wind roses', visual summations of the intersecting vectors of wind that blow over a particular location. The Weddell Sea ice fields had an ally in the winds above them – the west-turning sea was mirrored above by a west-running sky. Halley's wind-rose was compact, the petals of the north, west and south were short and neat, but it was supported by a long stalk that stretched far into the east – the direction from which the prevailing wind would collapse on us in recurring storms. Many of these winds are 'katabatic', from the Greek *katabatos*, 'descending'. Air high on the polar plateau is dense and very cold. Because the continent itself is a high dome of ice this heavy air 'falls' off the continent, rushing towards the coast until it gathers the momentum of a hurricane.

As the hurtling wall of air encounters an object – be it building, flagpole, or skidoo – the turbulence makes it drop its load of snow, leaving vast drifts to gather behind anything that had been left out on the ice. These 'wind tails' can grow as high as the buildings or vehicles that generate them, and made a contoured landscape out of our flat world. There were times when the wind tail behind the Laws platform grew so high it threatened to engulf the building, and Graeme and Ben would have to spend long days with the bulldozer, patiently removing thousands of tonnes of ice. When ice, sky and snow are all the same shade of white, shorn of the contrast provided by direct sunlight, these wind tails could be a hazard too. When the storm was over I took a short cut behind the west-facing side of the garage, and walked straight into the wall of an invisible drift.

But when the sun edged through the clouds the scene would transform, the way a photograph emerges slowly from the developing tray in a darkroom. Great beauty had been carved into the ice. Snowdrifts seemed sculpted in sigmoid whorls, peaked drifts were thrown into the sweeping contours of Saharan dunes. There was a pure, unlined magnificence about the wind tails. Though only hours old they had a polished sheen, as if rubbed smooth by centuries of pilgrim's fingers.

As the days ran to weeks a pattern emerged: awake by 7.30, half an hour of sitting gathering my thoughts, feeling my breath, listening to the great silence outside my room. By 8.00 I would be in the dining room eating breakfast, chatting with the others or eating in peace. By 9.00 I would be at my desk reading, writing, emailing, collating data for a science project I was involved in, or gazing out of the window. Sometimes I did a chapter or two of a language course in Italian. Still at a book or a computer screen by 11.00, my muscles would be stretching to be outside, to be skiing around the base, and I would look more carefully out of the window, gauging the clothing I would need to wear.

The temperature, wind speed and wind direction outside were constantly displayed in the radio room, and after glancing at this I would choose the wax for my skis. By mid-autumn this was no longer necessary – it was always below minus 15°C, and we had only one type of wax that would work at those temperatures. I would wax my skis, dress in my cotton Ventile suit and climb down the steps to the ice.

If there was sunlight the ice would be a carpet of rainbows, each granule a prism in miniature that kaleidoscoped through the spectrum with each shift in perspective. I would fill my lungs with gulps of clean air, shake off the stiffness of keyboards and computer screens, and fix on my skis. If contrast and visibility were poor I would need to follow a drum line out to the marked perimeter of the base. Only on reaching that perimeter, one kilometre from the Laws platform, would I ease into the rhythm of the skiing and the solitude.

The air and ice were cleanliness, purity, energy, life itself. A vast crystal wonderland into which my mind expanded every day. In a simple world of two elements I felt my mind, deprived of distractions, beginning to settle. Skiing the same route day after day for months I gradually drew my landmarks from the ridges of the sastrugi, from the position of the sun – there was direction and polarity to this landscape after all, it was possible to feel moored here. Moving over the ice I listened to the susurration of the skis, felt my mind gliding over the surface as if back in a Twin Otter skimming high over the landscape. I was a tiny figure creeping between a vast ice and an even vaster sky. What did I hope to learn from this place? I wanted patience, tolerance, endurance, stillness. The list reads like a job description of the emperor penguin.

Stuart had given me a cloud-atlas primer so that I could help him with the meteorological observations. I discovered the roll-call of clouds has a calming beauty about it, a meditative mantra of Latin description: cumulus (heaped up), stratus (stretched out), cirrus (curled up) and nimbus (storm cloud). Like the four constituent elements that make up DNA these four cloud types could be endlessly combined and recombined: nimbostratus, cirrocumulus, cirrostratus, cumulonimbus.

'It's not rocket science,' Stuart told me. 'Just describe what you see.'

It was not always so straightforward to me. One evening as I lay out on the ice the sky was so light and clear that only two or three stars could be seen along the darkest part of the horizon. From the west a barrier of spun-steel cloud sped towards me, its leading edge blown out like a billowing spinnaker. When its penumbra reached the moon there were rainbows, and then suddenly the moon was obscured (a pedant might say 'obnubilated'). The cloud mass slid over me like a hatch slid shut. I rushed to the Simpson platform to get out the cloud atlas, but drew a blank. 'Maybe it's a roll-cloud,' I said to myself. 'Or a speeding cumulus arcus.' The atlas had told me how to add descriptives to the cloud forms such as 'arcus', 'pannus' or 'radiatus'; names resonant of Linnaean classification. It was as if each cloud had its own genus and species – a taxonomy of the skies.

Along the Caird Coast there were no aeroplane contrails to disturb the atmosphere, no conurbations or power stations, and for days the sky might hang as open as an empty mind. It yearned for clouds. And then softly they would come; high cirrus drifting in from the South Pole, then the curds-and-whey lumpiness of altocumulus from the west. With time I realised flocks of cumulus were most likely to come from the north, and showed the greatest variety in forms; gaseous blooms like smoke from the bench of a cartoon scientist, or clambering over one another like unruly schoolchildren. Sometimes they were evenly spaced and disciplined, advancing south from the Weddell like a naval flotilla.

But the clouds were not always so fascinating. There were days or even weeks of smothering stratus; long, low and grey like the smooth stones that you find in a riverbed. They weighed on me.

Stratus, I read, was related to the Latin *sternere* meaning 'to stretch thin or spread out'. The days that it loured over the Brunt, stratus seemed to stretch time.

With my new-found enthusiasm for clouds I went through photographs I had taken around the base so far, using the atlas to name the clouds that formed a silent, and usually unnoticed, backdrop. I saw them with fresh eyes now that I paid attention to the skies within them. They were snapshots not only of events around base, but of the state of the troposphere and stratosphere above. I had captured crepuscular rays from breaks in the cloud, known to meteorologists as a Jacob's Ladder. There were castellated altocumulus, cotton-wool balls stretching skywards into turrets. Stratocumulus undulatus striped one sky in even bars of blue and white, and cirrus radiatus streamed another in fine-drawn pencil lines seven or eight miles up.

But the greatest find was in a photograph I took soon after arriving at Halley. A midnight sun swung over the South Pole. The ice was scored with sledge tracks, glinting in the sun the way that water glistens in the furrows of a ploughed field. The buildings of Halley, ten kilometres away, were just visible on the horizon. A band of cirrostratus moved from south-east to north-west, advancing into an empty quadrant of the sky. Waves had formed along the top of this cloud bank, miles-wide breakers formed by the shearing effects of high-altitude winds blowing off the continent. This phenomenon was, I read, known as a Kelvin–Helmholtz Wave Cloud. The physicists Lord Kelvin and Hermann von Helmholtz had both described the instability that occurs in any medium when flows of different speeds are forced to interact. Their description was not limited to clouds – I doubt they had Antarctic winds in mind when they described the phenomenology of turbulent fluids. The breakers I had captured over Antarctica are caused by the same process that surfers seek in the perfect rip curl, and that rolls through the cloudscapes of Saturn and Jupiter.

I remembered stopping a snowcat and standing on its roof to take that photograph. The air around me had been still, but in that moment the roaring currents of the skies, 20,000–30,000 feet above me, had been made suddenly manifest by a sharpened attention to the clouds.

For months the sun had circled day and night, hoisted high like an ostensory on a priestly circuit. By the equinox it had transformed into something more like a thurible, an ember swinging low along a smoking horizon.

On 21 March the earth teetered on its equinoctial axis, and we celebrated Nowruz, Persian New Year. Following the directions of a Kurdish friend of mine in London we built fires of old packing wood out on the bondoo then jumped over them as they melted down, sinking rings of fire into the elemental ice. There was something gladdening about the juxtaposition of fire on ice, and we all wished we had a fire indoors to gather around in the evenings, the way that Scott's or Shackleton's expeditions did. As tradition dictated, Craig cooked a celebratory Persian meal of rice and fish, improvising his ingredients in true Antarctic style. He made Turkish Delight from out-of-date dextrose infusions I found in the medical cupboards.

It was a waiting time, waiting for the darkness. The busy world in the north seemed impossibly distant. I found myself spending less and less time in the radio room battling the ionosphere to catch snatches of the BBC World Service. I built an igloo to fulfil a childhood ambition, and woke in it one morning to find my face coconut-dusted with fine crystals of ice. Saturn drew close to Earth and nightly I watched it through the old Halley telescope. Spinning low over the ice its rings shimmered like electron orbitals.

Each day I tried to draw as much light into myself as I could, skiing through the brightest hours around noon as if to charge myself for the long darkness ahead. I watched my noonday shadow, a snipped-out silhouette from the glare, change as the days grew shorter. It was not grey against the snow but blue, darkening as the days went by, reflecting the oceanic tranquillity of the sky. The broadening nights made it feel as if the year was drawing to a close, but for the penguins, like the Persians, the New Year was just beginning. Any day they would be returning from their three months at sea to join the great penguin jamboree down on the sea ice near the base.

By April the noon sky was ablaze in an arson of light. To the south it was a palette violent with dark angry purples, indigoes,

(*Above*) Antarctica at last!

(*Below*) Arriving on the sea ice at Halley

(*Above*) Halley Research Station: the Laws platform

(*Below*) Snowcat tracks between the ship and base

(*Right*) Waving goodbye to the ship, as the ten-month isolation begins

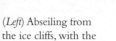

(*Left*) Abseiling from the ice cliffs, with the emperors on the horizon

(*Right*) Exploring the hinge of the continent

(*Above*) Sunset over the South Pole
(*Below*) Waiting for winter

FACING PAGE
(*Above*) A winter moon over the Simpson platform
(*Below*) The sun returns over the Laws platform

(*Facing page*) A female emperor returns after three months at sea

(*Above*) Newly hatched emperor chick

(*Left*) Fledgling emperor chick

(*Below*) Queuing up at the ice edge

(*Right*) Cases packed, ready for home

(*Below*) 80° South in the Shackleton Range

magentas. To the north the colours were hotter with furious reds and coppery yellows. This landscape was made up of the simplest of elements – light, ice, air – but an endlessly rich and varied beauty could be brought into being from them: the shapes in the wind-carved ice, the haloes and rainbows around the sun and moon, the diamond dust hanging in the air, the mirages that trembled along the horizons. The air felt brittle, stark, like a lens that might at any moment shatter into shards.

Russ and I tried to get down on to the sea ice to reach the penguins but were stopped by poor contrast and the rising wind-speed. After a day spent waiting in the caboose, our second morning was heralded by a 'sun pillar', a scarlet column like a searchlight shining from beyond the horizon. We took it as a good omen. Looking at the beam rising over the horizon I thought of the same sun climbing higher daily over Europe, falling like a hot coal over the tropics, and marvelled that it could be the same star.

The landscape had nothing of humanity in it, no life at all but that of the penguins, and our own. And instead of feeling that as a limitation I was flooded with a sense of potential. The sterile absence of humanity made it difficult to draw the landscape into myself, to feel part of it, but made me perversely aware of the defiant warmth of my blood, the life that sang in my muscles and bones.

Later that second morning we managed to abseil down on to the sea ice. The surface was crisp, a recently frozen skin that would now lie all winter. It was motionless, but occasional sounds like a whip-crack told me that the sea beneath the ice was straining in its lust for the moon. We made our way, dark figures in this world of light, from the ice-foot out towards the penguins.

They made way for us gently as we moved through the rookery. They tolerated us, unafraid, and I thought of how those Hebraic prophets could be so wrong: 'And the fear of you and the dread of you shall be upon every beast of the earth, and upon every fowl of the air.'

After three months out at sea, fattening themselves up, the males and females were returning to find mates and begin another year.

The air was filled with the yammering clamour of their reunion. Only about one in ten emperor penguins are faithful to the same mate each year, the lowest fidelity rate of any penguin. Perhaps time is so short they can't afford to wait for a particular partner to return, perhaps greater gene mixing improves their chances of adapting to this pitiless environment. Perhaps the demands of raising chicks mean that they do not spend long enough together to bond. As I made my way through the crowd I noticed several were resting, leaning back on their heels, while others were singing and bowing together, making their displays in groups of two and three. Their cries shook in my ears. One of Chaucer's most famous poems, 'The Parlement of Foules', has the narrator guided by Scipio Africanus to a place where every species of bird on earth, on St Valentine's Day, is choosing a mate. We were a couple of months late for Valentine's Day but otherwise I recognised the description:

> And that so huge a noyse gan they make
> > That erthe and see, and tree, and every lake
> So ful was, that unnethe was ther space
> > For me to stonde, so ful was al the place.

Edward Wilson, perhaps the first to see something grand and heroic in the lives of these birds, was also the first to call their song 'trumpeting', as if the courtship ritual merited bugle blasts. 'It is like a defiant trumpet-call, and can be heard at a great distance over the ice floes. This is its rallying call note, emitted with the head erect.' I listened to one call during what has become known as the 'ecstatic display'. Describing it as spiritually transported might be overstating it.

A lone bird, probably male, walked up to another bird and stopped a few inches away. The first bird dropped its beak down on to its breast, inhaled deeply then began to sing while squaring its shoulders and drawing itself up to its full height. It was a stuttering song, low, metallic and polyphonic, reverberating from the bird's chest like a bass harmonica. The stuttering seemed to divide the song into short syllables. Its pitch climbed gradually through the scale before dropping away after a couple of seconds. Experts in acoustics tell us that the 'song' starts at about 0.5 kHz, working up to 6 kHz at the soprano end of the scale. They are loudest at about 4 kHz.

Calling the emperors 'the most truly Antarctic of all birds', the American ornithologist Robert Cushman Murphy wrote as recently as 1936 that 'the courtship behaviour of the Emperor Penguin is unknown.' Even now the way emperors choose their mates is not fully understood. Unlike most penguins they do not preen one another. Many penguin species try to impress potential mates with the skill of their nest building and with presents of small stones, but the emperor has no nests and few opportunities to find stones. In keeping with their great dignity they prefer to stand face to face, beaks aloft, mirroring one another in mutual contemplation. Then they sing. It seems that the way they stand out from the crowd, the way they impress potential partners, is to sing better than their rivals.

Sonograms, frequency band images that look like cross-sections through strata of ice, show that there is great variety in the length and pattern of the call's syllables between individuals. Scattered through the song are breaks and pauses with a unique prosody for each penguin. In the waddling mass of 60,000 penguins, the song carries each bird's identity. Females have, on average, double the number of syllables as the males (about twenty as opposed to ten), but in both species the song is completed within about two seconds. Perhaps all emperors are poets in search of the perfect stanza.

The bird I watched swung its head sideways, making a horizontal arc with its beak, then looked up. There was no reaction from the other penguin; the song must have disappointed. The male inhaled deeply again then wandered away. Though the female seemed choosy they have a lower death rate than males who have that gruelling winter to contend with, and are at a surplus in the breeding colony. At Point Geologie, where the French have conducted the longest-running study of emperor penguins in Antarctica, the male/female ratio is 40/60.

Later, at a different part of the rookery, I saw a pair walk away from the huddle. Like humans, they prefer some privacy for copulation. After successfully mating, the birds will stay together until the egg is formed and ready to lay. French researchers have found that between courtship and laying it is usually the male who leads in these perambulations, perhaps testing the female's resolve. If she loses him she'll have no one to incubate the egg when she lays it in early June, long after the sun has gone from the sky, and still several weeks away.

The Ancient Egyptians hung eggs in their temples as totems of fertility. In the pre-Christian era, some Germanic and Slavonic peoples smeared their hoes with egg in the hope of transferring fecundity to the soil. In the Internet age cyber-witches sell 'egg rituals', promising anything from the return of a loved one to immediate pregnancy. That mere incubation can transform a gooey sludge into a living, breathing being still has the power to astonish.

Eggs are a traditional part of the Jewish Passover meal, but the Gospels are silent on whether Jesus included them in his Last Supper. Instead foil-covered chocolate ones are used to remember him every Easter, eggs being the perfect symbol for renewal, rebirth and even escape from the locked tomb. The word 'Easter' is Anglo-Saxon; the Venerable Bede tells us Eostre was a Germanic goddess whose month was celebrated each spring. Eggs were part of her rituals, too.

When I first visited the penguins in the summer I had found abandoned eggs scattered over the ice. Some may have been dropped several months earlier, but been shuffled around over the surface by the penguin huddle. Penguin biologists have estimated that about one in ten of all emperor eggs laid are lost or displaced in the huddle, and these frozen eggs lying out on the ice were the result. Some had cracked but the shell of an emperor penguin's egg is very strong, and most had not. I had gathered a few and taken them back to base. I kept them in the freezer though I could just have easily have left them outside. They would not have thawed.

As Easter approached I took one out. I weighed it in my hand – it was heavy, almost half a kilo, and smeared with pink and green guano. As it started to thaw it didn't smell good, like stale fish, so I scrubbed its surface back to a creamy cockleshell white. It looked like a dinosaur egg. Examining it closely I could see pores arranged over its surface, redundant breathing holes for the chick within. Emperor eggs have an unusually low number of pores because of the dryness of Antarctic air. Too many pores would allow moisture to leach out of the egg, too few and the chick would suffocate. Their shells are among the thickest in the bird world, and make up around fifteen per cent of the total weight of the egg.

I wanted to decorate an Easter egg – it had been years since I had painted one. With painstaking attention I drew a pastel wash of the Halley sky on my emperor egg, layered in colour, and allowed the paint to freeze on to it. Black silhouettes of the Laws, Simpson and Piggott platforms finished the scene, then I set it out on the dining-room table.

Craig had outdone himself, and prepared an egg-themed banquet. Down on the sea ice a few kilometres away the penguins were mating as we sat down to an Easter lunch. It seemed appropriate that the only two species left on this coast were on that day both celebrating life and the hope of new birth.

When Charlemagne rebranded the European calendar he decided to call May Winnemanoth, the 'month of Joy'. I know what he meant; May for me has always meant the anticipation of summer. Beltane, the Celtic festival to mark the midpoint between the spring equinox and the summer solstice, is traditionally celebrated on 1 May. Its name is linguistically related to Belenos, the name of an old Celtic sun-god. Belenos is like a butch version of Apollo, proud, strong and invulnerable. His myth developed in temperate zones and so like the sun of those regions he parades reliably through the sky.

For the Inuit the sun is more capricious, and a woman. After being raped by her brother, the moon, she cut off her breasts in disgust and took to the heavens. Before leaving she blackened his face with soot, and in his pursuit of her he often forgets to eat. And that is why the moon is dimmer than the sun, and seems to grow thin from time to time. The light and heat of the sun are explained through the incandescent rage of a wronged woman.

The ancient Norse were a circumpolar people, and for them,

like the Inuit, the sun is considered more vulnerable than it is to their southern neighbours. In the tumultuous chaos of Ragnarok the giant wolf Sköll ('treachery') will at last chase it down and consume it. Sköll's brother Hati ('hate') will consume the moon, while their father Fenrir (another wolf) and uncle Jormungand (the 'world serpent') will advance to a final battlefield and kill all the gods. Norse cosmology allows for rebirth and renewal following Ragnarok, the return of the sun indicative of that culture's belief in the cyclical nature of the universe.

During those weeks, as autumn slid towards winter, it was as if the sun fought a daily battle with the northern horizon. It grew visibly weaker, bruised and bloodied, struggling free of the ice for a few minutes less each day before slumping exhausted back into the ice. It was extraordinary to witness this and know that it had no mythology here, that the landscape had been invested with no significance. No indigenous human society had tried to explain it or integrate it into their cosmology. The scientific explanation, however elegant, seemed lacking.

The last days of April were our last days of sun. On 'sundown' day we saw it set; it would not re-emerge for 114 days. The sky that day was clear, we had been lucky. In the panoramic flood of red a single ember smouldered on the northern horizon. Only the topmost part of the sun had managed to nudge over the ice. I watched in silence as the point of light shrank, willing it to stay, knowing that it could not.

Mark S., the oldest base member, climbed up on to the roof and waved a torch. He wished us all a good winter, and lowered the British flag. It had been hoisted since 'sun-up' last year, now nearly nine months ago, and was tattered and faded by the storms and months of bleaching sunlight. The gesture seemed oddly final, as if we were abandoning the base. But it was the sun who had abandoned us, and the emperors, to winter.

# WINTER

CHAPTER EIGHT

# Darkness and Light

The stars are steel points; the glaciers burnished silver. The snow rings and thuds to your footfall . . . and over all, wave upon wave, fold upon fold, there hangs the curtain of the aurora.

Apsley Cherry-Garrard, *The Worst Journey in the World*

The door of winter did not slam shut on us with the sun's departure, but edged to a close over days and weeks. On base we adjusted to the rhythms of darkness. Every day I did some skiing, reading, sitting, studying, writing, walking, praying, sleeping. Not much talking. One day when sitting I noticed that my pulse had become timed with my breath; two beats for each breath in, and four beats for a breath out. I realised how rarely in my life I had had opportunity to notice details like that with such close attention. My old life was coming away like an unbuttoned shirt, and seemed increasingly unreal. When outside I often looked west into the gloom, wondering how the penguins were doing. They would be yet to lay their first eggs.

The others settled into the rhythms of their own work. I would drop into the garage to see Ben and Graeme as they worked on the vehicles, to the Simpson platform for cups of tea with Annette, Elaine and Stuart, to the workshop to joke with Tommo and Rob. It was normal now that I lived in a world with no money, no locks, no old people or children. There was little opportunity to vary routines, and none of us varied in our dress – we all wore identical BAS-issue gear. Craig prepared two meals a day so we never had to think about what to eat. Having so few choices in the day was not frustrating, I found myself relaxing into a delicious mental freedom. Not having to think about the practicalities of life meant I had hours free to think about whatever I chose. I spent hours in the library reading and rereading my favourite books, and turned again to one of the classic accounts of early Antarctic exploration: Richard Byrd's *Alone*. Byrd too luxuriated in the time that his Antarctic winter offered him, and wrote movingly about the way that for him, winter isolation was a great gift.

A US Navy admiral, Richard Byrd was the first to use aeroplanes to map large sectors of the Antarctic. In a single day's flying in the 1920s he surveyed more of Antarctica than all the land-bound expeditions before him had ever achieved. In 1934 he returned to fulfil an ambitious exploration programme, and during the winter that year spent four months alone manning a meteorological station on the Ross Ice Barrier. Like his countryman Thoreau eighty years earlier at Walden Pond, he chose to stay alone not because it was wholly necessary but simply to taste the experience of such solitude to the full. Rather than become paralysed with boredom, he became enchanted by the opportunities the winter provided:

> Thoughts of life and the nature of things flow smoothly, so smoothly and so naturally as to create an illusion that one is swimming harmoniously in the broad current of the cosmos ... My opportunities for intellectual exercise are virtually unlimited. I can, if I choose, spend hours over a single page in a book. I thought tonight what a very full and simple life it is – indeed, all I really lack is temptation.

Byrd was one of the first to seek overtly in Antarctica that sense of profound isolation that it offers, to be so frank about his motivations and, crucially, so articulate in describing it afterwards to a northern world. He used the geographical and political ambitions of his paymasters to pioneer a more cultural and intellectual evaluation of the continent. I read *Alone* with deep recognition, and now that I was living through an Antarctic winter myself, a growing sense of admiration.

\*   \*   \*

The winter blackness had its saving grace: now we would be able to see the aurora australis. Though the sun was buried beneath the horizon, evidence of solar storms flared regularly through the skies over Halley. There was wonder in this darkness.

This much is known about our sun: it is a hot ball of ionised gases fuelled by nuclear fusion. Deep in its belly, protons, neutrons and electrons are seething, moulded and transformed by unimaginable energies. From time to time mouths gape open on the sun's surface and, belching like a dyspeptic, our star vomits charged particles across the solar system. Magnetism shields us, the earth pushes through them like a boat nosing into a fast-running stream. But at the poles the hard rain of quantum energy finds a leak. Those particles reach our upper atmosphere, throwing off their energy into the gases that they find there. It is the 'cooling' of those gases, and the release of light as their electrons return to a normal state, that gives rise to the aurora borealis and aurora australis.

Those names, meaning 'northern dawn' and 'southern dawn' respectively, were coined less than four centuries ago by a French astronomer. To the ancient Greeks they were *chasmata*, great portals in the sky that yearned to be entered. To the Finns they are *revontuli*, 'fox-fire', reflections of a great fox scampering over Lapland. To the Chinese the writhing whorls of green could be explained only as dragons. To the Scots it is their movement that most inspires: they call them 'the merry dancers'. To the Norse they were *bifrost*, the great bridge between earth and heaven. To some Inuit they harbour the ghosts of dead enemies, and to be seduced into watching them too long is to court madness. Other Native American groups believed they are the work of the shamans, conjuring light from battles with elemental forces.

Like isotherms or isobars, in deference to the Greeks, zones of equal auroral frequency are still known as isochasms. The isochasm of highest auroral frequency meets the sea in only a few places, and one of those places is over Halley.

The first aurora I saw in Antarctica was a few weeks before sundown. Walking onto the ice not long after midnight, I watched an arc of light glow gently in the south. Under the pinprick precision of the stars it was hazy and green, and billowed silently like snagged gauze caught in the wind. I could see what the Norse meant – it seemed a bridge between heaven and earth. I learned that this was what is arrestingly known as a 'quiet arc', a band of light commonly seen in the south that stretches equatorward with the rising of the solar wind. It arched towards me, beckoning and welcoming me to the silence and grandeur of the winter.

A couple of weeks later I chanced on another, less timid aurora. Blades of green and red were shooting into the magnetosphere, stabbing the sky. A jagged cordillera of emerald and garnet, sky-wide, met high above me. The summits of that ridge were draped with stars, the diamond dust of the Milky Way hung between the columns of light like mist on mountains. It shook and snapped quickly, as if the fabric of the sky were a great flag flapping in the wind. I had a profound sensation of vertigo, lying on my back on the roof of the Laws I felt the depth of the stars, the infinite distances I would fall if gravity were to lose its grip. To look up into the aurora was to see space shift and bend, gather and spill depth. Though auroras have a base (they have been observed by astronauts to begin around 100 km above the surface of the earth), the depths they reach can't be accurately measured. I felt the truth of the Greeks' description, the chasms of space that are revealed to us in these lights.

As well as space, auroras bend time. They work to a rhythm which has nothing to do with hours or days; born of starbursts rather than the steady revolution of the spheres. Gerald Manley Hopkins, the Jesuit priest and poet, first saw the Northern Lights in September 1870. Only two weeks earlier he had taken his vows and moved to Stonyhurst, the great Jesuit college in Lancashire. From its windows he watched the sky pulse with light. The aurora was 'in a strain of time not reckoned by our reckoning of days and years . . . [but] dated to the day of judgement'. He was astonished by the lights, they were 'a new witness to God and filled me with delightful fear'.

Before flaming auroral displays, compass needles are restless. Mounted on ships, carried in pockets, locked forgotten in drawers, they tremble in anticipation. When the aurora comes it overwhelms the ionosphere with energy. Radios fall silent as they jam the airwaves. Shifting magnetic fields animate copper wires – it becomes possible, during a violent solar storm, to send telegraph messages through them without adding electricity.

Before leaving for Halley I had managed to get hold of an old science paper, the result of a year at Halley spent scanning the sky. Its author, Mike Sheret, spent the winter of 1959 crouched under a hatch in the roof of the first Halley base. On a gruelling regime of observations, sometimes every fifteen minutes, he would pop up out of the (at that time) subterranean base, switch off all the external lights, and assess the auroral state of the sky. His paper is a model of scientific understatement, but I did not believe that the man remained unmoved by the visions he had seen. Listing exactly how many clear nights he experienced, the only emotion Sheret allows himself is annoyance at the Brunt's tendency to cloud cover. Using a device mounted on the roof he assessed the height of the 'quiet arcs' and compared the colours and movements he saw in the sky with readings on a magnetometer. He came to some new conclusions: flaming displays are irregular, and often overwhelmed or obscured by competing forms of light. Undulating motion seems to occur close to times of reversal of the magnetic disturbance, and undulations of light from east to west seems to produce a more profound magnetic effect.

Two years later another man, George Blundell, continued the experiment. Performing observations every fifteen minutes through the darkest days he classified auroras as 0 = 'subvisual', 1 = 'bright as the Milky Way', 2 = 'bright as moonlit cirrus cloud', 3 = 'bright as moonlit cumulus cloud', and 4 = 'very bright, like full moonlight on snow'. He wore a pair of special goggles, transmitting only light of wavelength 5,577 Ångströms. This is the emission frequency of monatomic oxygen, 'auroral green', meaning that unlike Sheret he could see the auroras through the clouds. He noticed that they seemed to come on a twenty-seven-day cycle – like the moon – and compared the forms he saw with the records of an auroral observatory in Canada, noting that there were similarities but not complete agreement between the forms seen simultaneously in the Arctic and Antarctic.

For me the poetry of Sheret's and Blundell's experience is captured in their photographs. Both science reports are well illustrated with them: round images, smudges of black and white, miniaturised to fit several skies to a page. With the clumsy technology of their day the two men tried in vain to convey something of the magnificence they had witnessed. At first glance they did not seem to show skies at all; I was reminded of retinal photographs. When I first looked up under the aurora, fresh from Sheret's and Blundell's reports, it was as though the sky was the dark of a dilated pupil. I watched the stars as if even my eyes were agape.

*

The *Worst Journey in the World*, Apsley Cherry-Garrard's record of Scott's last expedition, has in some circles attained the status of a sacred text, beyond criticism. All the same, critics have consistently placed it among the classics of world literature, a remarkable achievement for a man who wrote no other books. The Worst Journey does not relate to Scott's trudge to the Pole and subsequent death on the Ross Ice Shelf, but to a 'weird bird's nesting trip' to the Cape Crozier emperor rookery made by Cherry-Garrard, Edward 'Bill' Wilson and Henry 'Birdie' Bowers through the darkest and coldest weeks of the year. Wilson's letters and journals, as well as Cherry-Garrard's book, imply that it was for this journey alone that Wilson had agreed to return to the Antarctic with Scott – he personally had no interest in reaching the Pole. Bowers and Wilson later died with Scott, and Cherry-Garrard mourned them for the rest of his life. His book is a grief-struck elegy to the humility, generosity and friendship of these men. 'They were gold, pure, shining, unalloyed. Words cannot express how good their companionship was.'

In 1910, when the expedition was setting out, Darwin's theory of evolution by natural selection still had a great many detractors. Links between species, genera and even between classes of life were still being tentatively tested. Discussions of the emperor penguin are dominated by superlatives, and Wilson, a skilled biologist, believed them to be the oldest, the most primitive, the most *reptilian* bird alive. Catching emperor embryos at different stages of development would, he hoped, clinch the long-suspected link between reptiles and birds. Scott himself developed grave doubts about the journey and urged Wilson not to go.

They left just after the winter solstice, 27 June, in a darkness so deep it was as if the sky had been bundled in velvet. On two nine-foot sledges they pulled 757 lb of weight – equivalent to more than 110 kg per man. They walked abreast of one another, harnessed to traces bound to the two linked sledges. 'Generally,' wrote Cherry-Garrard, 'we steered by Jupiter, and I never see him now without recalling his friendship in those days.' They made their way through the blackness from their base at Cape Evans around a peninsula called Hut Point (where Scott's *Discovery* expedition hut was still standing) then across the Ross Sea Barrier towards Cape Crozier. Seven years earlier Wilson had seen emperors congregate at the cape, and had even managed a few visits to the rookery. He had been astonished to find that on visits even very early in the spring the chicks had already hatched. He realised that emperors must be the only penguins who incubate and hatch their eggs through the winter.

Fuel was low, and matches were precious. Cherry-Garrard became plagued by a short phrase which would reverberate through his mind hour after hour, timing and urging on his footsteps: 'You've got it in the neck – stick it, stick it – you've got it in the neck.' For rest they would shiver for a few hours in their tent, the condensation of their breaths freezing their reindeer-fur sleeping bags stiff as coffin-board. Gathering warmth meant

closing the bags, and they became accustomed to slow asphyxia-
tion from re-breathed air.

The men were exhausted, malnourished and hypothermic. After
they passed Hut Point they had had to relay the sledges across
fields of deep granular ice, like pulling logs through sand. Often
they had had to pull ten miles to make three miles' progress. They
were blinded by darkness, and Cherry-Garrard by his severe short-
sightedness. They developed an acute sense of hearing; he describes
how, wearing light *finnesko* shoes of fur like the *kamit* of the Inuit,
they grew to recognise the change in the sound of their footfalls
as they moved over crevasses. Blizzards assaulted them, and once
on the way there they became confined to the tent for three days.
The experience, he writes, was almost pleasant: they enjoyed the
forced rest and the rise in temperature which a drop in atmospheric
pressure brings. For the first time on the journey parts of their
clothes and sleeping bags began to thaw.

As they finally approached Cape Crozier, Wilson grew more
apprehensive. The pressure ridges in the ice as it was squeezed by
the bulk of Ross Island seemed to have changed in pattern since
he had last visited them. They were later found to have lengthened
seawards three-quarters of a mile and the colony was sited precariously underneath regularly collapsing ice cliffs. Despite this they
proceeded down through the tortured ice towards where they
hoped to find the emperors.

'And then,' writes Cherry-Garrard, 'we heard the Emperors calling
. . . [they] made a tremendous row, trumpeting with their curious
metallic voices.' He is in awe at the horror of their lives, these birds
that yearly endure the conditions that were slowly killing the men.
They slaughtered three penguins for their oil, and snatched five
eggs. Cherry-Garrard was given two of these to carry, both of which
calamitously broke in his mitts. Up on the mountainside above the
cape they had built a stone igloo and covered it with canvas. Wilson
had intended to prepare the embryos there, and had pitched their
tent just outside in order to protect their stores. Carrying the three
remaining eggs they crawled back up to the makeshift camp. 'Things
must improve,' said Wilson, before they all tried to sleep. But things
did not improve. A storm-force katabatic gale blew down on them
from the mountain, and ripped away their tent. Shortly afterwards

the canvas cover of the igloo was also ripped away. The men lay in their frozen bags, shivering as if they had lockjaw, and waited for death. But still it did not come.

It took three days for the wind to lull. Each man was plotting how they could manage the seventy miles back to safety without a tent or canvas. They still had a groundsheet, and were thinking of digging a tray out of the ice every night to lie in, protecting themselves only with this thin covering. They knew they were fooling themselves: without the tent they would soon die. Still they had no thought of discarding the eggs.

When the wind finally abated they made a forlorn and seemingly hopeless search for the tent in the darkness. Against all reasonable possibility Bowers found it, half a mile down the slope towards the sea. The extraordinary vacuum pressure of the gale that pulled it up had also snapped it shut like an umbrella. It was so heavy with ice that Cherry-Garrard estimated its weight as approaching fifty kilos. The bamboos and the outer lining had tangled together, preventing it from opening again into the wind. If these three factors had not acted together the tent would surely have been lost. In stunned and grateful silence they stared at one another, until Bowers suggested they go back down to collect more eggs – a suggestion Wilson sensibly refused. They loaded the sledges and turned back towards home. From now on Bowers would sleep with the tent tied down to his waist by a rope.

Cherry-Garrard had not slept properly for over a month. It was at about this stage in the journey he began to sleep while pulling the sledge, waking only if he bumped into Bowers. He began to fantasise about what he might give to receive even one night's good warm sleep. Five years of his life, he concluded.

On the return journey they made better time – perhaps the wind had scoured away most of the deep snow that plagued them on the way out. Sometimes a thin shell lies over the surface of a polar ice surface, a brittle crust shielding an air gap that can be several inches deep. I have experienced the phenomenon many times on the Brunt: a step on to otherwise pristine ice would trigger a slump, and a large area around a footfall would collapse down with a sickening 'whump'. I had no fear of crevasses within the Halley perimeter, but

Cherry-Garrard did not have that luxury. On the return he describes the experience of digging a hole in the snow only to trigger a settlement of snow that dropped the sledges, tents, and all three of them about a foot. They waited with held breath to see if they would continue to fall further, but did not. Over these days of the return journey the air became stiller, but also much colder. 'I don't know why our tongues never got frozen,' he wrote, 'but all my teeth, the nerves of which had been killed, split to pieces.' One of their thermometers recorded minus 77.5°F, about minus 60°C.

Still they held their manners and their tempers. As they drew closer to Hut Point, where more stores were depoted, they even began to enjoy themselves. Cherry-Garrard wrote of the happiness of his memories of those days, joking with Bowers and Wilson, thinking of the food and warmth that awaited them. Wilson even suggested that when they reach the storage hut they camp outside it, so that they did not overwhelm their bodies with too much heat. This suggestion, however nobly intended, was quietly ignored. They found that no fresh oil or sleeping bags had been left for them and Cherry-Garrard's disappointment at the thoughtlessness of the main party a few miles along the coast at Cape Evans is thinly veiled.

On the final stretch to Cape Evans, Wilson told the men 'I couldn't have found two better companions – and what is more I never shall.' He urged them to spread out so that a watchman would see that all three had survived, but there was no watchman there to welcome them.

'This journey had beggared our language,' Cherry-Garrard wrote later, 'no words could express its horror.' He repeatedly states that the relentless physical misery these men had endured is not only unimaginable, it is indescribable. The only way to understand it would be to re-experience it and to do so willingly would be madness. As a legend among polar survival stories it stands with Shackleton's journey from the break-up of the *Endurance* to the arrival at Stromness in South Georgia.

Why do stories like these prove so popular? Perhaps it is the wonder they inspire, the sense of reflected glory we feel that despite everything that had happened to them these men stayed well in their spirits, and kept their peace with God and with one another. They are thrillers, fast-paced and exciting, but represent real events.

Part of the pleasure of reading them is of wondering how we would cope with a similar situation. And the secret of their endurance? Shackleton on the *Endurance* failed even to step on continental Antarctica, Scott died on the walk home, and Wilson's eggs added little to science. Cynics might suggest that, as the empire began to crumble, tales of heroic disappointment were more resonant with the British reading public, and more amenable to transformation into legend than triumphalist success stories. Other extraordinary survival stories, of shipwrecks, for example, or wartime PoW camps, have resisted canonisation in quite the same way. Perhaps these lack some sanctifying effect of the Antarctic continent itself.

A photograph taken soon after their arrival, as they had staggered into the hut and were brought hot drinks and sandwiches, shows something of the characters of the three men and the changes wrought by their experience. Bowers is blowing on his cocoa, and looks as if he is ready to step out and do the whole thing again. Wilson is on the left, there is a fire in his eyes; he was a deeply religious man and there is an intensity about his stare that speaks of transcendence, as if he has reached a new level of understanding with his God. Of the three men Cherry-Garrard has come off worst; his sunken eyes, taut cheeks, and blackened skin speak of a man taken to the limit of what the spirit can endure. His hollow gaze looks back at us, cosy in our armchairs, like a man reprieved from the edge of the abyss.

My copy of *The Worst Journey in the World* is in two volumes, a reprint by Penguin that came out in 1937, some fifteen years after the first edition. 'I am glad the *Worst Journey* is coming out in Penguin,' Cherry-Garrard notes at the start of it, 'after all it is largely about penguins.' The description of the winter journey is the final chapter of volume one. So it is that the last pages in the book jump forward two years to 1913, as the three embryos are presented to the Natural History Museum in South Kensington as Wilson would have wanted. It is a chilling postscript, and long after publication still has the power to shock. Wilson and Bowers are dead, buried in the Ross Ice Shelf. To their bearer the embryos have become symbols of the courage and self-sacrifice of the two men. Outside the office of the museum custodian Cherry-Garrard is ignored, then spoken to rudely ('This ain't an egg-shop'), then after finally handing them over is refused a receipt for them. On his return a few months later with Captain Scott's sister he finds that no one knows what has been done with them.

In the end, thanks no doubt in part to the fury of Scott's sister, the embryos were found. They were passed to a Professor Assheton who, owing to the distraction caused by the war, did little with them. Assheton then died and they were passed on to a Professor Cossar Ewart of Edinburgh University. In 1922 Cossar Ewart published a brief external examination of them which is appended to *The Worst Journey*, and which concluded that the feather papillae of the emperor embryos did indeed suggest a connection with reptilian scales.

In 1932 and 1934 an anatomist called Parsons published deeper studies of the three embryos and came to a different conclusion – the three specimens had not added greatly to human knowledge about penguin embryology or ancestry after all. It is in this context that, having crashed his aeroplane off the Antarctic Peninsula, Bernard Stonehouse made his collection of timed penguin embryos in 1949.

When Stonehouse brought his embryos back to the British Museum in 1950 he was accorded a more cordial welcome than Cherry-Garrard had received. The Department of Natural History put him in touch with the anatomist T. W. Glenister of Charing Cross Hospital, whose assessment was published by FIDS in 1953.

From the start it is clear that Glenister had a good idea not only of the potential scientific importance of the embryos but of the sensitivity that had to be shown in discussions about them, given what they represented. Cherry-Garrard was still alive at the time, but after decades obsessing over his part in the *Terra Nova* expedition, seemed to have lost interest. 'Cherry-Garrard was living largely in a world of memories when I met him over lunch in 1950,' Bernard Stonehouse told me. 'He spoke freely about the Worst Journey, but seemed not very interested in our findings. I sent him copies of my publications, but he did not acknowledge them.'

'It seems incredible', Glenister writes of the Cape Crozier embryos, 'that embryos of such rarity and biological importance, collected with such determination and under such appalling conditions, should have been treated with so little interest and sense of urgency.' The forty years since Cherry-Garrard had sat in an office in South Kensington had seen many changes: the British Empire was falling apart, two world wars had been fought, and of critical importance, the story of Scott's 'failed' expedition had been transformed into a national legend. Cherry-Garrard's book, in as much as it is an elegy for a vanished era and an unflinching appraisal of the merits and faults of Scott, played a large part in effecting that transformation.

Glenister writes that the pineal gland, that organ of darkness, is highly developed in Stonehouse's embryos but no more so than in budgerigars. He calls it 'comparable to the parietal eye of saurians'. Much of the report is highly technical ('the epibranchial placodes in relation to the first visceral furrow are particularly well developed'), but he does comment that the tails of the emperor embryos seem to develop in the same way as those of turtles, and the developing heart goes through the same series of convolutions as that of reptiles. He searches for evidence of a 'Jacobson's organ', that specialised tissue characteristic of reptiles that allows snakes to taste the air. But he cannot find one, concluding perhaps that Stonehouse had not collected a specimen from exactly the day in which a rudimentary Jacobson's may have appeared then disappeared. 'Its absence from these embryos therefore detracts little from the hypothesis that penguins are the most primitive of birds living today ... Wilson's conjectures appear to have been justified.'

Like the FIDS scientific reports I had read about the aurora australis, Glenister's report is well illustrated with plates. His embryos drift in a funereal blackness, like the Antarctic darkness from which they were taken. They look startled to be exposed to the dissecting lamp, their swollen pineal glands bulging towards the light. At several stages of development they seem to resemble crocodiles, the extant reptile thought to be closest in development to birds. In his choice of illustrations, Glenister shows himself to be sensitive to aesthetics, as if he is aware that his photographs should convey the beauty of the process he wishes to unravel.

He does not hide his admiration for Stonehouse. The conditions around Dion Islets in 1949 where Stonehouse worked were milder than those between Cape Evans and Cape Crozier in 1911, and Stonehouse had far better equipment, but they were still deplorable. Despite the weather the embryos were preserved in an excellent state. 'This is due in no small measure to the skill and enthusiasm of Stonehouse,' Glenister commented, 'who collected and fixed these specimens in very difficult circumstances in the middle of an Antarctic winter.' I like to think of Stonehouse, crouched in the clamour of the rookery at Dion Islets, and Glenister, crouched over his microscope in the white-tiled laboratories of Charing Cross. They inhabited different worlds, but worked with the same aim in mind – to complete the work that Edward Wilson had begun.

Wilson hoped that the dissection of the embryos from Cape Crozier would cement the link between reptiles and birds. The link seems arbitrary, but birds and reptiles are closely linked in phylogeny as well as in human ideas. When Wagner's Siegfried tasted the blood of the dragon he began to understand the language of birds. Some dinosaur skeletons show remarkable similarities with those of birds – a dinosaur called sinosauropteryx had hairs on the ends of its scales that may have been the earliest feathers. And penguins' feathers are as important for swimming as those of the albatross are for flying.

DNA hybridisation techniques have shown that penguins and

albatrosses, both primitive birds, are closely related. Over two centuries ago Linnaeus seems to have realised the connection: he initially included the jackass penguin in his genus *Diomedea*, a genus in which he had at that time placed only one other species: the wandering albatross. Penguins and albatrosses, or their common ancestor, were once thought to hold the key to how birds evolved from their dinosaur predecessors.

Through the nineteenth century a series of prestigious scientists added their intellectual weight to the question of penguins' origins: Thomas Huxley, a gifted naturalist who saw the world as a ship's surgeon, commented in 1867 on how similar they were to the Great Auk (*Pinguinnis impennis*, now extinct, its genus being one of the theories of the origin of the name 'penguin'). In 1887, however, Menzbier thought that penguins had a unique reptilian ancestor, different from all other birds, and Newton, in 1896, wrote that 'There is perhaps scarcely a feather or a bone [of a penguin] which is not diagnostic, and nearly every character hitherto observed points to a low morphological rank.'

In 1905 Ameghino, the Patagonian polymath and avid collector of fossils, expounded his belief that penguin ancestors passed through a flightless terrestrial stage before becoming aquatic. Lowe in 1933 was fascinated by the tarsometatarsus of penguins, the bones that in humans correspond to the joint just below the ankle. '[it] is absolutely unique in the class Aves,' he wrote, 'a similar modification is conspicuous in the bipedal dinosaurs'.

Whenever I looked at the scaly feet of an emperor I thought of the reptile beneath, of a child's fascination with dinosaurs, of the death of Siegfried's dragon, and wondered if I too might learn the language of birds.

I felt anxious about breaking into the first egg. I had no idea if the penguin chick within would still be microscopic, too small to see, or almost fully formed and difficult to get out. Even though any chick inside would have been dead for nearly a year there was a trepidation about cracking the shell that had something to do with reverence for life, and something to do with respecting the dead. It was early June; down at the coast the emperors would be laying. Thinking about the eggs and Wilson, Cherry-Garrard and

Stonehouse, I had wrapped my own stash of emperor eggs in a plastic bag and thawed them out. After a few moments deliberation I cut a hole in the base of the first one with a drill and peered in.

A tuft of black feathers surfaced. I widened the hole and, using some tweezers, managed to get hold of the chick's beak. I drew it out and, opening the hole further, delivered the crown. Its head swung down, neck spindle-thin, like a suicide on a rope. Its eyes were closed; black eyes with white patches around them, a panda cub in negative. Emperor penguin chicks have an egg tooth, and a special neck muscle which withers after hatching. Even so, it can take them three days to break through the armoured shell. Perhaps this one had tried to do so. I cracked the rest of the egg and admired the neatness with which the chick fitted, the tapering of the tail and hindquarters into the apex of the shell, the economy of nature. I had found some stainless-steel trays in the medical room and laid it out like a body in a morgue.

The next egg was easier. I punctured the shell and the albumen started to spill out, then stopped abruptly. Looking inside I saw a fleshy knob was blocking the hole, rounded like a fingertip in a dyke. I nosed it up and again caught the beak in the tweezers, delicate as a twig, and pulled it through. Its naked neck was ribbed like an earthworm and its skin was pale, almost translucent. It was rubbery and etiolated like grass left under a stone. It looked midstage, maybe a month's gestation. Through the thin skin of the head I could see the dark outline of eyes that filled the skull, eyes that would, if they had survived, have tracked the glint of fish half a kilometre under the sea. When Wilson collected eggs on those earliest *Discovery* trips to Cape Crozier he had hoped to find an embryo at just such a stage as this, but all of his eggs had been much further developed.

The rest of the body slipped out followed by the yolk sac and the remainder of the albumen. Its wings and feet were stubby and translucent, like tadpole tails, and pinprick feathers shadowed the skin around the abdomen and tail. They rubbed away in my gloved hands.

A third egg was addled, a turbid soup, coloured and fronded like Sargasso weed. I flushed it away for its sulphurous stink. A fourth was well preserved, but the embryo inside, a dark germ on the yolk, was too early to see properly. In the medical room I had an ancient microscope for performing blood counts on humans but none of the chemicals I would need to fix dead penguin tissue. I realised that I was wholly unprepared for carrying out any serious or helpful research on the emperors, alive or dead, though there is still a great deal unknown about them that I could perhaps have worked on.

In Wilson's day it was the doctor's job to be expedition naturalist in the Antarctic, but with the professionalisation of the sciences and the transformation of BAS from a flag-waving tool of the Foreign Office to a world-class scientific organisation, that role had been quietly dropped. It is now the work of postdoctoral research fellows and big-budget funding. At Halley the emperors were too low a priority, a worthy day trip for holidays and visiting dignitaries, but little else. Stonehouse himself told me of his disappointment that BAS had refused his requests to carry out any biological work on the emperors at Halley.

Despite my lack of equipment or direction I got on with studying them in my own quiet way, not contributing anything to the world's knowledge but attending to my own curiosity, sense of wonder, and gratitude that as human beings we were not alone in this place.

CHAPTER NINE

# *Midwinter*

And this is the tale the watchman
Awake in the dead of night,
Tells of the fourteen sleepers
Whose snoring gives him the blight.

Ernest Shackleton, 'Midwinter Night'

It is possible to lock the door in only two places at Halley: the toilet and the darkroom. As well as a digital camera I had brought a clunky old Minolta with me, a fully manual SRT model, because it didn't need batteries and wouldn't seize up in the cold. When I bought it I had asked if it was robust. 'Go ahead and try it,' the shopkeeper said. 'You can hammer in nails with that thing if you have to.' Long after the digital camera had died or whined or jammed, that camera kept going. Changing rolls outdoors became a fine and dextrous art, you had to weave the new film into the spool and wind it in quickly before the acetate chilled into rigidity and cracked. I became adept at picking broken pieces of film from the bowels of the camera mechanism. I had new respect for Scott's and Shackleton's photographers, Herbert Ponting and Frank Hurley, who worked with far more demanding equipment.

I alternated slide film and monochrome, but gave up developing slide film myself when the films emerged with psychedelic penguins. From then on I stored the exposed film in the surgery fridge, next to the travel vaccinations, until it was time to go home. I was more experimental with the black and white, and spent hours in the darkroom developing and printing images. Sometimes it was a relief just to go somewhere I could lock the door.

Photography involved resourcefulness as the winter darkness deepened and the temperature continued to fall. I had a wind-up timer that screwed into the camera. With ungloved fingers I'd mount the Minolta on a tripod then spring the timer, stand back, and wait for the click. When the temperature was lower than minus 40°C the shutter would sometimes stick open, but the exposures of stars, auroras or moonbeams always needed several seconds anyway. I'd count out loud and, lens cap in hand, sneak up on the tripod and pounce. A stealthy sleight of hand brought the exposure to an end, and winding on the film would usually bring down the shutter if it had frozen in place.

Back in the darkroom I'd develop the film. The negatives took time to dry out before they could be placed into the enlarger and, after fiddling with the focus, I'd shine light through them on to the baseplate and paper. The best moment was when they went into the developing bath. Silvered worlds, protected by their frames, emerged one by one into the darkness.

The darkroom was one way of being alone; going out to stay at the caboose beyond the Halley perimeter was another. In going so often to the caboose I'm not sure if I was being reclusive. The word 'recluse' has in its roots the Latin verb *claudere*, meaning 'to close' or 'to stop'. It carries the flavour of an active rather than passive decision, as in 'to make inaccessible'. The weekends I spent out at the caboose did not feel like a closing off from the world, rather an opening up. Leaving the base – the hum of the generators, the schedule of meals, the parties in the bar – was a way of looking outwards, a way to listen very intently to the powerful silence that lay between the elements of this landscape. Even the journey to get there was an exercise in the expansion of awareness. In the absence of moonlight the drums that marked the perimeter lines could only be seen from two or three metres away. Guided only by the white breath of the stars it was necessary to strike out tentatively, counting the drums as one went. Nine drums from the Simpson platform and you had reached the perimeter. At the ninth drum turn left, to the north, and count eleven drums more. From the eleventh drum the caboose lay to the north-east, at a distance of about fifty metres. The walk out to it was a journey of faith. A flapping flag off the perimeter line could be mistaken for the caboose on the darkest days.

Away from base the silence grew in power, and benevolence. It had a depth and ease which I grew to love and return to. Usually when I arrived at the caboose the door would be iced up. Kicking it free I would climb in and get the paraffin lamps going by the light of a headtorch. The air vents were often clogged with ice, but standing on the bunk beds it was possible to force open a hatch in the ceiling, climb out on to the roof and unblock them. Standing on the roof and looking back the base could be seen about a kilometre off, its halogen lamps like prison searchlights. Through the fog of my own breath I would fire up the stove and make some tea. By the time the cup was empty there would be a fierce temperature gradient in the caboose – above the waist I'd be naked, my head and torso in tropical heat but at my ankles the air would be around minus 20°C, and I would have to keep my mukluks on. Water dripping from the ceiling, sweat dripping from my forehead, would form stalagmites of ice in the buckets arrayed around the floor.

Hours slipped by. I had a stack of books on the bunk, a 'to read' list from the trunk of volumes that I had brought to Antarctica. It felt as if there was plenty to keep me busy – adjusting the stove, making tea, washing up dishes, looking out of the window. And when my mind could take no more printed words or my stomach no more hot sweet tea, I could put on all my gear and go to lie outside for a while. It had been months since I had had to contend with the flashbulb traffic of a 'normal' life. At Halley I had hoped that the background radio-chatter of my mind might be stilled. In that I had not been disappointed, though I still felt there was a long way to go. As far as working out what I wanted to do with my life after this long period of reflection, I was no further forward. The silence and space around me were so addictive I wondered if I would ever have enough of them. Perhaps I'd find ways of continuing this life in polar landscapes after all. The inclines and contours of my subconscious were rising up as other waters receded. Now deep into the winter I imagined how the lives of my friends and family were unfolding in the north.

My parents had written that they were experiencing the hottest summer for decades, and were out in the garden having barbecues every weekend. Careers of my colleagues were progressing while mine stood literally on ice. Esa had decided to quit her job in Milan and move to Beirut to teach. She had written that she was unable to imagine the darkness, the coldness and the silence of Antarctica, while for me the heat and the humanity of Arab cities seemed to be part of another world, and another, impossible life.

I had found a book on astronomy in the Simpson, and often took it out to the caboose with me. I'd lie on my back on the ice, far from base, acquainting myself with the unfamiliar stars.

There was Miaplacidus, a Latin–Arabic hybrid meaning 'placid waters'. And Achernar, a blue-white star 3,000 times brighter than the sun. It spins so quickly it appears oval. I picked out Antares, 'the rival of Ares' (Mars), bleeding crimson in the waist of Scorpio. It has been found to be a red giant whose girth, transposed to our solar system, would reach to the asteroid belt. I also came to recognise Canopus, visible to ancient astronomers low in the sky over the upper reaches of the Nile, it was named Kahi Nub or 'golden earth' by the Copts to reflect the glow of the desert horizon. The Arabs knew these heavens better than the Greeks, their knowledge born of long trading journeys into Africa and the Indian Ocean. Flourishes of Arabic twisted through the constellations: al-Suhail al Mulif, al-Suhail al Wazn. I knew the Southern Cross from trips to the Antipodes, but it was a shock to see it almost directly overhead. Sometimes on the northern horizon I would glimpse Orion, upside down, and I would feel a connection to the sky of my childhood, the arching continuity of space. Even from the bottom of the world he swung his club of suns; stars and nebulae dangled from his belt. Orion spans the poles – to the Inuit the stars of his belt are Siagtut, three hunters lost on the ice.

Often at the time I walked out on the ice Sirius, the Dog Star, could be seen flaring like a welding spark on the north-east horizon. Sailors talk of 'ocean stars' that skirt the ocean's rim. Some of my favourites I began to think of as 'ice stars', refracted through the horizon's glow. To the south-west Scorpio's sting curled into the galactic meridian. I watched for the Magellanic Clouds, woolly blushes of light called 'the Sheep' by the Arabs.

170,000 years ago, when mastodons and glyptodons still grazed in the north, a star exploded there. The light of that blast, the first supernova to be observed by modern astronomers, reached earth in 1987 and a pulse of neutrinos (most easily detected far from the contamination of man) was picked up in Antarctica.

Wordsworth said that stone held acquaintance with the stars. Thinking of the simplicity of the world around me, the quantum sliding into the stellar, I could think the same of ice. There was a quality to its brittle purity, its cold strength, that was echoed in the stars above. And in a world of ice starlight is often all the light you need.

I would tell myself that the universe is expanding, solar systems are collapsing and being born, that the stars were rushing away from me at unimaginable speeds. But all I could see was eternity. Lying out on the ice, watching stars at any hour of the 'night' or 'day', brought an appreciation of the messy, organic world that as human beings we inhabit; how frail and complex our breathing pulsing digesting organisms are by comparison. I'd try to focus on the infinite, imagine myself disintegrated into the simplest of constituent elements. But I could not give up the messiness of life or remain a recluse forever. I had to involve myself with Life, and in Antarctica that meant going back to the penguins.

I was not at the caboose, skiing, or messing about in the darkroom all the time. As the doctor on base I was involved in research examining the psychological and physical response to the pervasive darkness of our lives. Just as emperor penguins do, we humans have a pineal gland in the deepest kernel of our brains. Buried in darkness, the pineal learns about ambient light through stray nerve fibres that are diverted from the optic tracts; signals intended for our visual cortex are guttered off to a lower, more primitive place. The less light transmitted to it the more melatonin our pineal gland makes – in lower latitudes its secretion peaks at night. The hormone of darkness spreads through our bodies as we sleep like a drop of ink sinking through a glass of milk. It sets your body clock, telling the functions of our bodies when it is time to rest and be still, and when it is time to be active and wakeful.

Our bodies are not designed for high latitudes; we are tropical mammals. Through a polar night our melatonin gets out of kilter, causing chaos to our circadian rhythms. Without a night-time peak of the hormone we can become destabilised, 'free-running', our bodies falling into a twenty-two-, twenty-three- or even twenty-five-hour rhythm instead of the celestially ordained twenty-four. Whether we go short or long as free-runners is genetically determined according to things called clock genes; early risers tend towards a shorter day length, night owls to over run.

There are other *zeitgebers*, or 'time-givers'. Maintaining a pattern of food intake is important, as is the timing of our exercise, as is the hormone cortisol. But it is on melatonin that interest has focussed, offering as it does the promise of a cure for jet lag, insomnia, and quick adaptation for the toiling legions of humanity who work night shifts.

At Halley we all took a turn at a week of night shift, and adaptation to nights was one of the ways it was possible to study the effect of darkness on our body clocks. Fire-watch night shifts were another BAS tradition with its origins in the days of all-wooden bases and no sprinkler systems. Neumayer base, the German station hundreds of kilometres to the east, had done away with night shifts, but we carried on with them. I was glad we did.

Halley, despite its location, could feel crowded. Night shift offered the chance to have the base, and the continent, to yourself. There were a few tasks to be done through the night: make fresh bread to be ready for breakfast, make up jugs of powdered milk and get them into the fridge, walk outside at 0300 and 0600 to check the weather – Halley had a continuous meteorological log stretching back fifty years. The necessity of walking out on the ice, whatever the weather, meant seeing auroras you might otherwise have missed. Many times I popped out for a moment, only to spend an hour on my back watching the sky.

My research project was fairly simple. Everyone on base wore a wristwatch with a light and a motion sensor embedded within it. The data gathered meant I could calculate the light each individual was exposed to, when they were most active, and, crucially, how well they slept at night (restlessness in the night having been well correlated with other measures of poor sleep).

I also collected urine samples of everyone coming on and off night shift, to assess melatonin levels and see how quickly their body returned to a normal 'day' rhythm. Previous Zdocs had gathered this information on the base with normal background lighting. With fluorescent strip lights and old filament bulbs the lighting at Halley was sepia-toned, sickly sweet like caramels. The studies had found the poor light was barely enough to convince the pineal gland there was any light there at all. My project used supplementary lights, alternating white and blue-enriched bulbs, to assess whether boosting the light with short wavelengths would be more effective at convincing the pineal that there was a shape to the day.

The lights were not a huge success, though there were some benefits. I did manage to double the light exposure of everyone on base, but it was still not enough to convince the pineal that we were back in the tropics. Blue bulbs seemed to make everyone sleep better, but only marginally. As the weeks sank into a deepening darkness, sleep became increasingly disrupted, and a couple of people started free-running on to a new, internally determined body clock of their own. When someone becomes free-running, the discipline of base routine goes under strain, and Pat, as base commander, was keen to keep it running to order. Indiscipline in waking and sleeping, it might be said, could lead to other kinds of indiscipline, and that would not have been tolerated.

The northern Inuit once lit their winters with blubber lamps. Trapped Arctic explorers have lit wicks of cotton in tins of ski-wax. Wilson, Bowers and Cherry-Garrard, on their famous winter journey to Cape Crozier, gave up on the twenty-four-hour day entirely as they found it did not contain enough hours for their needs. In those situations a day's routine is irrelevant, and the only priority is survival. To us, too, day was a distant memory; our night would last over one quarter of a year. Perhaps the extra bulbs were a futile gesture, like striking a match on the dark side of the moon. No matter how much we turned up the brightness, light from our base fell away into the dark as it would into a collapsing star. The continent was always hungry for more.

Towards the middle of June it was not only dark all day but

the mercury on the old thermometers, housed in Stevenson screens outside the Simpson, plummeted. I had just acclimatised to skiing in the low 40s below zero, though breathing hard at those temperatures my chest began to hurt and I often returned with blooms of 'frost-nip', a precursor of frostbite, waxing pale over my cheekbones and nose. As ice crystals formed inside my face it felt like the skin was being tented up with tiny hooks.

A continental high-pressure system moved in and the anemometer eased to a stop. As the barometer climbed the thermometer fell, bottoming out at minus 52°C. Rob worked away in the heating room – our heating came from exchangers built into the diesel generators – but they could not keep up and the temperature inside the base began to fall. The generators themselves were diesel engines like those in the snowcats. Those who could moved to the top bunk of their pit-room, and we all began to wear mukluks indoors. A two-kilowatt heater, mysteriously christened 'Fergus', was found in storage and left burning on the main Laws corridor day and night. A vogue developed for rushing out on to the platform and throwing a cup of boiling water into the air. It froze at once with a soft and percussive 'whoosh', a noise that unfailingly satisfied. Water thrown down would not splash, but stuck instantly to the wooden boards of the platform like iron thrown on a magnet. It seemed fun at the time, less fun when it had to be chipped off again with a pickaxe.

Below minus 50°C another Halley tradition kicked in: a naked streak around the Laws platform. Total nudity was not required; hats, gloves and mukluks were considered the minimum essential to prevent serious cold injury. Five of the men took part. As we ran round the platform legs, it was not the skin but the lungs that felt the cold the most, as if the winter was reaching inside and pulling life out of our bodies at the source.

John Davis, an Elizabethan adventurer who tried to find the way through the North-West Passage, spent long winters in the Arctic and was well acquainted with such cold. He wrote: 'as the heat in all climates is indurable, by the eternal ordinance of the creator, so likewise the cold is sufferable by his everlasting decree, for otherwise nature should bee monstrous'. I did not share Davis' faith in the benevolence of the creator, but I was fascinated by his belief that all degrees of cold should be suffer-able. Dante after all had reserved ice for his most torturous circle of hell. Some 330 years after Davis, Richard Byrd would have a different perspective. For him the polar winter was a dead world, in which human beings were in grave peril: 'This was the polar night, the morbid countenance of the Ice Age. Nothing moved, nothing was visible. This was the soul of the inertness. One could almost hear a distant creaking as if a great weight were settling.'

The first night it dropped below minus 50°C I put on all the clothes I had and went to lie out on the ice. I put my giant 'bear paw' mittens down first, one under my hips, one under my shoulders. There was a subterranean stillness to the air. Exhaling gently into the silence I heard an unfamiliar sound: the vapour in my breath was freezing immediately as it left my mouth. It rustled and tinkled like the very distant breaking of glass. Breath not only had a sound here, it had a colour. As my breath transformed above me, the starlight beyond it was transmuted into haloes of rainbow and gold. By blowing hard or soft they grew and shrank, rising up from the chest and dissipating inches above my mouth. Some Arctic peoples have a word for the sound of breath freezing, but I have not heard that they have a word for the colours that breath makes against the stars.

I watched the increasingly familiar constellations. Two satellites crossed over one another, and a meteorite plunged icewards towards the Pole. The moon was almost full, marbled and cracked like an ice-shattered stone. Its light galvanised the ice, bending around the horizon from the north-north-east, the direction of Africa. A silver cascade spilled down from it, a 'moon pillar', like a flying buttress supporting the sky. Perhaps Davis was right, I thought, this was not the dead world that Byrd experienced. It was a living and changing part of our planet.

I thought of the hundreds of metres of ice below me, and below that, the cooled black crust of the Antarctic Plate soaking in a polar sea. Beneath that crust hot magma was coiling and flowing through unseen canyons. African gold mines have been sunk so deep that they approach that heat. From the summer heat of the veldt you can take an elevator into the cool darkness of earth, and then descend towards those magma chambers where the rock walls sweat and soften.

The coldest temperature so far recorded on the planet's surface, minus 89.2°C, was experienced at the Russian Antarctic station *Vostok*. In 1957, the year the Americans built their station at the South Pole, the Russians were one step ahead – that same year they built Vostok on the most inaccessible and austere part of the Antarctic plateau *and* put Sputnik into orbit. Vostok is higher, colder, and as it is closer to the South Magnetic Pole it is a better place than the geographic South Pole to make atmospheric observations.

For those of us at Halley, Vostok had a quasi-mythical status. The hardest base on a continent of extremes, it was spoken of in hushed and reverential tones. The *average* Vostok temperature in June is said to be around minus 65°C, making it almost impossible to go outside for more than a few minutes. Like the climate, its social problems were legendary. It was whispered that one summer the relieving team had arrived to find each wintering man barricaded into his own pit-room. For months each had been living on a private store of tinned food.

Vostok winterers would no doubt have found Halley a breeze, but after ten minutes outside at minus 50°C my hips and shoulders began to ache. My legs and jaw began to shiver, then my eyelashes rimed over and threatened to gel my eyelids closed. Delicate spicules of frost, fine as a baby's hair, were precipitating over the cotton fibres of my jacket. I was fortunate not to be hypothermic, undernourished, exhausted, demoralised, like so many in the earliest days of Antarctica's exploration. If I were it would have been so easy to be overwhelmed by the winter, to let my spark of life drain down into the ice and be lost in the enormity of the continent.

The twist in the spine of our planet had angled us into the dark for seven weeks. We had reached the winter solstice, now it would bend us back towards the light.

Midwinter on Antarctic bases is more than an excuse for a party. It means that the darkness has been half-endured, that we are moving towards the sun again. BAS stations declare a week's holiday from all routine work. All the Christmas decorations are put up, and everyone on base gives presents. The true meaning of Christmas is revealed: a festival of darkness in which we celebrate the promise of light returning. Pat called me into his base commander's office and gave me a Christmas card, signed by a Zdoc who'd been at Halley seven years previously. He must have left a stack of them in the office, time capsules for Halley doctors far into the future. 'Dear Zdoc,' it said inside. 'I hope you're having a brilliant winter, and if not, you're halfway there. Signed, Zdoc.'

For weeks we had been preparing presents for one another. We had each pulled the name of one other base member from a hat. I had drawn Mark S., the only other man on base who made a point of going outside every day, and had spent hours in the caboose beyond the perimeter knitting him a hat, scarf and attempting unsuccessfully to make him gloves. By coincidence he had drawn my name, and made me a picture frame holding an image of clouds in the Halley sky. The image itself was framed with different pieces of wood, made up to look as if the viewer gazes out through the window of a hermit's hut. In the centre of the frame he'd put a tree. For all his silences he had observed me closely, and given me what I valued most: a retreat, the Antarctic skies, and the possibility of trees. I was touched, and felt the hat and scarf I'd made for him, though well intentioned, were meagre gifts in comparison.

In the week's run-up to midwinter we received a series of 'personalised' faxes from world leaders. The British prime minister told us of his pride in the work we were doing. The president of the USA told us that he and his wife were impressed by our 'God-given scientific gifts to advance the knowledge of mankind'. The Chinese message was all in Mandarin. We received no less than five messages of support from Indian government dignitaries, including the prime minister and several cabinet secretaries. The minister for ocean development told us that we must all be extraordinarily inspirational people to live and work in such an un-Indian environment.

प्रधान मंत्री
Prime Minister
<u>MESSAGE</u>

**[For Station Commanders of all Antarctic Stations, Antarctica]**

On the occasion of 'Antarctic Mid-Winter Day, June 21, I convey my warm greetings to you all. The people of India admire your courage and determination in braving harsh conditions of Antarctica in pursuing frontiers of scientific knowledge. I wish you all a fruitful and successful stay in Antarctica and a happy journey back home.

---

Throughout the week we had only the dimmest of glimmers on the northern horizon around noon – all else was darkness. Every day of the 'holiday' there was a different activity planned: bungee races down the Laws corridor, quiz nights, fancy dress.

On midwinter's afternoon we crowded into the living room to listen to the BBC World Service broadcast a midwinter's message, organised for us by BAS headquarters in Cambridge. They had contacted our friends and families to record greetings. The ionosphere was uncooperative, and we strained over the static to hear the voices of the people we loved bend around the bulge of the planet. I heard Esa shout 'I love you' from an Italian phone box, then say the day was so hot her shoes were sinking into the pavement. Mark S. recorded the programme on tape, and later I played it over and over again, imagining that distant world where water could be liquid out of doors and where tarmac might melt. The temperature was more than 40°C with her, while for me it approached 40°C below.

We had all taken responsibility to convert a different room or space in order to have a themed pub crawl. Annette, Elaine and Stuart had turned the Simpson into a beach. I had made the library a forest, complete with hidden birdsong and trees made out of cardboard tubing and green paper. An ice cave had been dug out near the Simpson, and pints of gin and tonic were served on benches carved into the ice. The original Simpson, Scott's meteorologist, had had to conduct experiments in just such an ice cave. We finished up for the night on the beach at the platform named in his honour, sipping cocktails and talking about the five months remaining before our isolation would be broken.

On the way back from the Simpson to the Laws I stopped in the darkness, looking west. The moon was like the D of 'Darkness', a perfect semicircle. The sky was the black of the brain at the point of sleep, the stars glinting like neurons closing down for the night. There was no wind and the temperature was mild for midwinter, only minus 35°C. The beach party at the Simpson had been a reminder of another world that waited for us all in the north, a world that was daily growing closer. Down at our closest real beach the female emperors would all have left by now, their last eggs laid, and would be walking back to the open sea. The males were halfway through their four-month fast in the lowest temperatures on earth.

Shackleton's *Nimrod* expedition of 1907–9 was royally provisioned. Cherry-Garrard wryly commented that when luxuries were lacking on their *Terra Nova* sledging trips, you could usually find one of Shackleton's depots and dig down to some sheep's tongues, cheese or Rowntree's cocoa. At one depot they found a Primus stove in perfect working order which they used to the end of the expedition. Recently a trove of Mackinlay's single malt whisky was unearthed close to Shackleton's base hut at Cape Royds. It is often overlooked that in addition to all this luxury Shackleton carted a printing press to the Antarctic. On his *Nimrod* expedition he not only reached within a hundred miles of the South Pole, found the South Magnetic Pole, managed to make the first ascent of Mount Erebus, he printed the first ever truly Antarctic book, *Aurora*

*Australis*. It was printed in a limited edition of about a hundred copies, but I had managed to get hold of a facsimile edition, and brought it south.

The colophon on the inside cover showed two emperors, and the legend 'Printed at the Sign of the "The Penguins"; by Joyce and Wild. Latitude 77°..32′ South Longitude 166°..12′ East Antarctica. All rights reserved.' As editor Shackleton contributed a couple of heavily Tennyson-influenced poems and two prefaces. The first concludes: 'During the sunless months which are now our portion; months lit only by vagrant moon and elusive aurora; we have found in this work an interest and a relaxation, and hope eventually it will prove the same to our friends in the distant Northland.' The second apologises for the uneven quality of the inking, due, he reports, to the use of a candle to keep the inking plate of the printing press from frosting over. Going through the list of contents, my eye was immediately caught by a piece entitled 'Interview with an Emperor'. It was by one of the two expedition doctors, Alistair Forbes Mackay. It had been a couple of months since I had been able to visit the emperors, and I didn't know when I would next be able to make it back down to see them. I was intrigued that Shackleton's doctor too had been thinking and writing about their only neighbours during the long winter.

Mackay has a great love for the polar landscape, his prose lifts when describing the beauty that he sees in it. His piece opens with a description of a walk in the direction of Cape Crozier soon after midwinter. 'Such whites and blues! They were livid, ethereal, electric. Artists speak, I believe, of a dead white, but such an adjective could never be applied to the whites of the Antarctic snows by moonlight . . . it was like some lovely transformation scene, viewed by the wrapt gaze of childhood.' Despite the imperial aims of his expedition he goes on to describe what is, for him, the most intoxicating aspect of life in Antarctica: its un-ownedness. And then a note of comedy creeps in, hidden in the examination of a truth: 'This goodly portion of the Earth's fair surface was ours. No polluting foot save ours defaced its virgin solitudes . . . No uniformed park-ranger, or corduroyed gamekeeper could bar our way.' The only other life on this coast is the emperors, and he is as impressed by them as his surgeon predecessor Edward Wilson: they are 'the most majestic of living birds'.

But then from behind an iceberg steps a six-foot penguin with a truncheon made of seal bone under its wing. 'It must be a gamekeeper,' Mackay writes breathlessly, 'he is the most enormous Emperor Penguin I have ever met . . . I have had many a painful interview with gamekeepers and people of that kidney, but this one would take all my diplomacy to meet.' The penguin, astonishingly, has a broad Scots accent, and proceeds to frisk them for concealed eggs.

'"Weel Gentlemen," he says, "I'll jeest show ye aff the estate if he'll tell me whaur ye come frae, and what's yer beesiness?"'

Mackay goes on to offer whisky from a hip flask, gratefully accepted ('Man, yon's the richt stuff . . . it's gey scarce aboot here.') and parodies the conversations he must have had as a boy, chased by gamekeepers of the Scottish grouse estates of both the nouveau riche and the landed gentry.

'"Whose estate do we happen to have trespassed upon? I was not aware that there were any private grounds in this district."

'"Oo jeest Mr Forsteri, Aptenodytes Forsteri, a cousin o' the M. P., I'm surprised ye didna ken, man! It's a vera auld family."'

The giant penguin tells them that all the land that they can see is the property of Mr Forsteri. He becomes alarmed at their muttered excuses that they are only there to collect stone samples, because collecting stones implies to the penguin that they intend to build nests and breed there. Mackay quickly explains: '"Oh! no no," I said, "we merely collect the stones to take home, and show to people who are interested in them . . . Besides,"' he adds sadly, '"we've no hens with us."'

The penguin shows them off the 'estate', asking them not to go in the direction of Cape Crozier again. 'At any rate,' writes Mackay, 'we have obeyed his orders.' Wilson's, Bowers' and Cherry-Garrard's winter journey to Cape Crozier would not come for another three years.

Mackay's piece is surrealist, irreverent, and as a satire on land ownership, right on the mark. Giving the penguin a Scots accent and a penchant for whisky may have built on a private joke among the expedition members (perhaps when it was realised that some of the Mackinlay's malt whisky had been lost, it was presumed to have been taken by the penguins). But hidden within the narrative is a serious point: penguins are at home in this place and Mackay, like all humans in Antarctica, are interlopers. The creation of a mock estate shows up the concept of Antarctic land ownership for the illusion it really is. The emperors live, breed and die on those coasts. Mackay sums up the contrasting human position: 'we merely collect the stones to take home' and 'we've no hens with us'.

For our own midwinter publication Toddy drew on a similar theme with a design for a winterer's T-shirt. An angry emperor shoves one of us from a skidoo, and, twisting the accelerator, races for the horizon. It's their ice after all.

In our midwinter's photograph the Union Jack has been hung upside down. This may have been deliberate given that we hung upside down from the bottom of the planet. If not, it is an error that could never have been made by Scott or Shackleton's parties. In those days around midwinter I reread the official accounts of those explorers' more famous expeditions, to see what they had been doing at the coldest and darkest time of the year. It struck me again that two of those expeditions, Scott's with the *Terra Nova* and Shackleton's with the *Endurance*, were touched by failure and tragedy but also shone with the human capacity to transcend adversity. Perhaps that is the secret of their appeal after all. Much less attention is paid to those expeditions that run smoothly and successfully.

Shackleton's narrative of the *Endurance* trapped in the ice makes no mention of midwinter celebrations. The week of 15 June 1915 the men held an 'Antarctic Derby' with their dogs. Their main worry during this season, and an excellent distraction from more pressing concerns, was keeping the dogs well exercised. They knew their lives might yet come to depend on them. Across the continent in the Ross Sea some of the other half of his party, in the *Aurora*, had broken free of their moorings and were also drifting in the ice, somewhere around 76° South. Stenhouse, the acting captain of the *Aurora*, noted tersely 'to-day the sun has reached the limit of his northern declination, and now he will start to come south. Observed this day as a holiday.'

A year later Shackleton was in Punta Arenas, Chilean Patagonia, hosted by one Allan McDonald and trying to scrape together money and a ship to rescue his men trapped on Elephant Island. He had gone to Chile after receiving a frosty reception in the Falkland Islands, two attempts having already failed to rescue the men. Those men, meanwhile, barracked in two upturned boats, were enjoying a 'magnificent breakfast' of hoosh thickened with hot milk and a pudding of 'powdered biscuit boiled with twelve pieces of mouldy nut-food'. One of the items rescued from the wreck of the *Endurance* and carried all the way to the island was the 'practically unharmed' banjo of the meteorologist Leonard Hussey. Crowding into one of the boats the men had a sing-song, though they knew their chances of rescue were becoming slim.

Five years earlier on the other side of the continent Scott's party at Cape Evans were having a more traditional celebration. In his diary for midwinter's night, Apsley Cherry-Garrard noted that the men were all asked to make speeches, and instead of a speech Bowers produced a home-made Christmas tree of bamboo, ski-sticks and feathers. They all drank milk punch and danced together. Anton the Russian dog driver danced so well that 'he put the Russian ballet in the shade'. Where we had racks of DVDs to watch, they watched a slide show of Ponting's photographs. 'It was', said Cherry-Garrard, 'a magnificent bust.'

The following winter, 1912, their spirits were far lower. The polar party had not returned, neither had the geological party led by Victor Campbell. Campbell's party was meant to have been relieved by the *Terra Nova* but the ship had been unable to get through the ice to reach them. The men were forced to winter in a snow cave on a rock they named Inexpressible Island and survived on slaughtered penguins and seals. Most of the party contracted dysentery. The doctor in the party, George Murray Levick, managed to express his feelings about the experience like this: 'The road to hell might be paved with good intentions, but it seemed probable that hell itself would be paved something after the style of Inexpressible Island.'

Nine men had gone north on the *Terra Nova* to winter in New Zealand. Thirteen men were left at Cape Evans to go into another winter. Cherry-Garrard mourned the loss of Wilson and Bowers terribly. His book makes no mention of midwinter celebrations that year, noting only that he felt pressured to produce a copy of the *South Polar Times* in time for midwinter's day, which he managed to do. At Halley ours did not appear until August. Atkinson, another of the doctors, was 'base commander' in the absence of Scott. He convened a meeting through the winter to decide what the men were to do the following spring and summer. Would they go north and west, to find Campbell and his men who had been landed with some stores and so were thought to be still alive? Or would they go south, to try to find traces of what had become of the polar party who must surely be dead? Cherry-Garrard wrote 'it seemed to me unthinkable that we should leave live men to search for those who were dead', but later changed his mind. Around midwinter Atkinson put it to the vote, and only one member, Lashly, did not vote for going south. 'Considering the complexity of the question I was surprised by this unanimity,' Cherry-Garrard commented.

Campbell's men did return to safety in the end, and the southern sledging party in the summer of 1912 did of course find Scott's tent. The story of the journey, and the myth that has grown around it, owes itself to that vote. Scott's last diary entry had been made on 29 March 1912, only eleven miles from a depot that would have saved their lives. The papers found on him – such as the letter to Wilson's wife, to Bowers' mother, to J. M. Barrie, and his 'Message to the Public' – have entered British legend.

At Halley we were not living the life of legends. Our lives were extraordinary, privileged, extreme and very isolated, but after reading these accounts they also seemed very safe.

# CHAPTER TEN

# The Third Quarter

An almost monotonous discontent occurs in every expedition through the polar night . . . we are at this moment as tired of each other's company as we are of the cold monotony of the black night.

Frederick Cook, *Through the First Antarctic Night*

Through July the atmosphere on base began to change for me. It was as if a minor chord had been woven into the air. Thoughts struggled to rise as if they were slippery with oil. My mind went soft and buttery. For months we had eaten together two or three meals a day, and we began to run out of things to say. An uneasy silence would descend around the table, like a family dinner with a drunken uncle. Russ pointed out to me that I had begun to hum under my breath during the longer dinner silences. I had not noticed, and began to see why Mark S. avoided mealtimes – this was his third winter at Halley. He, Ben, Annette and Elaine were now going through their second consecutive winter, each coping in their own way. Mark had begun to train hard outside, jogging daily around the perimeter in mukluks and goggles, with a view to getting fit for a man-hauling trip in spring. Ben seemed almost unaffected by the darkness. Perhaps he drank a little more as the winter wore on, but he also began to use the base's tiny gym two or three evenings a week, lifting weights and doing pull-ups to a soundtrack of thrash metal that echoed through the Laws. Elaine and Annette were both managing well. Annette spent long hours outside, watching the stars from the steps to the Simpson as if she was trying to capture as many memories as she could before she left. Elaine took refuge in practical jokes – she began to sneak into the boot room at night, secretly filling mukluks with a variety of cereals. She was careful to choose a different victim every week, and for a while it was the talk of the base to uncover a pattern in the attacks, to guess who might be responsible. She even contributed an anonymous article to the midwinter magazine, leaving it in secret on Tommo's workbench one morning. 'Boot bandit,' he wrote in his editorial. 'We salute you.' It remained a mystery until she confessed by email, weeks after leaving Halley.

Outside, the polar night had lost some of its beauty for me. It became a pause, a limbo, a drawn breath between history and the future. Skiing around the base I began to see the ice differently. Instead of an untrammelled expanse of free space I saw the way that it imprisoned. I had until now looked to the moon as a welcome friend, glancing as benevolently over the tropics and the people I loved as it did over the ice. Now it squinted down on me like a jailer's eye. Messages from the north seemed to slow down. I noticed myself becoming irrationally annoyed if my emails were not replied to within a few days.

For news we were faxed a one page précis in which wars, natural disasters and political summits merited a line each. Now this printout seemed too paltry; hungry for news from the north I crouched in the radio room, again attempting to tune in to a hissing and stuttering BBC World Service all the way from Africa. I imagined the other listeners in equatorial darkness, their news accompanied by the humming and whirring of tropical insects while I strained to catch the headlines over the roar of an Antarctic blizzard.

In her meditation on silence and solitude Sara Maitland discusses *accidie*, a listless, apathetic state of mind that can descend on hermits and ascetics who have spent long periods in silence. According to Maitland, who has experienced the phenomenon, the state can afflict even those who have freely chosen their solitude and who have the means and capacity to leave it behind. Much more serious psychological risks, she says, are run by those individuals who have not freely chosen their isolation or whose way out is barred. Citing a variety of notebooks and journals, ranging from round-the-world sailors to self-flagellating monks, she shows how silence and solitude can steer some individuals towards madness. It is to diminish these risks, she implies, that monastic orders develop rhythms and rules. The same reason could be given for why most Antarctic stations hold to a strict routine.

I had a pile of papers from the BAS Medical Unit library touching on the psychology of what are known as 'Isolated and Confined Environments', journals including *The British Journal of Psychiatry, Environment & Behaviour*, and the *Journal of Psychology*. Antarctic winters were used in these articles as proxies for the closed communities of space exploration, oil rigs, submarines and saturation divers. The articles showed that although wintering brought benefits, it could become a profoundly negative experience for some.

In 'The Psychological Effects of Service in British Antarctica' a winter is described on the Peninsula in which a quarter of the men on base left early because of mood and anxiety problems. 'It is clearly to an individual's detriment to remain in the Antarctic when suffering psychological morbidity,' the authors wrote. 'Not only are facilities for treating him on a small remote base inadequate, but the Antarctic itself is often the root cause of the psychological problems, and leaving often appears to serve as both treatment and cure.'

Just as the French have carried out some of best longitudinal work on the emperors, they have some of the longest datasets looking at the mental health of wintering base members. A former winterer at the French base at Point Geologie, Dr Jean Rivolier reviewed twenty years of research on the subject and concluded that to a greater or lesser degree almost all winterers go through a series of negative reactions. He describes an initial 'alarm reaction' when a winterer encounters the pervasive lack of privacy on base, moving on to the individual questioning their motives for coming to Antarctica in the first place. This state, according to Rivolier, moves into resistance ('depression, aggression') and culminates in exhaustion ('tolerance, indifference'). Back in 1956 Rivolier wrote a book about the experience of wintering called *Emperor Penguins* though penguins make up only one thread of the narrative. I had brought a copy south. Despite killing a few for the table ('my desire for fresh meat won the day') Rivolier developed a deep love and respect for these birds that contrasted with the difficulties he had on base with his fellow humans. 'From the expression in his eyes he would appear to be remembering a love affair, or the death of a friend,' he wrote of the emperors. They were 'subjected to the worst storms the world has to offer ... [but] they face all this with the same wide eyes, the same majesty'.

When Rivolier arrived at his base none of the outgoing winterers would even speak to him about their experience. With matted beards and filthy clothes they avoided his questions, pushing past him on the way to the relief ship. Later in the winter one of Rivolier's party, left behind for a few days on a field trip, began hallucinating that zombies were poisoning his food. 'There are several causes behind what the psychologist would probably call the "mental syndrome" of a winter camp,' Rivolier writes. 'Loneliness, the feeling every member of a party gets at times of being struck off the register of the living, the climate, the trying difficulties of living so much on top of one another, the undeniable fact of being starved sexually. Taken together all this could so easily account for either a show of hysterics or a mental collapse to the verge of madness.'

Other psychologists have applied the 'Third-Quarter Effect' to winterers in Antarctica, which could help explain why only now, in July, I began to feel so trapped. The effect is one in which individuals find the third quarter of any isolated or arduous experience particularly difficult because of a realisation that despite all that has been endured the end is still a long way off. Later, when I analysed the psychological questionnaires my fellow winterers completed (as part of the base lighting research project), it was clear that they did not in general suffer a third-quarter effect, though I now think I did. In a large study of four Antarctic research stations over two winters, Joanna Wood wrote that 'if there is a third-quarter effect it is not universally experienced by all individuals in an extreme environment'. Why some individuals do and some do not was not clarified by the study.

When Richard Byrd arrived at the Ross Ice Shelf in 1928 he is said to have packed only two coffins, but a dozen straitjackets. He was one of the first to describe the 'Antarctic stare' brought on by months of isolation: a gaze into the middle distance with unfocussed eyes for minutes at a time. At BAS HQ in Cambridge it was called the 'Halley stare', and before I went south I had assumed it was just another Antarctic legend. But several studies have confirmed it. One researcher at the New Zealanders' Scott Base examined winterers for their 'hypnotisability' before and after their year. They not only stared more after their winters, they became easier to hypnotise, and their brain waves altered. The authors put this down to long months of sensory deprivation.

But study after study shows that true mental illness in the Antarctic is rare. Admiral Byrd was overcautious with all those straitjackets (though the Halley medical cupboards were well stocked with their modern equivalent, intramuscular injections of antipsychotics). Most winterers enjoy their experience, shown by the high number who reapply. Selection procedures seem to work. Base life and polar science go on, a permanent presence on the ice is maintained, and most people who go south benefit. Larry Palinkas, a psychologist who has interviewed hundreds of Antarctic wintering personnel, believes that former winterers will suffer less cancerous, nervous, metabolic and musculoskeletal diseases than age- and sex-matched individuals who stayed home. 'It's called stress inoculation,' says Palinkas. 'They think "if I can handle this I can handle anything".' Researchers at Scott Base found that the winter induced 'already self-sufficient, controlled, calm men to become even more so'.

If I wished for anything from this year now I wished that the solitude and silence that it offered would have the same effect on me.

The days followed a pattern, and the cycles of work and base life repeated themselves through the darkness. Each of us took a turn at being 'gashman', or base dogsbody, meaning that one day in thirteen (Craig was exempt) we'd spend cleaning the toilets, sweeping the floors, setting the tables and washing the dishes. In the evenings we would gather for a while at the bar in the corner of the living room, telling some of the same stories and most of the same jokes. Martha Gellhorn, the American novelist and war reporter, had a line for this kind of closed expatriate community in which intimacy is mingled with a guarded reticence: 'they all know each other both too well and too little,' she wrote, 'like jail-mates'.

Each day's gashman had the chance to choose a movie to put on later in the evening, though it was common enough to give the movie a miss and gather in some other space to talk, or even find some other place to hide for a few hours. Craig saved his most magnificent dinners for Saturday evening, and devised a series of games nights, quizzes and fancy-dress themes to go with them. Drinking was heaviest on Saturday nights too, and as the winter wore on, other evenings in the week began to soak in alcohol. First there was 'Workshop Wednesday', when the beer would be moved through to the Workshop and we would drink between the table-saws and angle grinders. Then 'Thirsty Thursday' back in the bar, and finally, as the monotony really set in, 'Pre-Wednesday Tuesday' in the garage. It was clear we were going to have to find something else to do as a group that didn't involve drinking.

On the *Discovery* expedition, Scott and Wilson had diverted the wintering crew by organising a series of debates – the most heated was on the relative merits of Browning and Tennyson (Shackleton argued for the former, Bernacchi the latter). Poetry would not have got us very far and Craig came up with a plan more suited to the interests of our wintering team – satisfying our stomachs. He designed a four-week cookery course, and in the evening we'd gather in the kitchen as he took us through the basics: sauces and soups, curries and risottos, meat and vegetables, breads and pastries. In addition to our duties as general dogsbody we also took turns to cook on Mondays, Craig's only day off. Most of us fell back on bangers and mash, spaghetti bolognaise or fish and chips, but now these dinners became more ambitious. I remember a Monday afternoon during the darkest months spent entirely in hand-mixing pasta, rolling it through a press then trying to crimp hundreds of tiny ravioli.

There were other evening classes on offer: Pat revealed himself to be a master practitioner of shiatsu massage. We spent evenings spread out on the carpet in the living room while he prodded our meridians and pressure points. I came up with a series of first-aid evenings and made sure everyone could tie a bandage, put on a plaster cast and stitch up a wound. The least popular was the evening I taught how to put a cannula into a vein; the most popular was when we worked our way through a bottle and a half of laughing gas.

There were so many opportunities to learn at Halley away from these organised evenings. Where else would you find astronomers, mechanics, physicists, musicians, cartographers, electricians, computer programmers and carpenters all cooped up together for a year? In the workshop Tommo had been teaching me some woodwork, and despairing of my squint boxes and misplaced hinges. Ben showed me how to strip down a skidoo carburettor. I spent a couple of days with Graeme in the generator room as he showed me how to service the big diesel engines we so relied on. His attempt to teach me how to drive a bulldozer was aborted when I almost drove it into one of the legs of the Laws. In the garage I had an ongoing welding project, a steel bookshelf advancing slowly under Graeme's and Ben's tutelage. 'Well,' I asked them when it was finished, 'do you think I'm ready to weld a skidoo chassis?'

Graeme shook his head, and took the bookshelf in his hands. 'Gav, I think you should stick to fixing people,' and dropped it into the bin for scrap. I had to agree it was the best place for it.

A labyrinth of service tunnels lay beneath Halley, worming through the ice shelf between the Laws and the Simpson, being buried deeper every year. In the bowels of the Brunt cables, pipes and fuel lines were slung to walls that were twisted and buckled by the contorting pressure of the ice. Summer and winter temperatures down there stayed fairly constant at around minus 20°C, and tunnel working could be a welcome respite from the colder days of winter. Some of our fuel was stored in tanks bolted on to sledges, and if it was warm enough for the bulldozer to operate (warmer than around minus 40°C) a tank would be pulled over to the Laws and pipes dropped down into the access hatch for the tunnels. They would be used to refill the 'flubbers', giant bags under the ice where the fuel for our generators was stored.

There were two jobs in 'flubbering'. Up on the surface there were the fuel lines to check, with the advantage of being able to watch the sky. As we moved into July the glow around noon grew daily, though the sun was still far below the horizon. The light slid from the north-west to the north-east, as if the sky was a turning bowl with a flame tint down one edge. The other job was down in the tunnels, which had its own beauty. Lace-like crystals of ice hung from every surface refracting the halogen lamps into rainbows of colour. Wrapped in many layers it was quite comfortable to sprawl on a flubber reading, listening for instructions from Graeme over the radio and checking the fuel level from time to time with an old broomstick handle. Once I spent a whole afternoon down there with Graham Greene's *Journey Without Maps*, and I can't read it now without recalling the smell of aviation-grade kerosene. One line from it in particular struck me; it could have described my own feelings about the penguins though he meant it of the scarce wildlife he encountered as he trekked through the isolation of the West African bush: 'You can grow intimate with almost any living thing,' he wrote, 'transfer to it your own emotion of tenderness.'

The most common reason to go down into the tunnels was not for flubbering, but to unblock the melt-tank shaft. The shaft was normally kept covered by a heavy metal lid, but if the lid was forgotten or displaced by a storm, blizzarded snow would whirl into the shaft, quickly filling it from the bottom up. It was a dreary trudge down the ladders to the bottom, where an elbow bend in the shaft was the usual site of the blockage. For some reason it seemed always to be Toddy, Russ and I who would be volunteered to stand on each of the steel mesh landings in turn, swinging a sledgehammer at the shaft until the snow shivered its way down, then repeat the exercise at the next level up. Our grey water and sewage fell separately into a giant cave, known as 'the Onion' for its pungent layers, where accumulated years of waste had excavated their own cavity. Luckily the Onion pipes blocked only rarely.

As much as getting the snow down into the melt tank, it was a regular job to haul dirty snow back up again. Ice accumulated from the air itself as well as entering through cracks in the hatches during blizzards, choking the tunnels. There was a well-established system: a pulley over the melt-tank access shaft allowed a rope to drop straight down to the base of the shaft. Thirty-gallon buckets were shovelled full of snow and hitched to the rope, and then runners, two or three to a rope, would pull across the bondoo as fast as they could to lift the buckets the equivalent of a six- or seven-storey building.

There was much of this hard physical work on base to be done, though less than in years gone past. Some studies have suggested that as bases have become more comfortable and their work increasingly mechanised, winterers have felt more, rather than less, isolated. Shared work, shared goals, shared exhaustion after a hard day, have all been shown to bring wintering groups closer together and alleviate the creeping unease of the 'winter-over syndrome'.

I tried to volunteer for any outside work whether raising snow, shovelling ice, flying weather kites, cranking the platforms higher, raising flags and drum lines or excavating fuel depots. It didn't always come naturally to me, given my preference for my own company, but I always felt better afterwards. Only those who wintered with me can say if I did enough.

If base commanders have Ernest Shackleton's example to live up to, base doctors have that of Edward Wilson. He is a hard act to follow. Thomas Hodgson, who wintered with Wilson on the *Discovery* expedition and shared his tent on the early penguin trips to Cape Crozier, wrote: 'I think he was more or less the confidant of us all . . . I have never met with a man so universally admired and respected in every way.' On both the *Discovery* and *Terra Nova* expeditions, Scott's journals show that while he may have led, it was Wilson who held the men together. He was 'the life and soul of the party, the organizer of all amusements, the always good-tempered and cheerful one', and elsewhere, 'the most valued and valuable of all'. His letters to his wife from the *Discovery* reveal that his calm exterior was only maintained with much effort: 'God knows it is just about as much as I can stand at times, and there is absolutely no escape. I have never had my temper so tried as it is every day now.' As a young man he had been prone to suicidal mood swings and used sedatives before public speaking; now he kept this anxious side hidden from view, and expressing it only in the letters he stored up for his wife. That he had experience of anxiety and depression is likely to have made him a more understanding doctor, and a better friend.

In the Antarctic summer of 1902–3 Scott, Shackleton and Wilson shared a tent on their reconnaissance sledge journey across the Ross Ice Barrier towards the South Pole. For entertainment in their tent at night they read to one another from Darwin's *The Origin of Species*. Wilson admired Shackleton, particularly the artistic side of the Irishman's spirit that had led him to memorise reams of poetry. The feeling was mutual; Shackleton could be ambivalent about Scott, but was unequivocal about Wilson – after their experience on the Ross Ice Barrier he could imagine no better companion for a hard southern journey. He pleaded with him to join the *Nimrod* expedition of 1907–9, the one that would in the end turn back only ninety-seven miles from the South Pole. When Wilson refused to join him – he was working on the biology of a grouse disease at the time – Shackleton wrote to him: 'Heaven knows how I want you – but I admire you more than ever for your attitude. A man rarely writes out his heart but I would to you. If I reach the Pole I will still have a regret that you were not with me.'

Wilson's character was a potent alloy of scientist, idealist and mystic, reinforced throughout with compassion for others and a profound reverence for nature. He was a follower of St Francis, and from his letters it seems he was an admirer of Spinoza. The Dutch philosopher was described by Novalis as a 'God-intoxicated man', and the same might be said of Wilson, who once wrote to his wife: 'Love everything into which God has put life: and God made nothing dead. There is only *less* life in a stone than in a bird, and both have a life of their own, and both took their life from God.' Elsewhere he wrote, 'So long as I have stuck to nature and the New Testament I have only got happier and happier every day.' Even when he lived in London his rooms were filled with bird skulls, chrysalises, sprouting saplings, bunches of bracken. Of all Wilson's qualities it is perhaps this reverence for nature, and by extension his particular affection for the emperor penguins, that most appealed to me. On base I had long since given up trying to be all things to all people, as he was.

One of his watercolour sketches, made on the *Discovery* expedition for the *South Polar Times*, best illustrates this passion. It
is reproduced in Scott's account of the expedition, *The Voyage
of the Discovery*. A leopard seal, teeth bared, chases two emperor
penguins through the water. The seal's movement is beautifully
rendered; Wilson followed Ruskin's maxim that paintings should
accurately reflect reality. It spirals from the depths like a coil
unsprung, fast and sleek, but looks frustrated by the chase and
very much of this world. The emperors by contrast stream seam-
lessly ahead, their wakes a blur of motion, their beaks like
compass needles pointing towards an inevitable and transcendent
escape.

Wilson's love for the emperors, and his desire to work out the details
of their lives, made him persuade Scott to try to base the *Terra Nova*
expedition at Cape Crozier where he would have easy access to the
emperor rookery through the winter. From memory he drew Scott
an accurate map of Cape Crozier, a place he had not visited for
seven years, outlining a projected site for their hut and a route for
the polar party on to the Ross Ice Barrier. He was still thinking of
how to get an emperor's egg, and thoughts of the polar journey
were secondary.

On 2 January 1911 as the *Terra Nova* approached Cape Crozier,
Wilson was one of the men to try to get ashore. Landing was
impossible and the plan was abandoned, but the reconnaissance
did give him the opportunity to get up close to the emperor
rookery and glimpse a fledging chick, at a stage of development
that had not yet been observed. Wilson's account shows no irritation at their failure to land, even though it meant that the winter
journey would now be necessary to reach the emperors. His journal
reflects only pleasure at a new discovery: 'about 6 feet above us,
on a small dirty piece of the old bay ice about 10 feet square, one
living Emperor Penguin chick was standing disconsolately stranded,
and close by it stood one faithful old Emperor Penguin parent
asleep ... The whole incident was most interesting and full of
suggestion as to the slow working of the brains of these queer
people.'

Key to appreciating his character is his lack of irritation with the often adverse unfolding of events; he was by now well practised at benevolent acceptance. Another important aspect of his personality was illustrated by his much debated, and much misunderstood, decision to detour on his way back from the South Pole to collect geological specimens from the foot of Mount Buckley. He was suffering recurrent snowblindness at the time, Scott had a badly strained shoulder, Oates was limping and Evans dying. When the men's bodies were found it was realised that Wilson had collected 35 lb of rather commonplace geological specimens and pulled them to the last. In his final scribbled notes, Scott took care to mention where the rocks were in relation to the tent, so that the search party who found their bodies might also be sure to find the specimens and take them back to England.

What kind of man would do this? One either foolish, foolhardy, or possessed of a drive to *know* that overwhelms all other needs, that places the appetites of the spirit far higher than the necessities of the body. It seems reminiscent of his winter journey to Cape Crozier, when common sense would have suggested he give up the journey or abandon the embryos. His actions seem to represent the implementation of the highest ideals into practice, an ascetic negation of the needs of the self in the service of, in this case, a high scientific ideal. The embryos he believed would cement the link between birds and reptiles, and the geological specimens contained fossilised plants that showed how, deep in geological time, Antarctica had experienced a much warmer climate. And for Wilson, as his letters show, understanding the lives of birds or the rocks of the earth was just another way of understanding God.

One Wednesday morning in July an urgent fax arrived from Cambridge. Kirsty Brown, a marine geologist carrying out research at the BAS station Rothera on the Antarctic Peninsula, had been killed by a leopard seal. The news was shocking, and utterly unexpected. Though leopard seals had been known to attack inflatable boats, attacks on humans were almost unheard of and in a century of Antarctic marine research there had never been any fatalities.

Her research involved surveys of the sea floor, looking into the destructive grinding effect that icebergs have on the marine life beneath them. It had been the first day that she had glimpsed the sun at the end of her own winter. She had been snorkelling close to the base with her diving buddy, carrying out her research, when the leopard seal grabbed her and pulled her under. Boats had been scrambled and it took fifteen awful minutes until she was sighted again on the surface. She was hauled into a boat by rescuers and then stretchered to the medical room on base. The doctor and a team of her friends and colleagues tried for over an hour to resuscitate her but she had been under too long, her injuries were too severe, and it proved impossible to bring her back.

Russ came into the medical room to tell me about it. We had both known Kirsty briefly in Cambridge; at the pre-departure conference we had passed time in the bar with her joking and chatting. She had been so excited about the job that she was taking on at Rothera, unfailingly cheerful, alive with enthusiasm and anticipation for her Antarctic adventure. She was rarely without company – already, before their journey south had even started, her colleagues were drawn to her warmth. It was an appalling and tragic waste of a young life, and I couldn't stop wondering about how the others at Rothera were coping. At the same time part of me was worrying how we at Halley would cope with a similar disaster.

That evening I went through for dinner at the usual time. I tried to talk about Kirsty I remember asking whether anyone thought HQ would try to get a plane down to Rothera – but was answered only in shrugs. One by one the others finished up their meals and left, and I ended my dinner in silence. It was as if we were so deep in the isolation of Halley, had become so myopic in our view of the world, that even events in Rothera felt too distant to be real.

Only two or three weeks earlier I had been contemplating how protected our lives were, how modern technology and a library of Health and Safety directives protected us from the dangers that the earliest explorers faced. Kirsty's death was a savage rebuttal of that position. The Antarctic is no less dangerous now than a century ago, I realised, it is just that we are getting better at being careful.

Slowly more emails came through from Cambridge. They would

try to get a plane in after all, both to repatriate Kirsty's body and to take out any winterers who were keen to leave. But getting it down to the Falklands and, crucially, getting the Rothera runway ready to receive it would take another six long weeks – a terrible time both for her family back in England and for the members on base.

Kirsty's parents, sisters and brother, as well as the families of all the other BAS winterers currently working in the Antarctic, were informed before the press took up the story. At Halley it was spoken of in whispers, in pit-rooms and once or twice in tiptoed visits to me in the medical room. No one mentioned that if something similar were to happen at Halley, there would be no plane coming to take the body, and no possibility of escape for those of us left behind. The tragedy of Kirsty's death, and imagining the horror of it for those left behind at Rothera, made our isolation feel all the more profound.*

Over the following week I felt a metalled morgue-like silence around base. The moon was a pallid skull. When I had first arrived I could barely manage one turn of the perimeter on skis, now I comfortably finished three or four and welcomed the opportunity to spend longer outside. Out in the western sector of the base, still within the perimeter, there was a wooden cross fixed to a sturdy sledge. I had not given it much attention before but now skied out to visit it. It was a memorial to the men who have died at Halley. Plaques with their names now stood through the same blizzards and under the same auroras that the men had once experienced. Neville Mann, surveyor, 'lost below this point 15 August 1963'; Jeremy Bailey, David Wild, and John Wilson, lost when their tractor fell into a crevasse in 1965; Miles Mosley, killed in an aircraft accident in 1980.

---

* Kirsty is commemorated with others who lost their lives in Antarctica on a plaque in St Paul's Cathedral in London, and on monuments in the Falkland Islands, and outside the Scott Polar Research Institute in Cambridge, dedicated to those who did not return. Her family began a fund to finance research into interactions between humans and leopard seals, to try to better understand the circumstances around Kirsty's attack, and help prevent similar attacks in the future.

IN MEMORY OF
JEREMY BAILEY
JOHN WILSON
DAVID WILD
KILLED IN CREVASSE
ACCIDENT 12 OCT. 1965
7°°°'S 18°41'W

Names and thoughts circled as I orbited the base, spiralling: how were the team at Rothera coping with the horror of what had happened, and the wait for the plane? How would we cope if someone was to die here at Halley? How well had I trained the others in first aid? I knew Jane the Rothera doctor well, we had trained in Plymouth together. For six months we had shared a house on the edge of Dartmoor. What must it be like for her? She had written hurriedly, strained but coping, answering my clumsy emails of support. How would it be to resuscitate a friend? Other thoughts edged in from the pragmatist in me: how much oxygen did I have in the medical room? Where, if we had to, would we store a body? Medical emergencies in the Antarctic might make good news copy, but I was glad to have had nothing more serious to deal with than infections, fractures and the odd rotten tooth.

Kirsty's death was the first BAS had suffered for decades. No one had died at Rothera since 1981 when two men, John Anderson and Robert Atkinson, had fallen into a crevasse. They were buried where they fell. The following year three men at Faraday Station on the northern Peninsula had been lost on sea ice. I had heard about the disaster and now looked up their names: John Coll, Ambrose Morgan and Kevin Ockleton. Since those three at Faraday we had been fortunate, those Health and Safety directives had done their job. I thought of the sea ice that still armoured the Weddell to the north, the crevasses that lay along the Brunt Shelf coast. These dangers were as real now as they were twenty or fifty or a hundred years ago. I stepped with more caution when I remembered Kirsty, and woke with more gratitude.

# CHAPTER ELEVEN

# The Promise of Life

Oh, how tired I am of thy cold beauty! I long to return to life.
Fridtjof Nansen, *Farthest North*

The sun was rising in my blood. I felt the promise of its return. One day while out skiing I saw the whole horizon spread with carmine and crimson; a widening garden of roses sprang up between the ice and the stars. Then a mirage started to flicker in the frozen air. The line of the horizon was obliterated, and the roses were replaced by a forest fire of black and scarlet flame. The prismatic air shifted the light depending on the height of the observer: if I crouched down the whole blaze moved to the east, if I stood up it rolled off to the west. I stood silent witness to a beauty that was suddenly precious, the way that something fleeting and transient is precious.

I had been asking to get down to see the emperors all winter, but the word was that it was too dangerous. One day Pat announced that approval had come through, those who were keen could go by snowcat down to the rookery to see the penguins before their eggs hatched. The idea was so popular that it was decided to make two trips, on consecutive days. 'This is your only chance,' he said, 'there are only a few people alive who have seen this.'

Ben and Toddy made a reconnaissance trip to the ice cliffs to check it was safe and hammer in new anchors for our descent to the sea ice. I rushed from my desk when I heard the snowcat coming back.

'Did you see any penguins?' I asked Toddy, meeting him at the door.

'Gav, I saw thousands,' he grinned, nodding and kicking the ice from his boots, 'thousands and thousands of them.'

Red light flooded the space between ice and sky. In a snowcat we drove to the end of the shelf's cliffs, twenty kilometres from base. The frozen ocean extended to the north, the fierce cold shimmering the horizon the way that heat bends light over African plains. The cliffs stood over the sea ice like grim sentries guarding the frontiers of the continent. I thought of how many hundreds of miles the sea ice continued over the horizon, how the gyre of the Weddell was pulled almost to a standstill by this primeval cold. Those hundreds of miles of sea ice seemed to cut us off from the warmth and life of the rest of the planet.

But not from all life. I walked out to the edge, not yet roped, and peered down to see the penguins. Toddy had been right, there were *thousands* of them. Their survival there on the ice, the very fact of their presence following the winter we had just endured together, was an astonishment. I hitched my harness to a rope and abseiled down the cliffs to join them.

I could just make out the dark smear they made on the ice, a kilometre away to the north. Noises made by other lungs, smells made by other bodies, the proximity of other living, breathing beings was intoxicating. I started walking towards them. Embedded in the sea-ice surface were the remains of old icebergs, caught at angles like shipwrecks frozen in place for the winter. There were emperor corpses too, freeze-dried and frozen in where they had fallen. The cliffs behind me captured the dull ruby light of the sky and held it, releasing it slowly as if they glowed from within. Approaching the penguin huddle at first I startled them, they waddled away when I came too close. But if I stayed still I was tolerated, accepted into their midst. They marched quietly around me, the only sound that of snow crunching underfoot and a rubbing of feathered body against body. Every so often a narrow head would extend like a periscope, silhouetted against the flame-red sky, and give a cry. Through the ice beneath me I felt the steady tremor of their footfalls, their ceaseless circling movement on to fresh ice. They circle not only to take their turn at the outermost exposed parts of the huddle, but to get away from the puddles generated by their great heat. Many seemed asleep, as if held in a hypnotist's trance, and almost walked into me as I kneeled amongst them. Penguin ornithologists suspect that emperors enter a sleep-like state for much of their winter, slowing their metabolism as well as their brain's activity in order to survive the frigid monotony of the dark months.

Most of the penguins had a bulge above the feet, a sign of a hidden egg. Those eggs were held as if in a velvet purse within the heated brood patch on the lower abdomen. From the epicentre of the colony rose a twisting cloud of steam; like many birds emperor penguins have a body heat two or three degrees higher than that of humans. Despite the cold that they inhabit, the long periods of inertia they endure, they live life faster and hotter than we humans.

The American naturalist Joseph Wood Krutch believed that in addition to their greater heat birds also live more joyfully. An admirer and a biographer of Thoreau, Krutch wrote that birds live in a series 'of almost discontinuous eternities'. The simplicity of their minds and the immediacy of their lives mean that for Krutch, those moments are 'eternities of Joy'. I enjoyed the idea of it, the penguins around me transformed from primitive bird-brains, phylogenetic idiots, into joyful ascetics lost in a reverie of the moment. Sharing their winter incubation, becoming one with their huddle, I caught a glimpse of Krutch's vision of that joy.

Leonardo da Vinci thought that once humans tasted flight they would forever look to the sky and feel bereft, as if grounded life would lose all flavour. To the penguins, who lost the power of flight long ago in evolution, the depth and form of their world is all directed downwards, beneath the sea. Perhaps anthropomorphism is catching, but after reading Krutch on birds I wondered how the emperors view the ocean; whether they feel it welcomes them with its tight embrace, or whether they pass through it on sufferance. In this world of ice where the elements of the landscape seemed to lose their contradistinction, the emperors seemed at ease. Perhaps flight would terrify them.

Even now, after months of frozen stillness, those elements of the landscape were in flux. The roiling currents of the Weddell and the ceaseless pull of the moon on the ocean had broken the surface in places, there were cracks in the shield of ice known as 'leads'. 'Sea smoke' is the name given to the vapour that can be seen rising from seawater exposed to frigid air, and wisps of it curled from leads to the north of the penguins. As late as 1936, when Robert Cushman Murphy wrote his classic text *The Oceanic Birds of South America*, these sparse leads were thought to be the way that emperor penguins accessed their fishing grounds through the winter. That the birds were fasting and needed no fish, and that it was only the males that incubated, was still thought too improbable to be true.

Moving gently through the huddle I thought of the first men ever to see this spectacle, and under what different circumstances. When Wilson, Bowers and Cherry-Garrard came among the incubating emperors of Cape Crozier they knew how privileged they were. But the men were too hungry, cold and in peril of their lives to fully appreciate what they were witnessing. If Wilson had had more time there, if the *Terra Nova* expedition had been able to base itself at Cape Crozier instead of Cape Evans, he would have observed that no penguins left the huddle to go fishing, that there was no transfer of eggs between pairs of penguins. 'We see distinctly only what we know thoroughly' was one of Wilson's maxims; with time and careful observation he would have seen clearly what would take decades more to be revealed. It is clear from Cherry-Garrard's account that Wilson was perplexed by the life-cycles of these birds. He could not understand how they lived because he could not yet imagine the truth: that all the birds he could see were male, and that they would fast until the chicks had hatched and the females had returned.

The sky was darkening. I heard Toddy shouting that it was time to climb back up the cliffs. No stone igloo covered by a tarpaulin for us tonight; I would drive my own snowcat home and sleep in a warm bed. *Five years*, I remembered, five years of life is what Cherry-Garrard said he would have given to be transported from his winter journey and given a single night in a warm bed.

On my way back towards the cliffs I passed a dead emperor penguin. It had died on the march, fallen on its belly and quick-frozen. The rest of its comrades had moved on, and it had begun to drift over with snow. It looked as if it had been bleeding – a bloody discharge streaked from its cloaca. I had an empty sixty litre rucksack on my back and on impulse I bent down and pulled the rucksack over the dead penguin's head. The bird must have weighed twenty-five or thirty kilos, was over three feet long, and I struggled to get it on to my back. Maybe back at base I can find out why it died, I thought.

As usual I was the last to arrive at the foot of the ice cliff, and there were still a couple of kitbags to be hauled up on to the ice shelf. When its turn came I tied on the rucksack with the dead emperor and gave the shout – the others pulled it up on to the shelf surface. Then I hauled myself up the rope.

'What the hell have you got in that bag?' Toddy asked me when I reached the top. 'It weighs a ton.'

'A dead emperor,' I said.

'You bloody idiot,' he smiled. 'Don't tell Pat.'

Back at the Laws platform I pulled the penguin from the rucksack. Its hook-like beak had ripped a hole through the nylon and I had to unsnag it. Its head had turned to the right as it fell, frozen in the attitude of glancing over its shoulder. 'I'll weigh it tomorrow,' I thought to myself, and propped it up against the gas canisters on the outside platform. Its ice-sharpened talons gripped the wooden floor and prevented it from sliding. My idea was to seal it in a polythene bag then thaw it out in the waste-compacting room; warm enough for the job of dissection but still separate from the base and cool enough to keep smells to a minimum. I would open it up, examine its bowel and cloaca and try to find out what had killed it. In the surgery I pulled out the booklet on penguin taxidermy, a relic of an earlier age when amateurs were appreciated. Maybe this was my chance to try it out.

Toddy was right, Pat was not happy. He heard about the penguin over dinner, and marched out at once to see it. 'Nobody will be cutting up any emperor penguins here!' he said when he came back in.

'It's dead, Pat,' I said. 'Cutting it up is not going to do anyone any harm.'

'I don't care if it's dead or alive, tomorrow you're taking it back to the coast.'

Rules are rules, and we were a long way from arbitration. The following day I found myself standing at the top of the cliffs, contemplating whether I was about to witness the first ever emperor penguin flight. The penguin lay on its front, the way that it had no doubt tobogganed hundreds or thousands of kilometres over the sea ice in its life. I nudged it gently towards the edge and watched it slip away, gathering momentum, accelerating towards the cliff top before launching out forty metres over the sea ice. For a moment I thought I saw it spread its wings. The streamlined contours that allowed it to flense its way through the water gave it an aerodynamic glide. It dropped into a snowdrift and disappeared.

The horizon to the north was brightening. It might have been my imagination but as I moved among the huddle the penguins that second day seemed a little more excitable, their necks strained a little more often towards the northern horizon. Perhaps they sensed the proximity of the sun, and the returning females. The next time I'm down here, I thought, the females will have returned and the chicks will have hatched. The rookery will have transformed, the sun will be back, and another season in the cycle of these birds' lives will have begun. I didn't want to hasten it, tried to live fully in the moment. But time among the penguins always seemed too short.

Three or four days after we visited the rookery a diarrhoeal illness ran through the base. At first I wondered if it had come from the dead penguin: like a Trojan Horse it had carried sickness into our sterile world. In the north we are surrounded by bugs and bacteria; in a teaspoon of garden soil there may be up to a billion of them. But we had lived now for months with only the bacteria we had brought with us, silent stowaways on our skins and teeming on the insides of our guts. We had become immune to those ones. The intruder must, I reasoned, have come from the outside. But I was the only one who handled that penguin, and I was one of those who did not get diarrhoea. Craig was adamant that it could not have come from his kitchen.

My medical work on base had been routine; now there was a real medical conundrum to solve. Twelve of the fourteen of us had visited the rookery, and crunched our frozen sandwiches down on the sea ice. Perhaps someone had laid their lunch down on a guano-streaked patch of snow. An enterprising Rothera doctor once rugby-tackled adélie penguins in order to swab them on the anus, looking for unusual bacteria. He was not disappointed – he found two or three species unknown to man. I gathered stool specimens from my base-mates to take back to Plymouth, dreaming of some new species of diarrhoeal bacteria. 'Perhaps we've been struck by a *Salmonella francisii*,' I said to the others, 'or maybe *E. Coli gavinii.*'

When the ship arrived, five months later, I loaded on the samples in a box bound for the laboratory in Plymouth. But they went missing, and my chance of Linnaean immortality was lost forever.

A few days before the sun was due to rise again the winter gave us one last blast, as if reluctant to let us go. It was a circumpolar wind, running the circuit of a continent as if the Pole was at the eye of the world's broadest hurricane. It arrived unexpectedly, knocking on the windows and doors of the Laws like a madman bent on revenge. Its gusts blew at over a hundred miles per hour. The world outside became an emulsion of blown snow. A sensor in the melt tank told us that the water level was getting low, and despite the weather we would need to go out and fill it. The melt-tank duty rota hung on the wall in the dining room. Everyone could see it was my turn, along with Rob and Tommo, and joked about when we were going to get up the courage to go out in it. As one who enjoys a challenge Toddy said he'd give us a hand.

We armoured up in the boot room as if preparing for battle. Long johns, fleece salopettes, sweaters, cotton Ventile suits, insulated nylon overtrousers, duck-down jackets, balaclavas, neoprene face guards, rabbit-fur hats and ski goggles. Mukluks on our feet and 'bear paw' mitts on our hands. Over the bulging layers we each strapped a VHF radio. Our voices were muffled as we checked with one another that we were ready to go; we knew that once outside we would be deafened by the steady roar pushing down from the sky.

Rob kicked open the front-door foot bar and we pushed out against the shoulders of the wind. The entranceway was arranged like an airlock, and exiting the building it felt as if we were stepping out on a space walk. The blast hit me like a shove, but because of the warm layers of clothing there was no chill in it. Pressing in on all sides the air found my skin only along a thin line around my goggles. In single file we made our way across the platform, down the steel staircase and, holding a rope strung to the base of the stairway for just this eventuality, made our way towards the melt-tank shaft. I could see the hand on the end of my arm, but no further.

Through gaps in the blasts of snow flurries it was possible to glimpse a red light ahead, the light by the melt tank which told us its level was too low. We moved on, buffeted by the wind, towards it. Around the melt-tank hatch there were ridges of bull-dozed ice, raised to make the job of digging the snow towards the hatch easier. The hatch itself lay in the shelter of those ridges and its hollow had filled with blown snow. We had to dig our way down before we could even reach the hatch.

Toddy and I tried to balance on the top of the piles of ice, leaning into the gale, hacking beneath our feet with a pickaxe and shovel then kicking blocks down the slope towards the hatch. The blizzard had robbed us of our senses, we worked in isolation barely able to see our feet. Rob and Tommo stood at the bottom of the bowl, guiding the blocks into the shaft as they rolled down the slope. If one jammed they would reach up and give us a firm pat on the leg, a signal to stop digging for a moment. The wind was so fierce that it caused a build-up of static electricity on our bodies; every couple of minutes I'd be jerked by electric shocks that sparked out of my hands into my steel shovel. My goggles kept icing up inside; I'd have to take them off, eyes screwed against the wind, and scrape them clear with a mittened thumb.

At last the red light blinked green, the tank was full. At first I had not noticed, had carried on blindly digging until Toddy slapped my shoulder and physically forced me to turn towards the light. Tommo was spread out on the snow at the bottom of the bowl, feigning sleep. Our clothes were so effective against the wind that he need not have been feigning it, sometimes I felt that I could have gladly lain down and slept.

We followed the hand-line back to the stair and, on hands and knees, climbed up onto the platform. The sky raced above us, still shrieking through the antenna assembly on the roof. When Richard Byrd wintered alone he had to leave his hut to clear his entry hatch after every blizzard. Cherry-Garrard's world 'having a fit of hysterics' perfectly captures the heaving chaos of the sky in a blizzard, but crawling up the steps I thought of Byrd's experience eighteen years later: 'There is something extravagantly insensate about an Antarctic blizzard at night . . . You are reduced to a crawling thing on the margin of a disintegrating world.'

Once inside the safety of base we looked at one another. Our neoprene masks were marbled in ice and our jackets rigid with snow. Toddy tried to struggle out of his clothes but found that two layers down his zips were still locked solid. He would need to thaw them out first. I went to take off my jacket then hesitated. How many more times, I wondered, would I have the chance to experience an Antarctic blizzard in the darkness of winter?

Near the melt tank was a miniature platform for launching weather balloons, known as 'Bart'. It was a meteorologist's joke – 'Bart' was the diminutive 'child' of the Simpson platform and was decorated with a yellow hairline along the roof. In high winds Bart was a safe place to find shelter, on its west-facing platform you could lie out of the wind, within reach of base, and enjoy watching the sky without being blown over. I moved back towards the door. 'What are you up to?' asked Tommo. 'Forgot something?'

'I'm just going outside,' I said, pausing for dramatic effect, 'and may be some time.'

In the 1890s, while still a medical student at Cambridge, Edward Wilson wrote to his sister: 'This is the most fascinating ideal I think I ever imagined, to become entirely careless of your own soul and body in looking after the welfare of others.' Twenty years later Scott wrote on his return journey from the Pole, 'Wilson, the best fellow that ever stepped, has sacrificed himself again and again to the sick men of the party.' Wilson seems like a man to whom a rare gift was given: the strength and perseverance to realise his ideals.

The story of Scott's return from the Pole is well known, but like all classic myths bears repetition. Seaman Evans, supposedly the hardest and strongest of the five who went to the Pole, died at the foot of the Beardmore Glacier on 18 February 1912. He had been weakening since they reached the Pole and found that Amundsen had 'beaten' them by a month. 'He has beaten us in so far as he made a race of it,' Wilson had written in his diary. Evans, an ox of a man, was pulling a sledge in harness the day that he died.*

Herbert Ponting sailed north on the *Terra Nova* in February 1912. Before Scott left for the Pole Ponting had taken a video cinematograph of Evans, Scott, Wilson and Bowers raising their tent, cooking their hoosh and getting into their sleeping bags. It was intended to be used for publicity on Scott's return. Watching it in the comfort of an Edinburgh cinema, more than a century later, I had a senseless flood of anxiety for the men's safety, and then of sadness at what we now know awaited them. Having read so much about these men and their characters, and having entered into the myth that grew around them, it was a shock to see them moving on a screen. It was like watching an authentic video of Odysseus resisting the Sirens, or King Arthur hauling Excalibur from a stone. Evans carefully assembles the stove, being cook for the day. Bowers strips off and snuggles into his bag. Wilson smiles gently and jokes with Scott as he peels off the layers of his socks and wiggles his toes. Though the scene was filmed to drum up public support for the expedition it now stands as a bleak and silent memorial to what became of these men.

---

* For weeks he had been struggling with an infected finger. It has been argued that he had picked up anthrax from the expedition's ponies or from the inside of his reindeer-skin sleeping bag. (See Falckh, R. C. F., *Polar Record*, 23: 397–403, 1987.)

On the Ross Barrier, down to four men, Scott had anticipated southerly winds to blow them back to Cape Evans. In 1908 Shackleton had found hard polished ice in this area, easy to glide sledges across, but they found only deep granular snow, headwinds and bitter temperatures. They limped on to the next depot, Middle Barrier Depot, which they reached on 2 March. Oates was an officer of the Inniskilling Dragoons who, like Cherry-Garrard, had paid the modern equivalent of about £50,000 to be accepted on the expedition. He now revealed that he had been hiding a badly frostbitten foot.

Both he and Bowers had been recruited from British India – this was a truly imperial expedition. Out on the ice, far from the empire that had nurtured them and for whose glory they felt they had marched, the men realised that there was not enough oil at Middle Barrier Depot to fuel them to the next. Wilson spent hours doctoring Oates' frostbitten foot, and by 10 March Scott was writing in his diary that Oates 'has rare pluck and must know that he can never get through'. He was by now unable to walk, and was being pulled by the others on a sledge.

The following day Scott demanded of Wilson that he hand out the opiate tablets that would allow them each to commit suicide. He may have been hoping that Oates would take the hint. 'Wilson had no choice between doing so and our ransacking the medicine case,' Scott wrote. The previous summer Oates had joked with Wilson, faking epileptic fits in an attempt to get a taste of the medicinal brandy. Now he had in his pocket the most potent drug in the medical case, but it took him five more days to decide to use it.

On 16 March Oates walked out of the tent to his death. 'I am just going outside,' he said, 'and may be some time.' A tragic epitaph, legendary for its understatement, sometimes mocked as characteristic of a certain period in British imperial history. When Francis Spufford wrote a book about the British fascination with exploration in high latitudes he called it *I may be some time*. His book unashamedly focusses on Scott and Shackleton at the expense of other, more successful Antarctic explorers, because it is Scott's and Shackleton's expeditions that have been most effectively transformed into myth.

The three remaining men, Scott, Wilson and Bowers, struggled on for another five days. On 21 March they pitched camp eleven miles short of the One Ton Depot that had enough food and fuel to restore them. Had they abandoned Oates earlier they would have made the depot in time, but now a blizzard set in for nine days straight. In those nine days the men simply wasted away from starvation and hypothermia.

It was seven and a half months later, on 11 November, that the physicist Charles Wright called the exploration party out of Cape Evans to a halt. He had spotted a small hummock of snow, off the line of cairns to the west. 'It is the tent,' he said simply. Atkinson later wrote of what they found inside. 'Wilson and Bowers were found in the attitude of sleep, their sleeping bags closed over their heads as they would naturally close them. Scott died later. He had thrown back the flaps of his sleeping-bag and opened his coat. The little wallet containing the three notebooks was under his shoulder and his arm flung across Wilson.'

Spufford has written that Scott's last expedition had all the features of classical myth, quest, or legend, but to some it is something more like a religion. Like other religions it has its own house of worship, the Scott Polar Research Institute in Cambridge, and its reliquaries. I too have gone to Cambridge to pay my respects, to look with my own eyes at the little wallet Atkinson found beneath Scott's shoulder, to see for myself the Book of Common Prayer that Wilson took to the Pole. There is even an old biscuit wrapper, found beside the tent, picked up by Cherry-Garrard and so accorded the same reverence as the other, more immediately romantic, objects on display. Most importantly the original letters of Scott can be seen; you can trace his handwriting for yourself as you imagine his pencil stub scratching the frozen paper.

Scott had written a last letter to Wilson's wife Oriana, an apology almost: 'His eyes have a comfortable blue look of hope and his mind is peaceful with the satisfaction of his faith in regarding himself as part of the great scheme of the Almighty. I can do no more to comfort you than to tell you that he died as he lived, a brave, true man – the best of comrades and the staunchest of friends. My whole heart goes out to you in pity. Yours, R. Scott.'

Wilson too had written a last letter to Oriana hinting that the mystical transcendence he had worked so hard for had at last arrived: 'My beloved wife, these are small things, life itself is a small thing to me now . . . God knows I am sorry to be the cause of sorrow to anyone in the world, but everyone must die – and at every death there must be some sorrow . . . I feel so happy now in having got time to write to you . . . All is well.'

Dreams so vivid: dreams of trees, dreams of beaches, dreams of sunshine. Dreams that go on through the night, gathering themes and elaborations as they spiral towards the morning. As we drew closer to sun-up, I began to dream viscerally, in technicolour. A straw poll of Halley-dwellers turns up a recurrent dream: the Brunt Ice Shelf has cracked, and is calving a giant iceberg. The Laws platform and all the buildings to the north are drifting off into the Weddell. The dreamer is caught on the wrong side of a widening gap, the sea below has already sluiced in. You must decide, instantly, whether to attempt a jump or hang back as the base floats away.

Perhaps it is something to do with what psychologists call 'sensory deprivation'; a mind so open with the emptiness of the ice that it will seize any stimulus or fear, and feast on it. Towards the end of winter if I ever watched a movie in the evening I would dream of it all night. If I listened to new music it would circuit on a loop. I grew watchful of what I fed my brain now that I would have to dream through the consequences. After watching a documentary on Alexander the Great I visited the oracle of Siwa three nights running.

The best dreams were those of trees. I had never lived so long without them. I would dream myself lying on beds of autumnal beech leaves, wrapped up warm and snoozing beneath the cross-linked arms of a northern forest. Or transported to Chiloe off the coast of Chile, into a dripping temperate rainforest I once explored: soaked in humidity, the percussive sound of Pacific breakers in my ears, the croaking of frogs in the undergrowth, the air so laden with mulchy organic richness that it felt edible. All the features of the dream were those elements of the natural world that I missed the most. But then I would wake from a nemoral world to hear the sigh of a polar wind or feel the background hum of the generator in my bones. Going to my pit-room window I'd see those familiar plains of sparkling ice, zinc titanium brilliance under moonlight, or watch again coiled ribbons of aurorae. I have been here forever, I thought to myself. Perhaps I will never leave.

Seasons felt meaningless without the testimony of trees. I waited for the sun.

# SPRING

CHAPTER TWELVE

# *Gathering Light*

We seemed to bathe in that brilliant flood of light, and from its
flashing rays to drink in new life, new strength, and new hope.
R. F. Scott, *The Voyage of the Discovery*

It is no coincidence that the flags of both Greenland and Lapland
– the only 'indigenous' Arctic nations – depict the sun. For peoples
who endure months of polar darkness the image of the sun holds
a power and a symbolism that most of us who live in lower latitudes can't imagine. Perhaps we appreciate most what we know
can be taken from us. In cultures where winter means months of
confinement the sun is a potent symbol of liberation, as well as
of strength heat and life.

On 11 August I was out skiing around noon. The sky above
me had a hint of blue for the first time in months. I had been
looking again that morning at photographs of the base in
summer; the white glare on the ice, the paintbox cobalt of the
sky, and still did not recognise what I saw. My mind's eye could
no longer associate Halley with full daylight. The photographs
seemed of a fabulous, alternative, impossible world. The northern
horizon was no longer the smear of oils that had accompanied
the winter trip to see the penguins, it was rainbow pastels, and
I knew that soon they'd stretch into wide watercolour washes of
light. And then, without expecting it, I saw the topmost rim of
the sun.

It was not expected for another couple of days. That it had
become visible meant that a layer of air was bending and moulding

its light, throwing a Fata Morgana around the curve of the world. The earliest Arctic explorers were baffled by this mirage-like phenomenon, and sometimes took it as an omen of God's goodwill. I did not care whether it had bent around the curve of the planet or shone directly. It was the *sun*. I stopped skiing, dropped my poles, pulled up my balaclava and let the first sunlight in three and a half months strike my skin. It was all I could do not to raise my arms.

In the half-light I reached for my radio to tell the others. It would be five months before I would leave this place, and for the first time I felt it as too short. There were so many things I still wanted to do here, but time was running out.

The next day a quilt of cloud pulled snugly up to the chin of the Brunt, and evidence of the sun's return was reduced to a thread of light like a copper wire along the northern horizon. The temperature rose with the insulating effect of the cloud to reach the mid-twenties below zero. To celebrate the end of winter we did the summeriest thing we could think of – an outdoor barbecue. To keep the beer and wine from freezing we stacked the bottles and cans to one side of the burning charcoals. Three and a half months ago Mark had lowered the flag; now Elaine, the youngest on base, climbed up on to the roof of the Laws and raised a new one. At the moment when the sun should have peeped over the horizon we all raised our glasses and cheered.

From *Beowulf* onwards the literature of northern Europe has treated the return of the sun as a pivotal, transitional time. Its celebration has something to do with relief and something to do with anticipation of the gathering summer. The corresponding literature of Antarctica has a far shorter pedigree, dominated by the writings from Scott's and Shackleton's expeditions. As at midwinter I wanted to turn to those as a way of marking another milestone in my journey through the year. The barbecue didn't last long – it was still too cold outside – but back inside, as the others went to watch a DVD in the lounge, I sat down in the library with a stack of books.

During Scott's second winter on the *Discovery*, in 1903, he struggled to find words to describe his relief on seeing the sun. It was 'beyond all power of description . . . grandeur and solemnity which no words can paint'. He had by now made his great southern journey with Shackleton and Wilson, and his thoughts were turning increasingly to home. The previous year he had been less circumspect, and his journal for that period hints at anxiety over the sledge journey that still lies ahead, and worries over how much of the continent he will manage to explore before the sun once more drops below the horizon. Perhaps he was even wondering if he would reach the South Pole: 'This glorious sun was bringing the light of day and some measure of warmth to the bleak, desolate region about us, and heaven only knows how far prophetic thoughts took us over its trackless wastes before those beneficent rays should again vanish and sombre darkness once more descend.'

It is another example of Scott betraying his dislike of Antarctica, its 'bleak, desolate' landscape, and 'trackless wastes'. As his sister Grace later observed, he 'had no urge towards snow, ice, or that kind of adventure'. He was altogether a curious choice to lead a polar expedition.

Five years later Shackleton saw the same thing, in almost exactly the same location, and was far more businesslike about it. 'On the morning of August 22, the day on which the sun once more appeared above the horizon, we started back for the winter quarters.' He was at the time preparing some of his men for a journey towards the South Magnetic Pole, and deeper into the Trans-Antarctic Mountains. Shackleton's *Heart of the Antarctic* is not a book to overindulge the emotions. In a nearby passage he even quotes an orders letter he received back in London in order to highlight the two main aims of his expedition under the auspices of the British Empire:

Dear Sir – If you reach the Magnetic Pole, you will hoist the Union Jack on the spot, and take possession of it on behalf of the above expedition for the British Nation.

When you are in the western mountains, please do the same at one place, taking possession of Victoria Land as part of the British Empire.

If economic minerals are found, take possession of these in the same way on my behalf as Commander of this expedition.

Imperial expansion and mineral wealth – it is historically interesting in a depressing sort of way that the two aims of Shackleton's expedition are now the same two considered so dangerous to the environment and to international politics that they are precluded by the Antarctic Treaty.

The *Terra Nova* had poorer weather. Cherry-Garrard in *The Worst Journey* complained that the sun's theoretical return was hidden by blizzards of blinding drift. Scott's journal too shows frustration at the weather, but that evening Ponting gave a slide show of his Indian travels. Scott felt himself transported to another world. On this day of sun-returning it is the photographs of Benares, now Varanasi, that most move him, watching through Ponting's lens thousands of Hindu pilgrims waiting on the banks of the Ganges for the rising of the sun: 'In the first dim light the waiting, praying multitude of bathers, the wonderful ritual and its incessant performance; then, as the sun approaches, the hush – the effect of thousands of worshippers waiting in silence – a silence to be felt.' I shared his longing not only to see the sun but to be surrounded by thousands of others.

It would be months before I'd be enveloped by the crowds of humanity again, but for now crowds of penguins would have to do. The emperors had no personal space; their world was to be enclosed within a huddle of thousands. Through our Antarctic winter it was only the humans who had marked out territories: Stuart, Annette and Elaine to their workstations on the Simpson platform, Mark M., Russ and Mark S. to the Piggott platform, Rob and Tommo to the workshop, Graeme and Ben to the garage, Pat to his office, Toddy to his kit-room, and Craig to his kitchen. I had moved between each of these spaces but always returned to the medical room, the library, or out to the openness of the ice.

Inuit peoples have developed more sweat glands on their faces than elsewhere on their bodies, because it is their faces that remain exposed whatever the weather. A Native American once told a curious European that he didn't need to wear clothes because 'I am all face.' When the temperature climbed enough for me to dispense with my neoprene face mask I was relieved. I prefer to meet the universe bare-faced.

These were the last of the dark nights. In August our planet moved through the Perseid cloud and nightly I watched the sparks of its meteorites flail through the sky. I was sure that some of them reached the surface, but too far away to seek them out. Classical and early Christian belief was that the heavenly bodies sang as they turned through the sky, and each had a unique tone that harmonised with the others. As I watched the planets over Antarctica for those last dark nights I did not hear the music of the spheres, only the continental whisper of blown snow. The auroras, too, were disappointingly silent.

The moon was fading, having lit our whole winter it grew pallid and sickly. I still looked for it whenever I came outside; sometimes drifting like a ship cut loose, sometimes moored to a bank of stars. I did not understand Scott's perspective on winter darkness. Though I was glad to see the sun again, the whiteness of the advancing summer was like a tyranny. In terms of appreciating Antarctica it was the winter skies that had depth and beauty for me. There was always something new to see in them. But the daylight had its advantages; it would be possible once again to make regular visits to the emperors.

One weekend after sun-up I asked Annette to skidoo down to see the penguins with me. The ice fell away from us on all sides with the curve of the planet; it was as if we were gliding downhill. There was a freedom in driving away from base in this way, a recognition that a new stage, and season, was beginning. After days of cloud it was as if a lid had been blown off the sky. The sun's rays, reliable now, had transformed our world; they cast the ice in relief with geometric precision. Every ridge and fissure seemed magnified. The sun still skirted the ice but the width of its arc grew wider every day, as if a brass wedge of light was being knocked into the horizon from the north. As we reached the ice cliffs above the rookery I was nervous with anticipation, wondering if the chicks had hatched.

They had. The tight huddle of male emperors had burst open, a spreading raucous reunion party had scattered over the bay. From the cliffs I could already hear the high-pitched skirling cry of chicks, invisible yet, over the clamour. Annette and I tied into our harnesses and abseiled off the cliff on to the sea ice.

We were engulfed by the emperors. To my eye they seemed sun-happy, delirious with pride and relief. One by one they waddled up and, pointing with their beaks towards their toes, hoisted the brood fold of their bellies to show me the grey-fluff squealing treasure inside. I saw shattered eggs discarded on the ice like Houdini's ropes, and some eggs turned prematurely to tombs. There were little corpses, too, isolated and drifting over with snow, of those chicks whose mothers had not returned in time.

Looking up I saw no predators in the sky, too early in the season for skuas or giant petrels to reach this far south, and understood why these birds have adopted such a gruelling breeding cycle. They were unafraid, as if in Eden before the Fall. The cries of the chicks all sounded the same to me, a high chiming whistle. Scientists have made sonograms of these cries, trying to puzzle out whether the adults, even from hatching, can identify their own offspring. While the adults' sonograms appear layered with strata of tones like chunks of sea ice, those of the chicks are like a child's drawing of a mountain range, high and pure with jagged contours. Though I couldn't distinguish differences with my ears, I saw on the sonograms that cries *did* vary between individuals; some looked Alpine, some more like the Karakoram. Emperor parents will run to a tape recording of their chick's cry, and will reject a chick whose call they do not recognise.

Most of those around me were females; I could tell them by the healthy shellac shine on their feathers built up by months of resting and fishing. The wasted and famished males I had seen in July had for the most part left for open water. Ornithologists André Ancel and Gerry Kooyman once arranged to track those males to find out how far they had to go to find food after their long fast. They were found to make for permanent ice-free polynyas where they can fish and rest at leisure, up to 300 km away from the rookery. One of the males they tracked took just over two weeks to make a journey of this length taking a zigzag course of over 450 km, an astonishing feat after a four-month fast (though they may make short dives for fish through narrow leads before they get there). How they find a polynya is not known; it may be that they sniff the air for the briny scent of open water, and like polar captains look up for 'water-sky' reflected in the clouds. Kooyman's team were also the first to strap video cameras to the birds and observe directly how they hunt. The emperors were seen to glide beneath the sea ice, camouflaged from above against the deep by their black backs, and camouflaged from below against the ice by their white bellies. From time to time they would stoop up towards the surface, plunging peregrines in reverse, to seize the fish that live within the melting labyrinth of the sea-ice ceiling.

A male will spend about three weeks away gathering his strength, then return to relieve his mate for six or seven days. The length of time they spend away grows shorter and shorter as the edge of the sea ice creeps southwards with the warming season. From hatching to fledging a chick might need as little as twenty meals in total, each one a bellyful of fish, krill or squid depending on what is available. It must grow quickly enough that it completes fledging before the sea ice breaks up in December or January. The race is on: these few feeds have to take it from a hatching weight of about 300 g up to a lumbering adolescent of 15 kg, a fifty-fold increase in just five or six months.

The penguins crouching on their parents' feet were a promise of life returning, but were closely stalked by death. Three-quarters of the eggs laid in June might hatch successfully but then a gauntlet of dangers await them: starvation, exposure in blizzards, burial by icefalls. Some of them would fall into leads and tide-cracks, others would be crushed by overzealous adults trying to foster them (there were gangs of these penguins, desperate for a chick of their own). Later in the season the giant petrels would come for them, and leopard seals and orcas as the sea ice begins to break up. Once fledged and free of the rookery the death rate would climb; only twenty per cent of chicks are thought to survive their first year. Despite these dismal statistics *Aptenodytes* are still considered the most successful penguins in terms of their chick survival.

Though I had been told that the dissection of an adult emperor was forbidden, for some reason the chicks were fair game. I took one of the dead chicks back to base and fished out the 'Guide to Penguin Taxidermy'. It had been hidden in the cupboard under the sink behind the body bags. Hand-typed on a blubber-stained piece of foolscap paper, creased and yellowed with age, it began with a list of necessary equipment. I would need a board to nail the penguin down, scalpel, tongs, forceps and scissors, wire netting to build inside the body and a bottle of borax salt for the skin. The nearest borax was several thousand miles away, so rock salt would have to do.

I hadn't done anything like this since medical school. Suddenly I was eighteen years old again, in my first week of anatomy class, faced with a skinned human body beneath a torn linen shroud. No white coat this time; I wore an insulated boiler suit stained with oil from my efforts helping Graeme in the generator room. I put on surgical gloves and pinned the chick down to the board with carpet tacks and a toffee hammer. The taxidermy guide directed me to make a cut from the cloaca out towards each thigh. The soft grey down slit open revealing shiny pink flesh beneath.

In Roman times a sacrificial animal would be cut open and the pattern of the revealed entrails used to predict the future. This process, known as extispicy, was conducted by a special class of priests; men who would prepare themselves, and the animals, in a ritual cleansing before the divining event. The blood on my gloved fingers had nothing to do with divining the future, but something perhaps about revealing the present. What were the penguins feeding their chicks? I felt for the stomach – it was lumpy like a bag of dice. Taking forceps and scalpel I made a hole in it and delivered three oblong pebbles of basalt. They were rounded, perhaps by years of grinding in the gut of the donor parent, or perhaps on the bed of the Weddell deep beneath the sea ice. Three featureless black rocks, but I placed them carefully to one side as if they were gemstones.

The patterns of its guts may not have told the future, but stones in the belly of the emperor penguin did predict the discovery of the Antarctic continent in a very real way. In 1840, Charles Wilkes' expedition from the United States collected samples of these stones from emperors pulled off the sea ice, and used them to argue the existence of an undiscovered land to the south. No one knows if the pebbles are there to act as ballast, or are needed to grind hard foodstuffs such as squid beaks. Some emperors have been found starving, their guts blocked with over 4 kg of rocks.

I turned the stomach inside out and found a fine greenish-pink mulch, the remains perhaps of the lowly krill, fish, or cephalopods that they eat (lowly but with exalted names like *Euphausia superba*, *Electrona antarctica* and *Psychoteuthis glacialis*). Closing the stomach back up again I began to look elsewhere in the abdomen.

The gall bladder seemed absurdly distended, with bile leaching out across the rest of the abdominal organs. I have seen the same phenomenon in human cadavers, and didn't take it as a sign of gall bladder disease. I stripped it out along with the delicate little liver, lobed like a human's, and then the intestines as far as the cloaca. I put the lot in a sealed bag before changing my gloves. The Australians have identified a micro-organism in emperor chicks which in humans gives rise to a sexually transmitted disease. How it got there is another of Nature's mysteries.*

I began to shell the body of the chick from its skin, opening a seam through the fat between the skin and the muscle. This chick was scrawny but an adult would have had two or three inches of subcutaneous fat all the way around. This layer is the secret of its survival in more ways than one: it insulates the penguin, but also within it are special cells that break down fat and release heat directly, without the penguin having to shiver or walk to generate warmth. They can turn this on like a switch when underwater, creating heat to replace what the freezing waters of the Weddell draw away.

At the feet and flippers the taxidermy guide directed me to cut through the bone, and through the net of blood vessels that act like countercurrent heat exchangers for the limbs. The blood going to the feet and flippers can be cooled by these vessels to approach the near-freezing temperature of sea water without any great loss of heat from the body's core. In summer, when temperatures around freezing are uncomfortably hot for the penguins, these blood vessels dilate, forcing blood to the extremities in order to cool the penguin down. Emperors are most comfortable between minus 10°C to minus 20°C; within that range they don't need to burn fat to generate heat. At more than 10°C above zero,

---

* It is a disease which in humans goes by the name *Lymphogranuloma venereum*. As a doctor I've only seen one case, picked up in a Latin American brothel.

temperatures they are exposed to in Western zoos, they become flushed, agitated and can die of heat exhaustion.

I separated the skin from the thorax where I saw that the ribs had interlocking ridges, probably to protect the lungs against the tremendous pressures of diving at depth. Opening the chest I stopped to marvel a moment at the lungs. They looked surprisingly like human lungs – pyramidal and spongy – but these ones, when mature, would be capable of a breath lasting twenty minutes. Teasing the whole thorax away from the skin I had to cut the spine, carotid arteries, oesophagus and windpipe just below the skull. With the windpipe severed I could look up from below the vocal cords of the bird, embedded towards the back of the tongue, and thought of the unique skirling whistle that once issued out of it. The tongue itself was hard and reptilian, coated with fine spines pointing stomachwards to guide slippery fish in the right direction. The puffins of the northern hemisphere, though unrelated, have developed almost identical tongues.

I began to strip the tight-fitting skin from the head, working the seam open towards the eyes. The broad clouded discs seemed disproportionate to the little skull, set with an iris capable of yawning wide enough to catch glimpses of bioluminescence half a kilometre beneath the sea. Those pupils can also narrow to a pinprick against the summer's glare. Edward Wilson had been astonished at the lack of bony prominences around the eye; they bulged proud of the skull in order to track prey either above or below the penguin as it swims.

I eased the eyeballs out, and with rolled-up tissue paper and wood glue stuck some marbles in their place. The plates of the skull behind the eye were horny and opaque, like fingernails knitted together. Behind the eye I'd read that there was a *rete mirabilis*, a 'miraculous net' of blood vessels that acted as a heat exchanger for the eye. And behind those blood vessels was the brain.

Hugh MacDiarmid, the Scottish nationalist poet and Republican sympathiser in the Spanish Civil War, begins his poem 'Perfect' with a Spanish phrase about the dead opening the eyes of the living – '*Los muertos abren los ojos a los que viven*' – only to go on to describe the wonder of holding a Hebridean bird skull in his hand. The fineness of the bone, the neatness of the space where once lay a brain, he associated with the bird's mastery of the air: 'twin domes like bubbles of thin bone,/Almost transparent, where the brain had been/That fixed the tilt of the wings.' The brain held within this penguin skull had developed with an instinctive mastery of the sea, along with other useful information: how to avoid leopard seals, how to find food, how to find your way back to a breeding rookery.

At the spinal cord in cross-section it was just possible to make out the dipterous pattern of grey matter on white, shaped just as it is in humans. Brains – either penguin or human – are so delicate that without fixing them with chemicals they are unable to support their own weight out of the skull. I peeled back the thin plates of bone carefully to examine the brain without moving it. Birds also 'speak' with their left hemispheres, and despite the received wisdom of their stupidity there are many other similarities between the brain of a bird and that of a human. Once thought to be much more primitive than their mammalian counterparts, anatomists gave names designed to give a sense of ancient and unevolved simplicity: *paleostriatum primitivum*, *archistriatum*, *paleostriatum augmentatum*. But those flat-earth anatomists have been proven wrong, and those parts of the bird once thought to be primitive have been recognised as essentially the same as those of mammals. The habenula, which Descartes took as the seat of the soul, is as present in birds as it is in humans.

It had none of the convolutions of a human or a cetacean brain, it was as smooth as an unworried brow. Painstakingly I tried to lift it out intact, but it fell apart like soggy toothpaste. The expansion of human brains has moulded out our skulls; our frontal lobes are cradled on a crib above the eyes, the temporal lobes scoop out twin hollows behind our ears. The blood vessels draining our enormous human brains are so large they imprint our skulls with a relief map of rivers and tributaries. The emperor skull was not mapped and sculpted in this way, it had the pearly smoothness of the inside of a mussel shell.

Into that opalescent holy ground that so excited MacDiarmid's imagination I stuffed some pieces of ripped-up toilet paper. I replaced the thin plates of skull bone and pulled the skin back over the head the way you pull a sock over a foot. The inside of the skin was scrubbed with rock salt, which stiffened and set it solid, and I wondered if this was why borax had been recommended. Working fast as it set I shaped some wire into the neck and filled out the sack of the chick's body with paper and wood glue. The rent in its belly was closed with surgical sutures and I left it in the waste room to cure.

The pebbles I put in my pocket to keep, but was dismayed to discover later that they had fallen out. They must have dropped on to the ice through a hole in my pocket. Even now they will be working their way down through the ice shelf, moving at glacial pace back towards the seabed from where they had been taken, and where another emperor, perhaps centuries into the future, might one day find them.

The air temperature was still far below zero every day, but as spring advanced the steady hail of sunlight on the brightest days could heat black surfaces enough to melt snow. I emerged from the Laws one morning to find an icicle hanging from the edge of the platform. From its tip I watched a drop – tiny, glinting, precious – fall to the ice below. It was a transition point, as if the Snow Queen had been banished. During a low-pressure storm towards the end of September the temperature rose to a sweltering minus 4°C. We lay panting in the heat after melt-tank duty, remarking on the new sensation of soggy clothing.

I took off my gloves and felt with my hand the warmth of a black oil drum in the sunlight. When I lifted my hands to my face I saw that my fingertips were wet. I had been drinking water made from melted shelf ice for nearly a year now. Human beings are almost three-quarters water, my body was by now composed of the stuff of the continent. It bathed my brain, pulsed in my heart, nourished my limbs. I realised that my skin must have renewed itself entirely since I had arrived in this place; it had known no other environment than the Antarctic. It was as if now, even as I began to think about returning home, I was becoming more at one with my surroundings.

In early September we had a fancy-dress night, themed 'come as your favourite star'. Tommo and Graeme were the Blues Brothers, Annette dressed as a Spice Girl, Pat the shiatsu masseuse and karate fan dressed as Bruce Lee, and Toddy, who is a passionate fan of westerns, was Clint Eastwood. Rob and Mark M. revealed a secret love for hip-hop music, and came as gangster rappers. I constellated a black suit and came as the stars of the northern hemisphere. It felt like a long time since I had seen them.

As the days moved into October I no longer went skiing around lunchtime. Like a prisoner emerging from solitary confinement I found the midday sunlight smarted my eyes. I waited until evening when its light was kinder, softer and more oblique. The schedule of outside work accelerated and we began to prepare the base for a still-distant summer. I took a sledgehammer around the perimeter, knocking the drums from the ice and setting them up on the newer, higher snow-surface. The drum lines to the emperor rookery, the Relief Creeks, and towards the N9 relief site all had to be raised. For this, long loops of rope, fixed to the back of a slow-moving snowcat, were dropped over the submerged drums. The drums shattered out of the ice as the vehicle pulled past. It took days of this work to raise all the drums. The meteorologists ran another 'kite-flying campaign', working shifts day and night for which they advertised for volunteers. Each kite was up to twelve feet in diameter, as wide and buoyant as an albatross wingspan, and lifted instruments to measure temperature, windspeed and humidity through the layers of air sheeting off the continent. Another long day out was a GPS survey of the Brunt. Markers placed many kilometres out on the shelf had to be found and their positions measured with a sensitive GPS computer. The information gathered meant we could see how the ice flow varied across the shelf, the way the surface we lived upon was being twisted and distorted by its flow. The distortions we measured across miles of shelf ice also had effects on a local scale – the ice between the legs of our base was moving too. Pat and I spent afternoons up ladders with a theodolite. Each leg of the Simpson, Piggott and Laws platforms had to be jacked or lowered to compensate for changes in level, and the shearing effects of the legs being pinched together or separated had to be quantified. Pat would gather all the data together for the steel erectors, welders and engineer who would be brought in for the summer to straighten out the most rickety legs.

Ben had serviced all of our skidoos, and now that the temperature was in the minus twenties said that we could start to use them again around base. I had one of the newest models, capable of seventy miles per hour, but a limiter had been placed on its accelerator wire inside the carburettor. Early one Sunday morning when Ben was still asleep I remembered his carburettor tutorial and managed to remove the limiter. It was not that I wanted to go faster – it was just that the limiter made the accelerator stiff and it had started to give me cramps in my hand. At least I think that was the reason.

I was found out. Ben had to move the skidoo (no one ever took the keys from the ignition – why would they?), noticed the ease with which the accelerator on the handgrip turned, and confronted me later that day. It was at lunchtime, and he, Graeme and Russ were all eating soup in the dining room when I came in to join them. Their conversation stopped when I sat down.

'Did you open up the carb on that skidoo?' Ben asked me, tensing all the muscles in his shoulders. The spoon in his hand was trembling slightly.

'Yes,' I said, trying to look him straight back in the eye, 'keeping the revs up was starting to hurt my hand.'

'I don't give a shit why you did it,' he said, 'do I go into the medical room and mess around with your stuff?'

'No, but—'

Russ and Graeme, who had been looking carefully at their soup, both got up and left the room.

'No but nothing, you could have fucked it up, if you can't be trusted to use one of our best skidoos then I'll take it off you.'

We finished the rest of our lunch in silence, and afterwards he took my skidoo back to the garage. It meant I had to do a little more skiing around base, but after a few days, and a couple more apologies on my part, he gave it back to me. I didn't mess with it again.

Visits to the coast were easy now. Dark leads in the ice, angled like blades, had appeared around the edges of the rookery and whittled away at the area still fast to the cliffs. The advance of spring had brought other species to these coasts – I saw my first Weddell seal of the year. She was spread out on the ice, half a tonne of blubber and fur, dozing peacefully in the sun. I tiptoed carefully towards her but need not have bothered; even when I got close enough to feel her breath on my face she did not stir.

Weddell seals, *Leptonychotes weddellii*, are the largest seals to haul out on these coasts, and the earliest. Her girth was immense, and in stretched-out form she reached up to my chest as I kneeled beside her. I was in awe of her size but could not imagine her causing me harm, except perhaps by rolling in her sleep. A smile twitched at the corners of her lips. Weddells live most of their lives under a frozen ceiling, maintaining breathing holes in the sea ice by scratching at it with their teeth. A seal whose teeth have worn out is doomed. In spring they come onto the sea ice to give birth, and this one's size suggested she would do so any day. With the emperor chicks fattening daily and the seals returning, there was evidence that the sterility of the ice around me was only surface-deep. Underneath was a world flourishing with life.

Antarctic seas teem with one of the most populous species on the planet. Some sources suggest that Antarctic krill, *Euphausia superba*, has *the* greatest single-species biomass of all living beings. There are an estimated 500 million tonnes of them in the southern oceans and under the sea ice, or about the same combined mass as all the domesticated animals on the planet (human beings, by contrast, add up to a risible 150 million tonnes). The krill subsist on a turbid soup of phytoplankton, those unicellular organisms that float freely in the sea, blooming over our blue planet's surface, staining and phosphorescing the ice.

In *Encounters at the End of the World*, film-maker Werner Herzog delighted in the contrast above and below the ice, as if the sea ice was a barrier not only between elements but between worlds. Like Alice down the rabbit hole he follows divers through a break in the sea ice into a fantastical wonderland: Weddell seals sing their otherworldly songs, giant sponges, feasting on oxygen-rich water, waft in the currents' breeze, and the melting ice of the continental shelf forms a glassy ultramarine labyrinth of such breathtaking beauty that Herzog feels emotionally and spiritually transformed by it. The divers, he says, call diving under the ice 'going down into the cathedral'; he likens their preparations for a dive to that of a priest preparing for Mass.

Leaving the sleeping Weddell seal I approached the edge of one of the leads; I wanted to see down into the cathedral. Adult emperors erupted from the surface in bursts, scattering jewelled drops of water over the ice where they froze on contact. The penguins crash-landed on their bellies only inches away from me and slithered away into the rookery. Lying on my belly and peering down into the lead I caught brief glimpses of them speeding skywards, streams of bubbles trailing in their wake.

Up on the sea ice the chicks had begun to herd themselves into crèches, freeing up the adults to go fishing for longer periods of time. Eight or nine weeks old now, the age at which human babies are just beginning to smile, the emperor chicks were starting to strike out on their own. There was something very human about the way that they wrestled together, playing in the snow, slapping and cuddling one another with their wings.

I moved back towards the ice cliffs, preparing to climb back up on to the Brunt, and passed an exploratory expedition of chicks trying to do the same. They had climbed up the ice foot in single file, led by the biggest among them, and three had already reached a vertical section of the cliff. They scrabbled against it using beak, wings and claws, squealing in indignation, until they all fell tumbling down the slope.

Elias Canetti, the Bulgarian Nobel laureate, wrote that the earth hates men for their trampling feet, but that the air is well disposed to the birds that pass through it. As I reached for the rope I wondered if emperors might yearn for the sky after all.

Some years all of the emperor chicks die. One sunny afternoon in Guildford, a lifetime ago, or so it seemed, I had met a doctor who wintered at Halley some years before. He described going down to the coast in spring after a storm to find that all of the sea ice had broken out. The chicks cannot swim until they are at least partly fledged, and all of them had drowned. I had by now grown so attached to the emperors that even imagining that event was like a bereavement to me.

Almost nothing is known about the rise and fall of different emperor colonies. Only fifty years ago just four emperor rookeries were known. That number has edged up slowly as ever more comprehensive surveys, mostly by air, have cross-hatched the continent. For rookeries to be visible they must be counted in late winter or spring, a time when most of the continental fringe is inaccessible. Groups of penguins are invisible from sea level more than a few kilometres away. By 1993 it was thought that there were perhaps thirty-two emperor colonies worldwide, but this estimate was said to have a significant 'location bias' – biased towards locations that could actually be reached.

Enter Peter Fretwell and Phil Trathan of the British Antarctic Survey. Based in the Mapping and Geographic Information Centre (MAGIC) of BAS headquarters they work surrounded by extraordinary images of the continent. I visited the office once and had to be prised away – it is a map-lover's paradise. Maps of rocks, maps of species distribution, maps of winds, maps of sea ice and maps of ozone. There were rainbow-coloured thermal maps and maps of the availability of maps. One of my favourites was a map for the air unit, the continent strung up by a cat's cradle of air routes drawn between deep-field fuel depots. Each depot was marked with the number of fuel drums available there at the start of the season, and each flight path by its distance, flight time and fuel consumption at 600 lb an hour. I admired it for so long I was given one to take away.

These map-makers have also turned their attention to the emperors, and have published a paper with the unlikely title of 'Penguins from Space'. Rather than describing extraterrestrial visitors it analyses satellite images of the entire circumferential coastline of the continent, tracking colonies by their tell-tale faecal staining on the ice. *Euphausia superba* are red, like shrimps, and that redness is thrice-useful – to the krill themselves as protection from UV radiation, to the penguins to help them find their prey underwater, and when passed out as faeces the pigments become visible to satellites as stains on the ice. Edward Wilson would have been captivated; sitting in their offices in Cambridge the authors use electronic eyes in the sky to describe the first 'synoptic pan-Antarctic assessment of the colony distribution of emperor penguins'. It represents an innovative direction in ornithological science, 'the first satellite-based study of a vertebrate that captures almost the whole breeding distribution of the species'.

There are a few surprises. They found thirty-eight colonies large enough to be seen from space, including ten new ones never before described, mostly along the rarely visited coastlines of Ellsworth Land and Marie Byrd Land. Some historical colonies had moved, others shrivelled away, including Wilson's at Cape Crozier – recent visitors have found it reduced to less than a hundred pairs. More worrying was an identified trend for colony reduction and even disappearance north of the 70° latitudinal line, which the authors tentatively linked to climate change through a gradual reduction in the viability of sea ice. In another paper, this time with Bernard Stonehouse, the authors explore the reasons for the disappearance of Stonehouse's old colony on the Dion Islets. The increasing instability of the sea ice due to regional warming is their conclusion. They call Dion Islets a 'sentinel' colony, in that its demise may be a warning of more serious threats to come.

In Edward Wilson's time there was the widespread belief that emperors were primitive throwbacks to the dinosaur age, clinging on by their scaly feet to life at the bottom of the world. Over time that perspective shifted to one of easy confidence; the emperors were well-adapted, robust survivors, the ice on which they lived was going nowhere and their food supplies were abundant. Species are classified according to their vulnerability by the International Union for the Conservation of Nature (IUCN). Given these new findings Trathan and Fretwell repeat the proposal that emperors should be moved from the 'Least Concern' IUCN category into 'Data Deficient'. In only a few years the 'eternal ice' of the Antarctic has been shown to be more vulnerable than was thought.

Climate change on our planet, in addition to all that carbon-footprint anxiety, is intimately linked to the ozone hole over Antarctica. A ring-a-roses of oxygen atoms, ozone has the chemical formula $O_3$. The ozone layer that protects us is kilometres up, undulating in miles-wide banners more than twice the height of Everest over our heads. When I arrived in Antarctica I had tried not to think about climate change. In the same way I avoided dwelling on the ozone depletion above me or my nakedness beneath it. I slapped on the factor 30 though, just in case.

It was at Halley in 1985 that the ozone hole was discovered. On the Simpson platform, named for Scott's meteorologist, Stuart had shown me the instrument that had picked it up, the grandly named Dobson spectrophotometer. It looked like a museum piece, a box of dials and diodes suspended by an iron gantry beneath a hole in the roof. Light within the spectrum range affected by ozone fell through filters and lenses into the dark interior of the machine. He explained how it worked but lost me along the way. 'The Americans have got a fancier system,' he added, 'at the South Pole. They had noticed the same trend as BAS, but thought there must have been a mistake.' He chuckled at the folly of those clever Americans and their computerised equipment. 'They just recalibrated the machine to adjust for the newer, lower ozone level every year!'

George Simpson was a quiet, reclusive Derbyshire man, and a meticulous and perfectionist scientist. He was helped by Charles Wright, the physicist who later found the polar party's tent, and who said of Simpson that he had 'a supreme contempt for everything but meteorology'. Simpson would have been glad to hear that his platform was now contributing to global climate models, and that it scooped ozone depletion – perhaps one of the most important scientific discoveries of the century.

One of my discoveries in the Halley library was the book of a British expedition to Greenland, called *Northern Lights: The Official Account of the British Arctic Air Route Expedition 1930–1931*. Within it was an account – spare, direct and unromantic – of manning a meteorological station alone through a polar winter. The man who wrote it was Augustine Courtauld, and his published account predates Richard Byrd's *Alone* by six years. When I reread Byrd's book at the beginning of my own winter my impression had been of an unprecedented elemental struggle, man against nature. Byrd's months of isolation were profoundly transformative. He had emerged convinced of the paramount importance of family ('an everlasting anchorage'), the existence of a God (an 'all-pervading Intelligence'), and that few men, himself included, come close to tapping the resources that lie within them. 'Part of me remained forever at Latitude 80°08′ South,' he wrote towards the conclusion, 'what survived of my youth, my vanity, perhaps, and my scepticism ... I live more simply now, and with more peace.' Ample reward indeed for a few months on the ice.

Courtauld's account of nearly five months in a tent buried under snow, with no communications and few supplies, is tucked modestly away in Chapter 10 of *Northern Lights*. The result is a very British reflection on isolation; his conclusions do not dwell on the experience itself, but consist of some fairly dry descriptions of stores and closing advice to others that might try to repeat what he had done. But a great presence of mind shines through his account.

It begins by warning against over-dramatisation of the risks involved. 'There are many men, trappers and the like, who live by themselves for most of the year. An accident is very rare among these men, nor are their minds usually deranged.' He had arrived mid-December, and the first weeks he occupied himself daily with drying out his sleeping bag and digging his way out of the buried snow tunnel to read the meteorological instruments. By early January the access tunnel had completely filled with compacted ice, and he was reduced to cutting himself out with a penknife (he had left the spade outside). He decided to dig a new passage from his tent through to a nearby igloo and force a hole through its roof to the surface. It was all tediously laborious, he pointed out, as he had nowhere to put the snow but elsewhere inside his tent. He spent much of February digging for supply boxes that he had mislaid.

He passed the rest of his time in reading, playing chess against himself, concocting menu plans for sumptuous dinner parties, and planning sailing routes with the help of an atlas. On 22 March, the spring equinox, he had been alone over three months when a severe gale blocked his access shaft. He was trapped, and surveyed the potential outcomes: 1) he might now suffocate as the air became stale, 2) accumulating drift might crush him to death, and 3) the search party from the coast might miss his tent when it came because he could no longer keep watch. 'It was clearly futile to get anxious,' he notes, 'when by no possible endeavour on my part could I make any difference to the course of events.' Throughout this maddening ordeal Courtauld kept his peace. 'There were times', he wrote, 'when the Bible made very good reading.'

Courtauld had estimated his rescue date as 15 March and had budgeted his rations accordingly. So it was that by mid-April he was permanently in darkness, eating margarine mixed with uncooked pemmican, and smoking tea instead of tobacco. Smoking tea he seemed to consider the greatest hardship. Icicles gathered in the tent and fell on his head. He had no gramophone or radio to break the silence, and for that he was grateful. 'For the first month or so I was very averse to the least noise. The complete silence all round seemed to urge one to keep in tune with it by being silent oneself.' As the weeks went by without rescue he nevertheless became increasingly convinced it would come. 'I will not attempt any explanation of this but leave it as a fact, which was very clear to me during that time, that while powerless to help myself, some outer Force was in action on my side.'

At times I felt keenly the lack of human history in the Antarctic. There were days when that absence seemed Antarctica's greatest gift, and days when it rendered the continent wasted and sterile. Humans lived here on sufferance, I thought, with foods and fuels imported from a parallel, temperate universe. Sometimes the solitudes it offered seemed hostile, as if it were a continent better left alone. Like Forbes Mackay, Shackleton's doctor who had joked of being evicted by a six-foot penguin, I felt at times as if I was trespassing.

The indomitable Captain Cook, the leader of the first men known to have approached its shores, said the Antarctic was not worth the bother of reaching it. He wrote, 'should anyone possess the resolution and fortitude to elucidate this point by pushing yet further south than I have done, I shall not envy him the fame of his discovery, but I make bold to declare that the world will derive no benefit from it.' It was an entirely impassive continent, a world apart from the peopled Arctic, but I did not agree with Cook. Benefit there was here, in abundance, but for me that benefit was in the solitude it offered, a whitewashed primordial backdrop against which ideas, memories, ambitions, regrets, could be examined without distraction. To travel in the Arctic is to be part of a frontier human society. Travelling in the Antarctic, I found, is very different. There is a great emptiness there, unlined by cultural history, and what you see in the landscape is all about what you carry with you. I began to question what I would take away, and what direction I'd now choose for my life.

The stories of the *Northern Lights* expedition appealed to me because, unlike the grand old men of Scott's ponderous expeditions, or the ragtag band of Shackleton's, its members were all young men like Courtauld, straight out of university, making up the rules as they went along. Those young men seemed poised on the edge of the same decision I felt myself wrestling with: whether to continue in this life of travel and expeditions, in increasingly extreme destinations, or settle down to a profession while they still had the chance. In the end the expedition leader, Gino Watkins, chose the former, while Augustine Courtauld and *Northern Lights'* author Freddie Spencer Chapman chose the latter. And taken on its own Courtauld's experience struck me as one of the most enthralling polar survival stories I had ever read, and one of the most enviable.

Towards the end of October I had begun to prepare for a more extended trip away from base. I wanted to spend a longer period on my own, but for safety's sake it was not allowed. Mark S. and I would instead make a journey together across the ice shelf on skis, pulling a sledge each with tents and all our supplies. This was why Mark had been training for the last two months – he too preferred solitude, but to travel as a pair was the closest either of us would get to being alone away from base. Into my sledge I packed all the books I could find in the Halley library on Watkins, Courtauld and Chapman, and set off thinking about solitude, of the peopled Arctic and the empty Antarctic, and what can happen when a young man, driven by ambition, is given free rein to realise his dreams.

As Courtauld had imagined, Watkins did have great difficulty finding the buried tent. The first attempt, in March, had to turn back after a month of searching. The second attempt, expecting to find a tomb rather than a tent, set out on 21 April. Watkins himself had almost given up hope when, on 5 May, a black dot on the ice was spotted. The Union Jack had shredded away to a scrap. Chapman wrote 'we began to have certain misgivings. The whole place had a most extraordinary air of desolation.' Watkins rushed across the ice and began to call down the stove pipe. No one expected a response.

But Courtauld did respond. 'The voice was tremulous, but it was the voice of a normal man.' His last drop of paraffin had burned out only minutes before. The book has a series of plates showing him emerge from his oubliette, tangle-haired, smoke-stained and gaunt. I realised with a shock that I had passed the same number of weeks at Halley since midwinter as Courtauld passed alone. My experience in comparison had been luxurious and pedestrian.

There is a photograph of, from left to right, Rymill, Watkins, Courtauld and Spencer Chapman leaning back together on a Nansen sledge, soon after the rescue. Watkins radiates a ruddy health, with tanned face and clean white clothing. Courtauld appears like his photographic negative, his clothes are soot-stained and his face has a subterranean pallor. But despite all that he had gone through there is a remarkable composure about his manner. He sits back with his body at ease, hands folded in his lap, and his face wears the confidence of a man who has faced down his demons and won.

Unlike Byrd, Courtauld was not interested in generating a myth around himself. He returned from Greenland to get married and take up his inheritance. His interest in polar exploration extended to just one more expedition (to climb a mountain in East Greenland in 1935), and in later life to edit an inspired and broad-ranging anthology of polar writing. He did not take part in Watkins' second expedition to Greenland, though he wrote a generous introduction to its book. Like Apsley Cherry-Garrard, another sensitive and moneyed individual who paid his way to polar regions, he had no interest in making a career of being an explorer, but drew strength from the memory of his first expedition for the rest of his life.

At the end of Courtauld's brief account he provides an outline of the prerequisites for repeating his experience, which would do well as a guide for prospective Halley winterers. The individual should, he writes, have an 'active, imaginative mind, but not be of a nervous disposition'. He must volunteer himself and be secure in the knowledge of his stores, his base, and the arrangements to take him out again. He must have books and a plentiful source of light. If so, Courtauld writes, 'there is no reason why any normal person should not live in perfect peace of mind for an indefinite period'.

CHAPTER THIRTEEN

# Freedom of the Ice

At times I'm enormously aware of myself moving among this
vast, elemental indifference, the only breathing thing for miles . . .
yet it's oddly uplifting, like looking up at stars in the blackest of
nights.

Andrew Greig, *Summit Fever*


Our clothing was light, fine-twilled cotton, resistant to wind
and wear, flexible even at the coldest temperatures. We wore
soft leather boots, fixed at the toe to waxed skis. The Brunt is
flat and the access slopes to the sea ice for the most part are
gentle; there was no need for the skins that give grip on a steep
incline. The sledges themselves were fibreglass, lashed with
tarpaulins and nylon rope. Elastic cords don't work at those
temperatures, they quickly become brittle and crack. Each sledge
was stacked with about 60 kg of gear. Mark too had brought a
pile of books.

There was a hypnotic rhythm to travelling in this way, the
emptiness of the ice washing into the mind until it felt filled up
with light and sky. I felt as empty-headed as a minim. We skied
over a plain of frosted silver, Mark far ahead, the sounds of my
breathing lost in the whisper of the skis on the ice. I had never
before been so fit – my work in the north had always been seden-
tary – but now every day was bringing jobs that required great
physical effort. There was a pleasure in the use of my limbs, an
ease with which I lifted and carried weights, or skied for hours
on end, that I had never before experienced.

As we left Halley the *Shackleton* left England on its way to relieve us. It would be two months in coming, but hearing of its departure made this journey feel like a farewell. On our first day out we pulled past the sunken tomb of Halley IV, buried in the ice. Perhaps mankind did have a history here after all, even if only the faintest trace of one. Halley I, II and III had each been witnessed jutting out of the cliffs years after they had been abandoned. The metal staircases and radio antennae of all three, embedded in icebergs, had each in their turn calved off and sailed north into the Weddell.

In November 1967, at the inception of Halley II, a Zdoc called John Brotherhood together with another man, Jim Shirtcliffe, made a man-hauling trip like ours the length of the Brunt. Pulling along the edge of the ice cliffs they misjudged their path in poor contrast and dropped over on to the sea ice, falling thirty feet on the way down. Shirtcliffe twisted his ankle, and limped over to find Brotherhood moaning in agony with a broken back. He managed to rig up their tent as best he could over the casualty, and together they waited for rescue. It took thirty-six hours to come.

The rescuers strapped Brotherhood to a sledge and pulled him back to base where, lying immobilised on a spinal board, he had to interpret his own X-rays. He had crushed two vertebrae in his spine, broken his cheekbone, and two of his teeth had been forced through his lips.

The British didn't have reliable aeroplanes in those days, and it was the Americans, once again, who flew in to the rescue. They crossed the continent from McMurdo with two C130 Hercules aircraft, and landed with the help of arrows drawn on to the Halley ice with cocoa powder. The doctor on board confirmed Brotherhood's opinion of his own injuries, and loaded him on to one of the aircraft. About twelve hours later, more than five days after the injury, he reached a hospital in Christchurch.

That story stood as a warning to us of the risks we ran in being here. But it also served somehow to highlight for me the special nature of this place, and how much I had grown to love it: its paradoxical space that liberated as it imprisoned, its brisk clarity, its harsh lessons in closed-community living as well as in survival. It had given me insights into the way individuals can work together, how the qualities of a personality are not always what they seem, and how people can always surprise you. It had given me a solitude I hadn't dared hope for, and it had given me the emperors. After a few hours' pulling I reached the cliffs above the colony. Mark was already there, ready to abseil over the edge.

The sun was an unblinking eye to the north, the only witness to our journey. Only a few days before it had thrown out the largest solar flare yet recorded, but with skies so illuminated there had been no auroras. High chevrons of cirrus stood over the Pole, like brush strokes on a porcelain glaze. To the north colossal tabular icebergs along the horizon appeared tall and thin, stretched skywards by mirage effect.

Down on the sea ice the air was crisp and still. The leads had frozen over and glittered in the sunlight. Frost flowers, tiny precipitations of salt squeezed from the water, bloomed over the new ice. Opalescent brash ice piled in aimless heaps at the foot of the cliffs. I put my foot through one of the tide-cracks to see real seawater again and watched it well up obligingly. It was the gentle but unstoppable respiration of the ocean that had cracked these breaks in the ice.

To one side of the colony penguins gathered at the ice edge, jostling together, anxious and expectant. They were waiting for one of their number to jump in first, so that they would see if there were leopard seals beneath the ice. Leopard seals are the penguins' greatest threat in the water. Though over three-quarters of the emperor eggs that are laid make it to hatching, only one in five of them will survive their first year out on the open sea. But once they reach a year of age their survival rates are good; they have a long and leisured adolescence. Able to breed by three or four years old, emperors seem to follow Montaigne's maxim that one should wait for greater maturity before facing the realities of parenthood. Most are six or seven by the time they come to breed, some older. The chicks around us were bigger now, squat and ravenous, and they had more of the reptilian serenity behind their eyes that I had grown to recognise in the adults. Their fearlessness as I moved through them was a kind of acceptance, but it seemed also an expression of their otherworldliness – my irrelevance to their lives.

Their minds were of a simplicity that was unknowable and incomprehensible. For the first time since arriving I began to yearn for other creatures, other minds – the greater abundance of Life that lay in the north.

We spent days down on the sea ice at the penguin rookery. The shadows of the locked-in icebergs rotated through the day like sundials. One day I came upon a leopard seal stretched out asleep in the middle of the colony. The penguins stood back, silent and watchful, and I followed their example. On our last day at the colony, as the shadows stretched to the east, Mark caught my eye with a wave towards the cliffs. As I turned towards him I saw my first flying bird of the spring, a snow petrel heading south towards its nesting cliffs deep in the continent. With the petrel's arrival it seemed the northern world was rushing towards us, the year's circuit drawing to a close. The sun would set only briefly that night, and soon would not set at all.

I tunnelled into my sleeping bag and slept, but woke at 3 a.m., groggy and dehydrated. I buried my head in the bag again to get away from the violence of the light. I had been reading more about Courtauld, and imagined him now in his ice-cap prison, how he spent weeks in darkness and silence, plotting dinner parties and sailing routes. And then of Watkins' immense and solitary ambition – before even finishing his first expedition to Greenland he had been planning a dog-hauled crossing of the Antarctic continent. But Watkins' plans came to nothing; he died on his second Greenland expedition while hunting seals alone. His capsized kayak was found, but his body was never recovered.

Mark slept soundly nearby, earplugs in his ears and a blindfold over his eyes. I gave up trying to sleep and lay thinking about the north, and what I would do with my life when I returned. Esa and I still wrote to one another regularly, but now questioned openly how much we would still have in common when we managed to meet. At times I felt fear spread through me like an oil slick, fear that the experiences we had gone through over the last fourteen months had been so different that our lives would no longer be reconciled.

\*   \*   \*

Like Nansen and Amundsen, Gino Watkins had believed the best way to survive polar environments, and train for further expeditions, was to learn the ways of the Inuit. His mistake was to go hunting alone. In Greenlandic Inuit culture a lone hunter is a *qivitok*, a supernatural figure to be feared, usually said to be an old man who has tired of village life and gone off into the wilderness to prepare for death. To be a *qivitok* is to be in a liminal state, on the fringes of the human world, at the threshold of the animal and spiritual and able to understand the speech of animals. Only the *qivitok* and the Inuit shamans, known as *angakoks*, are presumed to be able to manage the silence, the solitude, and the danger of living alone in such a landscape. Their social purpose in that traditional polar society seemed to encompass doctor, magistrate and priest, and they went through intensive training before taking on such a demanding role.

As a young boy, barely walking, a future *angakok* was chosen for quick-wittedness and fostered by an older shaman. His earliest memories would be of bright summers learning the names and the ways of the animals, and dark winters lit by blubber lamp, learning chants on the knee of his master. He had to learn a new language, of allegory and metaphor, and the different songs for each of the sicknesses of man. Some were low and soft like the song for the dying, sung by the deathbed for days on end and telling of the happiness to come in the world beyond. Some were louder, like the exorcism of *suilarkinek*; that state of grief where the sufferer seeks danger to deaden the agony of living. He learned that selfishness is the worst sin and that the soul is shaped like the body – and like the body it too can be healed. As he grew older he had to spend ever-longer periods in silence and solitude, fasting and meditating.

If he succeeded he would be rewarded by the appearance of a spirit animal to guide and guard him. On his return to the village, the clairvoyants among his peers would see how he had been changed, that he walked with new bearing and confidence, that his breath now seemed to flicker with flame. If he failed in his training he became instead a *kilaumassok*. Though always to be considered a useful individual in the community, it was recognised that a *kilaumassok* had turned away from the path of solitude and asceticism that led to higher spiritual training.

It struck me that the Inuit *kilaumassok*, who had 'failed' his ascetic training but was able to return to his community enriched, had a better deal than the *angakok*, who had succeeded and would forever live a life apart.

The ornithologist Graeme Gibson wrote, 'Paying attention to birds, being mindful of them, is being mindful of Life itself.' The act of watching birds can 'encourage a state of being close to rapture – the forgetfulness that blends the individual consciousness with something other than itself'. During days down on the sea ice with the penguins, then in hours hauling between camps on the ice shelf, a sense of solitude brought me back into my body but also turned my awareness outwards. Emerson wrote of this feeling, a sense of becoming interwoven with what he called 'wilderness': 'Standing on bare ground, my head bathed by the blithe air and uplifted into infinite space, all mean egotism vanishes. I become a transparent eyeball; I am nothing; I see all; the currents of the Universal Being circulate through me.'

The days were flooded with a sense that soon I would leave this place. At night I dreamed of populated places; busy hospitals I had worked in, teeming cities I had visited, crowds at stadiums and concerts that I had pushed through. Something within me was in preparation for my return, anticipating the sensation of being among people again. And with those dreams there was the realisation that a life like this, of solitude or of polar living, meant giving up all of the richness of a life in community, abandoning diversity for the sake of something simpler and purer.

It was as if the greatest lesson to take from the sterility and uniformity of Antarctica, and from the only other species with whom I had shared this winter, was in the end to turn away from them both. The poet Louis MacNeice tried to pin down that sense of the overflowing abundance that pulled me northwards – he called it the 'incorrigibly plural'. Antarctica is a singular place; I began to feel my life in need of some plurality.

I returned from hauling with Mark straight into a week of 'nights', though by now the sun never dipped below the horizon. Night shifts at Halley were like guarding a museum that nobody visits. My mind felt like a well-swept room, large and airy and filled with light. It was a welcome return, a gentle recalibration to the society of base.

A day after the end of those night shifts, my body clock staggered and stunned by the twelve-hour switch, Toddy asked me to be up early. He wanted me to go down with him to the shelf edge north of base, to make a reconnaissance of potential routes on to the ice shelf for Halley Relief. The *Shackleton* had already crossed the equator; soon it would be upon us.

On skidoos we followed the drum line to the north, out to the creeks where the barrier of the Brunt had been splintered into bays. Stopping well back from the cliff edge Toddy and I roped up in case of crevasses. At the head of each bay a winter's worth of storm drift had filled in a ramp of snow. It was possible to walk down a gently sloping boulevard, lined by grottoes and caverns, onto the sea ice. The sea ice itself was polished by winds, grey and dimpled like hammered iron. The sky, though, was soft, with light clouds like down feathers that seemed to drift gently icewards.

We walked west beneath the cliffs, steel crampons scratching on the metalled sea ice. We edged towards a crab-eater seal enjoying the sun, and sat down to eat lunch nearby. It did not mind us. Isolated emperors, deep in their stillness, were dotted along the ice, and I saw more snow petrels swoop low overhead on their way to the south.

After examining each of five potential creeks, Toddy shortlisted two – gently sloped enough for the snowcats to haul their way on to the Brunt – and crevasse-free. 'Now,' he said, 'we can go and play.'

He clambered towards one of the caves in the side of the cliffs, breaking off icicles that stretched across the entrance like a portcullis. Inside were glassy walls that poured with a cold light. It was utterly silent. The cavern tunnelled deeper, leading us in, and further inside widened to a broader space of luminescent blue. As the passage narrowed in again Toddy began to climb, swinging the ice axe into the walls. Whites and yellows on our clothing, the whiteners in the toothpaste on our teeth, began to shine with a purplish nightclub glow. 'Let's see if we can tunnel our way out,' Toddy said.

The end of the cave narrowed to an apex where the walls met a ceiling hung with intricate chandeliers of ice crystals. I swung my axe into them; they shattered like toffee glass. The light that filtered through the ceiling now seemed a little brighter, a little whiter. When the last layer of ice fell away I poked my head through the hole to find my eyes level with the surface of the Brunt, the base just visible on the horizon. I felt like a child who'd managed to dig his way to Australia.

We slid back down chutes of ice, then made our way out towards the cave entrance. Two emperors blocked our path; they must have followed our tracks to the cliff face. I asked them to excuse me, and they fussed awkwardly to one side. Their plumage was immaculate, they looked like young birds at the peak of health. I nudged past them on to the sea ice. As we left I glanced back; they still stood at the edge of the cave, like teenagers daring one another to go in first.

Strung out along the coasts in November the penguins we came across were youngsters, free from the demands of chick-feeding. They were inquisitive, but never seemed playful in the way that the smaller penguins, the adélies and the chinstraps, seemed to play. It was as if having fun was beneath their imperial dignity. Perhaps they were gathering strength for the hard years ahead.

On the plain of shelf ice that surrounds Halley there is only one feature on the landscape besides the ramp of the continent to the south, one contour to catch the eye. To the north-east, beyond the aerial array, lies an irregularity along the horizon; the fractured ice called the McDonald Ice Rumples. The following day Toddy and I drove out to visit them.

From the air the Rumples are seen to spread through the ice shelf like ripples on a pond. There was a map of the Brunt on the wall at Halley, drawn by some of the first men to winter there. The Royal Society surveyors had called the rumples 'Great Waves in the Ice Sheet', and though the area had changed a great deal in fifty years, they had drawn the same sixty-foot spires of ice and shattered patterns of bergs that we saw from base today. The underbelly of the Brunt, hundreds of metres below, is snagged there on a rocky outcrop. As the continental ice flows seawards some of it is held back by this rock, while the ice to either side of it carries on at the same speed. The difference in motion causes a buckling and tearing of the sheet. The glaciologists who study the Brunt's flow, trying to figure out when Halley itself might calve off, would visit it later that summer. Toddy needed to find the safest routes around it in advance of their arrival.

We drove the skidoos between the torn ridges of ice, our two vehicles roped together in case of a fall into a crevasse. On a flattened patch between ridges we pitched a tent and stepped back to enjoy the view.

If I had been silenced by the beauty of the caves along the creeks to the north of base, the scale of the Rumples was even more astonishing. The Brunt's solidity was taken for granted, it was the given on which our lives depended. But here it had cracked over a rocky fulcrum beneath us, and the evidence of the shelf's fragility was terrifying. At some point in the past the sea had broken through these cracks, valleys had welled up with water, and then that water had frozen. The new sea ice had spread in like an advancing army. Caught in this new ice were giant icebergs, collapsing under their own weight. One had yawned apart and the split, once open to the sky, had closed over with a roof of fine-blown snow that was suspended like an embossed ceiling. A staircase of ice blocks led up to it as if to a cathedral door.

The floor inside was as smooth and polished as tile. The passage walls narrowed as we walked deeper inside, guiding us on a gentle bend to the right. After a couple of hundred metres the daylight reaching us from the doorway had lessened but the walls still gave a cold shine, as if refracted from the glow of a dying star. It was possible to climb up inside the passage, a cramponed foot on each wall, and hang motionless high in the heart of the iceberg. Its transience was part of its beauty. By next winter this whole iceberg and the glorious hallway running through it would be gone.

The Rumples are named for one Allan McDonald, a Patagonian Scot who, during the years around the First World War, was the British representative in Chile's southernmost region of Magallanes. In those days of the British Empire, Scots emigrants seemed to seek out the coldest, wettest and most wind-blasted habitats. They nurtured a nostalgia for high latitudes the way others might nurture a grudge.

McDonald would have looked out over the Strait of Magellan as storms beat in from the south Atlantic, and sipped his whisky beneath the *Casa Inglesa* in Punta Arenas' main street. In 1916 he took pity on Ernest Shackleton, whose government had deserted him, and through the generosity of the British Association of Magallanes raised £1,500. There had already been two failed rescues of the men on Elephant Island, and there was no guarantee that this time Shackleton's luck would be any different. It was a substantial sum for the times, reflecting the wealth of that sheep-farming community. But the ship *Emma* that it funded, a forty-year-old oak-hulled schooner, didn't make it through the pack that still stiffens the seas around Elephant Island. It was only on the fourth attempt, with a steel ship loaned by the Chilean government, that the crew of the *Endurance* was finally rescued.

Shackleton named a glacier spilling out from the Caird Coast in gratitude to Allan McDonald. I never found out whether McDonald was proud of this honour, or if he might have wished for a more prominent feature of Antarctica. Later, when the British returned to the Caird Coast, the placement of this glacier was uncertain, and as the Rumples were the most prominent feature of the landscape in the area the name was given to them instead. Perhaps to get a whole coast named after him rather than just a glacier or some 'rumples' he would have had to come up with a lot more than £1,500.

Shackleton was following a strong British tradition: blank polar landscapes had been overwritten with the names of the rich and influential for centuries. In 1775 James Cook called his new island South Georgia for George III, and in 1852 a Franklin-searching expedition named Ellesmere Island for the Earl of Ellesmere (president of the Royal Geographical Society at the time). Scott doffed his cap to the big money behind his Antarctic expedition when he gave the peaks of Victoria Land the lumpy title of Royal Society Range. Its highest peak, Mount Lister, was of course named for the president of the Society, and lesser peaks for lesser dignitaries. The Americans turned this convention on its head. Richard Byrd named about a quarter of the continent after his wife Marie (perhaps as compensation for all those long absences), and Lincoln Ellsworth, another of the pioneering aviators (who crucially held his own chequebook) had another massive chunk named Ellsworth Land.

This buy-a-landscape tradition was magnificently mocked by the American artist Rockwell Kent. In the early 1930s Kent spent a year in Illorsuit, western Greenland, finding some release from the neurosis of New York society for a while. His book about his time there, *Salamina*, named after his Greenlandic mistress, is a love letter to a country. It is illustrated throughout with Kent's etchings, for the most part drawn in ink; crisp, muscular and traced with evident affection for the landscape and its people. For the directness of the portraits, the curve of their lines, their lack of affectation, the haunting ability to catch something of the soul behind the eyes, they have something of the paintings of William Blake.

Each is appended with a punchy caption. On the opening page, the map of the area around Illorsuit, Kent shows his irreverence for cartographic convention. The new age of the 1930s along with a heavy dose of American informality means that the heavyweight traditions of polar 'exploration' are starting to give way. The map is captioned:

> Discoveries of the Kent Greenland Sub-Polar Expedition of 1931–32. Lest the backers of the expedition be disappointed with its results it must be explained that someone, unfortunately, had already given names – and what names! – to the larger bodies of land and water . . . Should there be generous souls or corporate bodies desirous of furthering the aims of the expedition we should feel that it would be advancing the glory of America to write their names upon the map.

He has already penned in The General Electric Co. Ice Cap, perhaps in anticipation of future patronage (in 1939 they commissioned a fifty-foot mural from him). Nearby is a feature named for his publisher, the Faber & Faber Ice Cap. Other ice streams and mountain lakes stand blank in the hope of future corporate sponsorship.

The 'McDonald Ice Rumples', recalling the sleepless nights of Allan McDonald in his bid to rescue Shackleton's men, seemed like a name worth commemorating after all.

Towards the end of November, shortly before our winter isolation was due to be broken by aeroplanes, there was a solar eclipse in Antarctica. The shadow cone of the moon, over a hundred miles wide, would score a stubby line across the blank page of Antarctica.

The word 'eclipse' comes from a Greek root meaning 'abandonment' – the sun abandons us to the terror of a day turned suddenly, disastrously, night. The shadow of the moon as it passes over the sun casts a fleeting shroud over life on earth. Though few now believe our lives are governed by the heavens, our language perpetuates the fears of an earlier age. 'Disaster', another astronomical calamity term, means 'the stars are against us' – *dis-astra*. And it seems that all our learning has not lessened the shock of an eclipse; modern minds have shuddered at them as much as the mediaevals ever did. Virginia Woolf wrote in her diary shortly after witnessing one that 'suddenly the light went out. We had fallen. It was extinct. There was no colour. The Earth was dead . . . I had very strongly the feeling as the light went out of some vast obeisance.' Hold your hand at arm's length on a cloudless day and you'll see the sun is about the size of your smallest fingernail. But to see it extinguished is to confront the mortality of all things, including ourselves.

From the perspective of the earth, the moon once loomed larger than it appears today because it was closer. Total eclipses must once, deep in pre-history, have been commonplace. But the relentless drag of the tides over billennia have slowed our moon. The arc of its orbit has slipped away from the earth, as if held by a string that is gradually stretching at a rate of about an inch and a half a year. We live in an age of astronomical coincidence when the sun, 400 times the diameter of the moon, appears from the earth's surface exactly the same size. As the moon slips further away in future ages, total eclipses will become a thing of the past.

We gathered on the Laws platform to watch the moon consume the sun. Some had on welding masks, the rest of us watched through the dark parts of X-rays I had pulled from the medical archive. As it began someone shouted over to me, 'This is God's punishment on you, for cutting up those penguin chicks!' Another yelled, 'Maybe the emperors will all die of shock.' Though the eclipse was still a few minutes off we glanced skywards every few seconds, joking nervously.

As the bow of the moon edged over the sun's disc the depth of the sky was made suddenly manifest. The moon, the impossibly distant moon, was seen to swing low over the earth – no number of book-explanations could prepare the mind for that immediate and incontrovertible proof that there were layers to the sky. And if the moon could be closer than the 'sky', then the sun must be too – I saw the abyss of space that hangs behind it imaginable as never before.

The shadow of the moon moves at around 1,500 miles per hour; it passed over like a lid blinked shut. As the eclipse approached its maximum, it spilled a platinum light that seemed to deaden by the minute, the brightness on the ice sinking through a desolate spectrum of silver and grey. It was as if the laws of nature had been suspended; like oil made miscible with water, the darkness of night was suddenly made miscible with day. I looked for flashes of glare at the margins of the sun, those pinpoints called Baily's beads that are formed as sunbeams tunnel between the ridges of the mountains of the moon. If present at all they were lost in the grain of the X-ray films.

I willed the sun back. Though at times since its return I'd felt its glare as too strong, and had looked back with longing to the darkness of winter, I shuddered at the threat of losing it again.

It may be true that eclipses auger badly. Two days later the aeroplane that was originally to break our isolation had to turn back. Lez the pilot had met a great storm over the Ronne Ice Shelf, and retreated to Rothera. Once at Rothera he was sent out on other missions, and the date of our relief was postponed. 'Don't worry,' we were told by HQ, 'he'll get there eventually.' Later we heard that it would be the Germans, on their way from the Peninsula through to Neumayer base, that would be the ones to bring our ten-months-late post.

I was skiing on the perimeter, swinging past the eastern arc of the base, when I heard an unfamiliar sound. It was a steady drone, just above the threshold of hearing. Perhaps there was a problem with the generator, I wondered, or with one of the bulldozers. Then with a sudden jolt I realised where it came from. An aeroplane!

It was as if I had forgotten about the possibility of aeroplanes, that our base could ever, would ever, be reached from the air. I looked west, and up into the clear translucence of a sky that had been empty for three seasons. There, unmistakably, was a dark smudge on the blue, an aeroplane. It was growing, getting closer. It was a shock as sharp as a slap; in a moment our empire of ice and isolation collapsed.

I left the perimeter and, pushing hard on the ski poles, hurried north towards the ski-way to meet it.

# SUMMER AND WINTER

CHAPTER FOURTEEN

# Of Endings and Beginnings

Devotions over, the ice mountains'
jagged edges met his gaze. He smiles, 'Life!
Wo! *That* straggling caravan . . .'

Kathleen Jamie, *The Autonomous Region*

'I can tell the moment I step into the base whether it's been a
good winter or a bad one,' Lez told me, 'even by the way they meet
me at the ski-way. If it's been a bad one then the atmosphere hits
you like a wall.'

'What did you think this year?' I asked him.

'Pretty good, I'd say,' he replied. 'I've seen a lot worse.'

Lez had been working as a BAS pilot for years. He preferred
Halley to the other bases. 'This is my Antarctic,' he said, 'the Peninsula
is a lot busier, too many people telling you what to do.' A couple
of days after the Germans arrived he had made it across the Ronne
Ice Shelf to Halley, carrying staff from HQ, and more bags of mail.
He had also, and for this he could be sainted, brought a box of fresh
fruit and vegetables. Craig almost wept for joy and we ate tomato
salad for the first time in a year. It tasted so extraordinary I wondered
that the tomatoes had not been artificially enhanced.

Living so long in a sterile world our immune systems had
become lazy – a few days after the planes came in we all caught
heavy colds. There were just three weeks left until the ship would
arrive and Lez said he had a lot of work to do. There were fuel
depots deep in the continent to be replenished, and their buried
drums dug out. 'I'm going out to the Theron and Shackleton

Mountains tomorrow,' he told me. 'Weather permitting. Want to come?'

The Therons and the Shackletons are mountain ranges deep into the continent behind the Caird Coast, about a third of the way down a line between Halley and the South Pole. Vivian Fuchs discovered them back in 1956, while making reconnaissance flights in preparation for his traverse of the continent. Rather than named for the original Theron, an obscure Greek–Sicilian tyrant, the Therons were named for the Canadian sealing ship that had carried Fuchs and his men south. Fuchs had named his base camp 'Shackleton' in honour of the man who had tried to cross the Antarctic continent before him, and decided to give the second range of mountains the same name.

'Mountains?' I said to him. 'It feels like a long time since I have seen mountains.'

The plane's skis shuddered over the ridges of the ice, the propellers tore the air in roaring spirals and, as if suspended on the strings of a marionette, the Twin Otter jerked into the sky. We took off towards the east, into the wind, and looped back in a wide orbit over the base. Within seconds I could take in the whole of the Brunt. The bleached whiteness of the ice mirrored the clouded sky, and the base shrank until it became just a scrawled hyphen and some commas on an empty page. The drum line to the emperors was just visible, and to the north-east the Rumples roughened the horizon. As the aeroplane turned towards the Pole I reflected that I had never lived life constrained for so long to such a small area. Fourteen months earlier I had sailed through the tropical Atlantic wondering whether my mind would be made clear and uncluttered by a year on the ice. My mind did not feel clear or uncluttered; I wondered instead how amidst so much emptiness it had managed to stay so full.

A minute or two later and the plane was climbing over the Hinge Zone, striking south and west as the ice ramped beneath us. The cloud base began to break up and washes of Michelangelo blue streaked between its layers. Searchlight beams of sunshine played over the ice, as if God had dropped something and hoped that in Antarctica He might find it. I'd seen meteorites fall over this sector, and I glanced down now in the hope of seeing one embedded in the snow.

It was not long after leaving Halley that the nub of the Therons could be seen splintering through the ice sheet. They stood in the way of its flow from the south; little mountains, hunched shoulders of rock with their backs towards the Pole. They leaned into the pressure of the polar plateau like children on a beach bracing themselves for a wave. Beyond them was a river of ridged and fissured ice, twice as wide as the Amazon at its mouth, known as the Slessor Glacier for the chairman of Fuchs' expedition. And beyond the Slessor I could just make out the slate-grey shimmer of the Shackleton Range on the horizon, at 80° South.

When we reached the Therons, Lez took a spin between their summits. Grey and brown stripes of rock had been shattered into sheer cliff faces. The Therons have rich seams of coal, strata laid down during Antarctica's time in more tropical latitudes. Between the sediments the rocks were stepped with basalt sills. Geologists brought out here from Halley have spent weeks in those mountains, and have calculated that the sills match up with others in southern Africa, suggesting that the Therons were once bound to the Lubombo mountains of Swaziland and Mozambique.

Ice poured between the peaks, frothy as spume, and tumbled to the mountains' feet. As we approached the cliffs I stared in wonder – snow petrels were billowing in their hundreds around the stacks of rock. It was a desolate 200 miles to the coast, but these birds commuted it to bring back food for their young. The petrels nested on ledges in the Therons, huddled against katabatic winds, in order to get as far as possible from predators such as skuas.

Lez pointed out the fuel-drum depot in the lee of the ice flow, and the Twin Otter swooped in to land. As the skis hit the ice and we bumped towards the pile of fuel drums I saw that a south polar skua had beaten us to it. Even here, at the end of the earth, the snow petrels were not safe, and neither was my lunch. I shooed it away; I prefer to eat my sandwiches in peace.

Back into the plane, and we continued on towards the Pole to leave fuel drums at the depot beneath the Shackleton Range. The Shackletons are made up of ancient rocks, Precambrian sediments from the dawn of the earth that have been twisted and transformed by billennia of pressure and continental drift. Geologists have wondered at their orientation, as they lie across the grain of the Trans-Antarctic Mountain Range. Fossils of some of the world's earliest life forms have been chipped from them – petrified molluscs that are so primitive they became extinct nearly 500 million years ago. The mountains themselves are now low-slung peaks, clogged with ice, slouching ever lower into a frigid horizon.

Fuchs had trundled past here in his snowcats, negotiating icefalls with aluminium bridges. From here to the Pole there are only a couple more rocks that peep through the ice sheet, nunataks that Fuchs called Whichaway as he figured out the best way around them. As we flew over the mountains I looked south towards the Pole – it was unlikely now that I would ever see it. That realisation didn't bother me; I felt I had seen enough empty plains of ice.

After digging out the fuel depot I sat down to watch the Shackletons for a while. That they were almost submerged in the polar plateau now made me oddly, inexplicably sad. I was glad to have wintered at the coast rather than among this sullen and arid range. Perhaps the feeling came over me because no snow petrels whirled between the peaks – no life at all made it this far south. The mountains themselves were slope-shouldered and looked as if they had been defeated. The only evidence of life here were fossils dead half a billion years, and their barrenness was like a memory of loss.

When Icarus and Daedalus feathered their wings they were thinking only of escape; escape from Crete, escape from Minos and the Labyrinth, escape from a life controlled and restricted by others. The fall of Icarus is a warning not against transcending the boundaries of our lives, but against letting that ambition make you reckless. When you aim high, the myth tells us, remember you might come a cropper.

Icarus' fall has proven one of the great themes of Western art, perhaps because some artists fear being overwhelmed by their ambition. One of the most celebrated, Pieter Bruegel's *Landscape with the Fall of Icarus*, is unusual in that Icarus himself cannot be seen; a few feathers flutter earthwards and a leg thrashes in the waves. As viewers we look down from the sky, momentarily winged, as if we have mastered flight at the moment that Icarus falls.

There are three bystanders in the painting, and the artist has made all of them look the other way. One is ploughing his field, one is herding his sheep and another, just a few feet away from the drowning Icarus, appears to be fishing. If Bruegel wants us to take a moral lesson from his work it must be that we can't expect bystanders to step in to help us if we push the limits of the possible.

The poet William Carlos Williams was fascinated by this idea and used the painting as an opportunity to meditate on the simultaneity that exists, the wealthful abundance of life but also of death surrounding us, and how we are so often oblivious to tragedies unfolding right before our eyes.*A Pulitzer prize-winning poet as well as a doctor, Williams spent almost his whole medical career in the small New Jersey town in which he had been born. Through his art he tried to overturn conventional ideas about provincial life, to show how the lives of ordinary people were as filled with drama and passion as those of the gods of classical myth. In his autobiographical essay 'The Practice', he wrote that his medical work fed his poetry, which in turn nourished his compassion and insight as a doctor. Poetry, he held, was fundamentally concerned with mankind, and there was no better work than medicine for confronting humanity in all its complexity, vulgarity, ugliness, nobility and beauty.

Facing return, I was glad that Williams found inspiration in the sort of conventional medical practice that awaited me. Maybe it was time for me to get involved with people again. I began to understand the *zugunruhe* of the migratory birds – if I had had wings they would have been trembling to fly.

The earth had spun a full circuit of the sun and in December, almost a year since I had arrived on the coast of Antarctica, the emperor chicks I had followed since they were laid as eggs were beginning to fledge. Soon they would leave for the north. After gaining weight for nearly five months they were losing it again,

* W. H. Auden's 'Musée des Beaux Arts' describes the same painting and meditates on the same theme.

burning off fat to make feathers, though they had only reached half the size of a full-grown adult. The biggest chicks had already been abandoned as their parents took their own chance to moult. The chicks' bellies were the first to gain true adult plumage – the downy fluff was rubbed off as they tobogganed back and forth over the ice to reveal a slick white gleam of adult feathers. They looked like half-blown dandelion clocks. The wings of these birds too had fledged to a sleek black, and they would soon be put to the test as they were pulled by their hunger out to sea. The only down that remained was on their backs, hanging from their shoulderblades like a cashmere cape. Their heads were still piebald; the buttercup-coloured auricular patches would not develop until after the first full adult moult.

From the sea ice I saw a large floe break free from the edge, with two chicks as passengers. As it cracked it set them off on the first journey of their lives. They were only half-fledged, their feathers still too undeveloped to risk a dip in the sea. The window of opportunity to hatch, grow and fledge was so narrow, and the continent so merciless. If they had not fledged further before the floe broke up they would be unable to swim and, like Icarus, would drown.

I too was preparing my wings. Through an agent for BAS in the Falkland Islands I had already booked my flights home – a Chilean airline would fly me from the military base on the Falkland Islands to Punta Arenas in Patagonia. From there I'd connect to Santiago de Chile for a day, before flying back into a European winter. The speed of my return would be startling; after having had months to acclimatise to the idea of arriving in Antarctica, I would have only a few days to get used to leaving it. Of the fourteen of us who had wintered I would leave first with Craig, as soon as the ship had finished unloading its cargo. The others would have to wait until the ship's final call in February.

There was a bittersweet sense to the final days. I wanted to gather as much of the continent into myself as I could, though I knew it was not possible to take it away with me. At the same time there was an itch to leave, to be on my way north and on to a new season in my life. When I looked out over the Brunt the ice was overlain with memories, of hard afternoons working outside, of those hundreds of circuits of the perimeter I'd completed on skis, of trips to the Hinge Zone, Rumples, the penguins and the creeks. Most of all I remembered the beauty of the ice through the darkest months, the platinum reflection of moonlight and the silent depth of the auroras in the sky. I felt a gladness and a sense of privilege to have lived through the cycle of a year here, to have seen each season pass through.

All that remained for me to do at Halley was to write a final report for my bosses at the BAS Medical Unit and at HQ.

Before writing it I read through the pile of medical reports in the surgery. Soon after my arrival I had put them away, afraid to poison my experience with the negativity of others. Now I read methodically, charting the progress of the base from the have-a-go era of Fuchs and Dalgliesh through to the modern day with its instant communications, its ponderous bureaucracy, its unprecedented comforts. Modern Antarctic bases are the heirs of the primitive huts of the Heroic Age, and in the early years of Halley there was still a great deal of heroism. Men went out with dog teams for months in the field, and there must be hundreds of untold stories of narrow survival against the odds, as well as those tragic deaths. I read through reports written about winters of misery, where almost no one on base got on with one another and the days to the ship's return were crossed off on hidden calendars. I also found reports of happy winters where by and large everyone worked and played together, and even had a few jokes at HQ's expense. There was a story of one official back in Cambridge, sending a telex to a wintering team that they had 'all better polish up their reasons for being in the Antarctic'. He arrived to find the cliffs of the Brunt crowned by a giant bottle of Brasso crafted out of packing cases.

Halley's dining-room walls were covered in photographs of winterers past, many of them with hairy faces grinning alongside hairier dogs, photos I had seen so often now that I barely noticed them. Each group had tried to make their wintering photo unique. Perhaps it is natural to want your experience to stand out from the others, though so many have wintered at Halley before you. Some groups lined up in front of the bar, pipes in hand. Some were in fancy dress. Some stood on the tops of bulldozers and snowcats. One had lain a camera on the ground and crowded round it in a circle, their faces forming a halo around a circle of Antarctic sky. Another had lined everyone in a row, thumbs out, doing a Monty Python silly walk. I carefully examined those photos from years that I knew had turned sour. There was no way of telling from their faces, no sign of the tension they must have carried inside. I looked for the years in which someone had died at Halley, and saw the sad, late inclusions, faces snipped out and inset to one side of the group. Now it was time to add our own group photo to the wall.

We had chosen to take it on the platform of the Laws, looking up to a camera positioned on the roof. Pat is up on a pedestal in the middle of the picture. Ben's in a T-shirt to his right; he had been two and a half years in the Antarctic now, and no longer notices the cold. Craig edges into the background to Pat's left, as if he might make a break for the kitchen at any moment. In the middle row, from left to right: Stuart plays it straight, Graeme has been dragged from the generator room and still has his boiler suit on, Tommo looks as if he is being kicked up the backside, Mark M. slides into a shadow, Toddy wins the prize for the most dirty, worn and therefore authentic-looking Ventile suit, and Mark S. has been pulled out from behind a computer terminal – he is still wearing his sandals. In the front row Russ has clearly been working on his tan, while Rob to his left is geared up as if he is setting out for the South Pole. Elaine has carefully brushed her hair – you wouldn't know that it's nearly three years since it's been styled in a salon. Annette, crouching to her left, has given up on her Antarctic clothing and is dressed as if already liberated into the mountains of Latin America. That leaves me, radio slung on my chest like Elaine, I must have been called in from work on the perimeter for the occasion.

We printed it off, framed it carefully in the workshop, and added it to the rows on the dining-room wall. There was a blank space next to it for the following year's photo. We were far from the first, and would be far from being the last to see through the isolation of winter on this patch of ice.

\*     \*     \*

Reading through the medical reports, the experience of individual Zdocs was difficult to divine. They are official documents and each was understandably circumspect about revealing the winter's effect on their state of mind. I knew that some Zdocs had struggled with the isolation of Halley, both socially and professionally. I had heard of doctors in the past returning to find their marriages failed through the long absence. Jobs were sometimes hard to come by, and some had the sense that their medical skills had rusted through disuse. Many took a few months off on their return to try to get back into the tempo of British life again. I'd heard of one doctor, a long time ago, who had found the silence and isolation too much. The solitude had unearthed grievances and sadnesses from the past, long suppressed, and once open to the light he had no choice but to take a year or two off on his return to deal with them. But I had heard stories too of doctors bounding back into their careers, refreshed from the break and finding themselves pushed up the shortlists at every interview because of their unusual job history, the originality of having worked in the Antarctic. Some of them had looked back on their time in Antarctica as a golden age of freedom (no boss! no waiting room!) and used the memory of it as a resource and a touchstone in their lives back in the north.

'Everyone has an Antarctic', wrote Thomas Pynchon, some presumably a more literal Antarctic than others. Only now, after twelve months at Halley, was I starting to get the sense of what Antarctica would mean to me. It was too early to predict how my return to the north would be, but I felt strengthened by my time on the continent, emboldened even, and having seen through the winter sensed a confidence that I would be better able to face hardships that might be waiting in the future.

I had wondered if in Antarctica I might learn something from the emperors, from the silence and simplicity of their lives. Although we had shared the same stark environment and the same relentless darkness, comparison is impossible. I had been cosy in my artificial base while they had walked on the ice in temperatures down to minus 55°C, I had eaten three square meals a day while they fasted for four months. After the winter I felt closer to understanding something of their lives, but realised of course that there was an unbridgeable gulf between us. They are seabirds, but I had never followed them into the sea. On the ice they seemed at peace despite their lives being so much harsher and more dangerous than mine could ever be. They had welcomed me into their huddle, had no fear of me, and that in itself was a treasure worth remembering as I returned to the fearful and hesitant birds that would surround me again in the north. Perhaps I had learned something of patience, of tolerance, of stillness and of endurance, but these qualities are survival skills for the emperors, life-or-death matters carved into their behaviour by millennia of breeding and dying. For me they were experiences to help me on my way, attributes that I hoped to develop further as I moved back to an environment that is shaped by humans rather than by ice.

I typed up my report for HQ, printed and bound it, and added a copy to the pile on the shelf in the surgery. Then I went down to sit with the penguins.

By 22 December the *Shackleton* was stuck in obstinate ice seven or eight kilometres away from the nearest accessible ramp up the cliffs. There were two large cracks in the sea ice that the snowcats with their heavy sledges of cargo would be forced to negotiate, and it took almost a week to build bridges over those cracks using whatever spare materials we could find around base. It would mean a drawn-out process to unload the cargo, but after a week it was under way.

I picked up Frank, my replacement, on the back of a skidoo and took him on the same white-knuckle tour of base that Lindsey had taken me on one year before. He was surprised to find me focus as much on ski-way duties and the waste-compaction room as I did on the X-ray equipment and the anaesthetic machine. 'Medicine,' I told him, as I showed him how to rivet lids on to waste drums, 'is likely to be the least of your concerns.'

I realised that my gait had adapted to moving over the collapsing surface of the bondoo; those of us who had wintered outpaced all the newcomers as we walked between platforms and the depot line. They panted to keep up. The base was crowded with new personnel, and it became difficult to find a space to be quiet.

Those of us whose time in Antarctica was coming to an end found ourselves hiding together in odd corners, whispering about what we would do when we went home, where we would travel, whether we would ever come back to the ice.

After a week of this work around the clock the *Shackleton* was unloaded. She was behind schedule now, and the captain was in a hurry to leave. The message came through on the radio that if I did not want to spend another year at Halley I had a couple of hours to get myself down to the ship.

My cases had already been loaded. I sped down to the garage on my skidoo to say goodbye to Ben. He had a hard season ahead of him, fixing up the snowcats and getting them ready to over-winter again, as well as training up his replacement. He had never really forgiven me for tampering with the skidoo carburettor. 'See you round, Danger Doc,' he said, looking up from welding a broken chassis. He had six weeks left at Halley, then a long trip home via Argentina and Chile with Elaine.

I found Toddy at the depot line, digging out supplies. A year saving us from falling down crevasses hadn't been enough for him, and he'd agreed to winter again at Rothera looking after an even bigger crowd. 'Enjoy being back in the mountains again,' I told him, 'and I'll see you in Scotland?' At Rothera he did enjoy being back in the mountains, and a couple of years later as we climbed in the Cairngorms together he told me that BAS had asked him to sign up for regular seasons. Like an arctic tern he now lives in perpetual summer, travelling from the Highlands of Scotland to the Antarctic Peninsula and back each year.

Annette and Elaine were on the Simpson, crunching numbers on the computer with their boss who had arrived fresh from Cambridge. Both of them looked stressed. After two years on the Brunt they were ready for home. 'What will you miss most?' I asked Annette. She looked out of the window and sighed: 'I'm never going to have an office view like it again.' Elaine laughed, 'I won't miss being surrounded by MEN all the time!'

On the Piggott building Mark M. had decided to stay on another winter, and Mark S. was ready to go. For the last couple of months he'd been studying a Spanish phrasebook, in anticipation of travel-ling towards home through Latin America. He nodded a brief goodbye, and told me I seemed like one of the happiest BAS doctors that he had met, a rare compliment. His words made me realise that I *was* happy at Halley, and would stay longer if I had to, but I still felt drawn back to the colour and possibility that waited in the north.

Russ was staying on, and had been unanimously appointed the new winter base commander for the year ahead. I asked him how he'd taken to his new responsibility, and he smiled. 'You wait,' he laughed, 'I'll get this lot whipped into shape as soon as the ship has left!'

I found Pat, Tommo and Graeme in the workshop. After having helped build Halley, then winter in it twice, Pat was going back to Cambridge to take up a permanent job as a Halley manager. Tommo was wintering again at Halley ('Maybe I'll stick to the diet this year, Doc,' he said, slapping his belly), and Graeme too had decided to stay on another year – his six-week secondment on the ship turning into a two-and-a-half-year epic. His mother was starting to despair of him ever coming home. 'I'll see you in Anstruther for a pint,' I said to him, but later lost his email address. Two years later I happened to be in Anstruther, and bumped into him near the harbour. He was driving a forklift truck, and was wearing the same boiler suit I'd last seen him in.

Stuart was locked in the darkroom and I knocked on the door and shouted my goodbyes. Rob was going home. One winter was enough for him, and plumbers were still earning a fortune back home. 'Thanks for everything,' he said, 'especially for these,' gaping his mouth to show as many of his teeth as he could. I'd given Rob four temporary fillings, glad that my dentistry training hadn't gone entirely to waste.

And Craig too was going home, on the ship with me. He'd lined up a new job in the Caribbean, and had arranged a complex series of flights routing him from the Falkland Islands through Chile, Venezuela and Grenada to the hotel on a tiny island that would be his new home. I had run down the flight of stairs from the Laws, after saying goodbye to Rob, only to find him already waiting on the back of the snowcat. 'Hurry up Gav,' he said, 'I'm not spending another year in this place.'

Ice and sky that day made a formless and depthless panorama, a blank dreamscape into which I had poured myself long enough. On the northern horizon we glimpsed the red streak of the *Shackleton* miraged up over the cliffs. We drove north, the Laws sank below an undulation in the ice, and then quite suddenly was gone. I wondered if I would ever see it again.

Driving across the sea ice by skidoo I scanned the horizon for a last glimpse of an emperor. I needn't have bothered: there were a couple of them loitering at the water's edge, not far from the bow of the ship. I stepped off the skidoo, walked over towards them, and sat down on the ice. They waddled over, as if for a farewell chat. 'Thanks for everything,' I said. 'I couldn't have done it without you.'

Winterers returning from the Antarctic have been found by psychologists to show remarkable similarities to returning prisoners-of-war. Both groups show 'cognitive slowing, emotional withdrawal, indecisiveness, and poor communication', and both are said to have profoundly disturbed sleep and abnormal patterns in their brainwaves. The individuals concerned do not, on the whole, complain of these problems; it is their colleagues and their partners who notice the difference. For the Antarctic winterers, difficulties persist for up to a year; for the prisoners-of-war, they often persist much longer. Research has been sparse but has shown that many individuals, having lived with almost unlimited professional freedom in the Antarctic, struggle with authority when they return to more conventional work. Reintegration, it seems, can be as difficult a process as the original adaptation to the Antarctic.

The ship felt almost empty. BAS employed a ship-bound dentist, Ben Molyneux, to service the teeth of base personnel through the summer. In conversation we realised I had once worked in the same African hospital as his sister. A world of social connections opened up to me. That Africa still existed; that it might be possible to work there again seemed too unlikely to be true.

Apart from brief conversations like these I kept my own company. I felt as if I was under a bell jar, separated from the world. The crewmen on the ship were the same ones that had sailed with me from England as far as Montevideo fifteen months before. 'You were much nicer last time,' they told me when they were drunk. 'That place has screwed you up.' They listed Zdocs of the past who had sailed south as happy-go-lucky optimists but returned sullen, introverted and irritable. I knew what those individuals had been going through – they just wanted to be left in peace to adjust. In the bar one of the permanent BAS staff told me gruffly that I had developed a classic Halley stare.

I spent hours in the sauna below decks, watching the steam pucker the skin of my fingers and toes, and feeling the heat surge back into them. When I had sat in there long enough I went up on deck to look out over the steadily thinning pack ice. After a few months at Halley my breathing had eased gently into time with my pulse. Now my chest felt sprung tight, and my heart thudded unpredictably within it. Though the *Shackleton* nudged north at just eleven knots, I felt as if it was clattering down the rungs of latitude, out of control, or like a space capsule scorching with the force of re-entry. Potential futures lay ahead as if my life was a child's choose-your-own story book; I knew I'd soon face a bewildering labyrinth of choices. The slick of fear had eased, replaced by a fatalistic sense of acceptance of whatever would come. I had no idea what to expect on my return.

At first we cut through rafting fields of heavy floes, gradually thinning to ragged doilies of ice. Only four days out of Halley we crossed the Antarctic Circle. Colour edged back into the sky; it was a delight to see the sun set once more after the months of bleaching sunlight. I wrapped up warm and lay out on the helideck again welcoming the now-familiar southern stars. Two days after we crossed the Antarctic Circle the icebergs thickened again – the *Shackleton* ambled through boulevards of them towards Signy base.

The sea floor rises around the South Orkney Islands; giant bergs pouring north with the gyre of the Weddell Sea are sieved by the archipelago like boulders on a storm drain. At Signy I went ashore and spent an afternoon in astonishment at the feel of rock beneath my boots. After a year of cushioning snow it amazed me how much it jarred my knees.

But it was north of Signy that something magical happened: albatrosses gathered like kites trailing the ship, and while watching them out on deck I caught the smell of grass on the wind. Grass! At Halley the only smells were of penguins and kerosene. The Falkland Islands were still twenty-four hours over the northern horizon, but months of olfactory deprivation must have sharpened my nose. I strained my eyes and my nose towards the source of that delicious smell, and the reality of my return fell in on me. Just then rain began to fall like a benediction – a light mantling rain that softened the sky. I realised I had not felt rain since South Georgia, over a year before.

The *Shackleton* reached harbour in the Falkland Islands; I had arrived with only a day to spare before my flight. There was a road near the dock, and, wondrously, I could see traffic on it. I hitched a lift into town with a woman who told me she had a boyfriend once who had been to Halley. '"Hot off the ice" they used to call men like you,' she told me, and winked. 'Some of those boys hadn't seen a woman in nearly three years.'

The rain still felt magical. At the Mount Pleasant military base I swam in a swimming pool, ate fresh vegetables and flicked through a year's worth of news. There was even a movie theatre, and I queued up with teenage squaddies in combat fatigues to watch square-jawed Americans kill the Viet Cong. I had forgotten about the use of money, and kept handing over twenty-pound notes for every purchase then walking away without waiting for change.

And it was at Mount Pleasant the following day that I presented my rucksack and passport, and asked to be accepted on to a flight for Chile. 'Have you really been here over a year?' the military official asked me.

'Er, no,' I told her. 'I've been living in Antarctica in the meantime and they must have forgotten to stamp my passport.'

'Don't worry about it,' she said, spreading even rows of disciplined teeth. 'I'll let you go just this once.'

'Once is all I need.'

In Santiago the warm air cloyed at my throat and slicked my skin. There were palm trees on the roadside and I stood mesmerised by the fact of them – the heat that sustained them and the light that nourished them. I walked stunned by the profusion, the beauty, the iridescence, and the variety that surrounded me on an ordinary Latin American street. The smells in the market alone had me immobilised for an hour. I gazed at the fresh fruit like a devotee at a shrine, and almost postponed going home.

But as evening fell another aeroplane took off with me on board, looping once over the city then turning east and up over the stone wave of the Andes. I watched sunset light catch the summit of Aconcagua, then lightning storms play over the Argentinian pampas. The plane moved on into Brazilian skies and I looked down over the Amazon basin, another of Nature's unknowable immensities. When the plane reached the Atlantic I slept.

It was lunchtime the following day when I cleared immigration. Snow was falling on the black-lacquered bonnets of taxis outside the airport. A driver leaned out of a window. 'Not too cold, son?' he asked, and I realised I had on only a T-shirt.

'No . . .' I said, then wondered if I should explain. 'I'm just back from Antarctica.'

I climbed into the taxi and closed the door behind me. We moved off into the traffic.

'See any polar bears?' he asked, glancing in the mirror.

'No polar bears,' I replied, 'but a hell of a lot of penguins.'

# The Memory of Antarctica

> These days are with one for all time – they are never to be
> forgotten – and they are to be found nowhere else in the world
> but at the poles . . . One only wishes one could bring a glimpse
> of it away with one with all its unimaginable beauty.
>
> Edward Wilson, *Diary, Jan. 4, 1911*

In my first months back from Antarctica I felt like a monk broken
free of the cloister, enchanted by the world and eager to get
involved. I carried the memory of Antarctica like a mantra or a
prayer, an inner place of space and tranquillity when my days
seemed cramped or chaotic. After spells working at hospitals in
India and West Africa, and a trip half-way around the world on
a motorbike, I finally went home to take up a job as a city doctor.
The girlfriend that I flew back from the Falklands to meet had
since become my wife. We have three young children now and the
noise and laughter, colour and messiness of our lives are about as
far from the empty silence of Antarctica as it is possible to imagine.

But sometimes I stop in traffic, on a playgroup run or at a
dinner party and think of the great silence that lies unbroken in
the south. I think of the simplicity of that world of ice and light,
of the beauty that I saw conjured from those two elements. I think
of its limitless skies, and how they brought an awareness of rhythms
that operate on a vast, celestial scale. I am glad to have seen the
interior of the continent – to have experienced that cold purity
– but glad too to have spent my year at the coast among the
emperors. In the dead of winter they reminded me that I was part

of a community of the living. The warmth and energy of their lives were a welcome and unexpected comfort through the months of darkness and isolation.

My winters are different now; they carry the memory of deeper cold, of a more pervasive darkness. There is a heightened awareness too of the balance of the seasons across the broad reach of our planet. When the Christmas lights are glowing now I imagine the emperor chicks fledging, midnight sunlight around them refracted into haloes and rainbows. In a northern July, playing with my children in the warm evening light, I picture the male penguins in the darkness, eggs on their feet as they huddle through the lowest temperatures on earth. As time goes by those images don't fade, but remain, as if an invisible connection spans our parallel lives.

# Acknowledgements

Antarctica might be a good place to find solitude, but getting to it, living on it, and then managing to write about it has only been done with the help of a multitude of people.

I am immensely grateful to Creative Scotland, back when it was the Scottish Arts Council, for their belief in this book and for giving me the means to write it. I never would have got to Antarctica without the trust of Iain Grant and Pete Marquis of the BAS Medical Unit; from their offices in Plymouth their imperturbability has calmed many a jittery Zdoc. Richard Hanson and Nick Cox of BAS gave me their hospitality, confidence and stories from the south. Thanks also to their colleagues James Miller and Mandy McEvoy for their invaluable advice. I'm grateful to the family of Kirsty Brown for giving me their blessing in telling a small part of her story. Bernard Stonehouse gave me the freedom of the Scott Polar Research Institute as well as guiding me through the recondite but endlessly fascinating world of penguin ornithology. Alan Francis has saved my computer, and early versions of the typescript, from my own technical incompetence too many times to count. Tam MacPhail and Duncan McLean in Orkney gave the project the thumbs up in its earliest stages and helped me on my way more than they can know. Will Whiteley cast his unsparingly honest eye over the early drafts. Other Zdocs have helped – in particular Lindsey Bone with her recollections and Jenny Hine with her photograph of the Halley memorial sledge. The ink sketches of the emperor on a skidoo and the aurora over Halley are used with the kind permission of Paul Torode, who also made a beautiful job of the maps.

To paraphrase Cyril Connolly: the writer's greatest enemy can be the pram in the hall, and so immeasurable thanks go to all those who took the pram (or the triple buggy) out from time to time: Rachel Avery, Wendy Ball, Michelle Lowe, Ruth Marsden, David and Sally McNeish, Rita Connelly, Giovanni Aldegheri, Jack and Jinty Francis, Elisa Manera and Dawn Macnamara.

I'd like to thank Parisa Ebrahimi, my editor at Chatto, for her enthusiasm, humour, rigour and intelligence. The editing process is often a hidden one, but no one else knows this book as well as she does. Her care over it, as well as her breadth of vision, have been a pleasure to deal with. In David Milner I had a copy-editor of extraordinary attentiveness and sensitivity. I'm grateful too to my agent Jenny Brown for her wit, tact, knowledge and the trampoline in her garden.

Last of all I'd like to thank the Halley winterers who share the dedication of this book, as well as those 60,000 emperor penguins. Without them this would really have been a book about solitude.

With grateful acknowledgement to: Elizabeth Chatwin for permitting me to quote from her late husband's work *The Viceroy of Ouidah*; Richard E. Byrd III of Massachusetts for allowing me to quote from his grandfather's book *Alone*; Kathleen Jamie for permission to quote from her work *The Autonomous Region*; Peter Matthiessen for allowing me to quote from his *End of the Earth*; Deirdre Grieve for permission to reproduce parts of Hugh MacDiarmid's poem 'Perfect'; Cecilia Esposito of the Plattsburgh State Arts Museum, New York, for permission to reproduce the work of Rockwell Kent; to Hilary Shibata for permitting me to quote from her translation of the account of the Japanese National Antarctic Expedition, 1910–1912; Pia Simig, Ian Hamilton Finlay's executor, for permitting me to reproduce his concrete poem 'Horizon', David Higham Associates for permission to quote from Graham Greene's *Journey Without Maps*; the Wylie Agency for permission to quote from Vladimir Nabokov's *Speak, Memory*; Curtis Brown Agency for permission to quote from Graeme Gibson's *Avian Miscellany*, Andrew Greig for permission to quote from *Summit Fever*, and Barnaby Rogerson for permission to quote from Martha Gellhorn's *Travels with Myself and Another*.

# Notes

**Preface – A Glimpse from the Ice**
'It is a wonderful place . . .' Shackleton, Ernest, *The Heart of the Antarctic*. London, 1910 (William Heinemann)
'it seems far-fetched . . .' in Seaver, George, *Edward Wilson of the Antarctic*. London, 1938 (John Murray)
'It is no easy matter . . .' Scott, R. F., *The Voyage of the Discovery Volume I*. London, 1905 (Smith, Elder & Co.)

**Chapter 1 – Imagining Antarctica**
'Some deeper quest . . .' Matthiessen, Peter, *End of the Earth: Voyages to Antarctica*. Washington DC, 2003 (National Geographic) Reprinted by permission of Donadio & Olson, Inc.
'until we resorted to . . .' Ross, Sir James Clark, *A Voyage of Discovery and Research in the Southern and Antarctic Regions During the Years 1839–1843*, Vol. II, Chapter VI. London, 1847 (John Murray)
'Several modern authors . . .' Sclater, P. L., 'Notes on the Emperor Penguin', *Ibis: A Quarterly Journal of Ornithology*, Vol. VI (Fifth Series), 325–34, 1888
'Some day this . . .' from March 13, 1904 edition of the *New York Times*
'It is in vain . . .' Thoreau, Henry David, in *The Journal of Henry D. Thoreau Volume IX*, edited by Bradford Torrey and Francis H. Allen. Cambridge, Massachusetts, 1949 (Houghton Mifflin)
'I learned this, at least . . .' Thoreau, Henry David, *Walden*. Boston, 1854 (Ticknor & Fields)
'He seemed a little . . .' Emerson, Ralph Waldo, 'Thoreau', *Selected Essays*. New York, 1982 (Penguin)

**Chapter 2 – The Axis of the Atlantic**
At the start of the . . .' Chatwin, Bruce, *The Viceroy of Ouidah*. London, 1980 (Cape)
'turned his stern . . .' Alighieri, Dante, *La Divina Commedia, Inferno*, Canto XXVI. Author's translation.
'As when two Polar . . .' Milton, John, *Paradise Lost*, X: 290. London, 1688.
'Though we were pretty much . . .' Shelvocke, George, *A Voyage Round the World by way of the Great South Sea*. London, 1726.

'it is significant to note . . .' Pirie, Rudmose Brown, Mossman, *The Voyage of the Scotia*. Edinburgh, 1906 (Blackwood & Sons)

'as if the storm . . .' Darwin, Charles, *The Voyage of the Beagle*. London 1838–43 (issued in parts) (Smith, Elder & Co.)

'At intervals it arched . . .' Melville, Herman, *Moby-Dick*. New York, 1851 (Harper & Brothers)

### Chapter 3 – Of Kings and Emperors

'A penguins finds . . .' Kennedy, A. L. 'On Having More Sense', in *Now That You're Back*. London, 1994 (Cape) Reprinted by permission of the Random House Group.

'that was all we brought . . .' Shackleton, Sir Ernest, *South: The Story of Shackleton's Last Expedition 1914–1917*, annotated edition edited by Peter King. London, 1991 (Pimlico)

'presumably as a result of . . .' Stonehouse, Bernard, 'The King Penguin *Aptenodytes patagonicus*', FIDS scientific reports No. 23, London, 1960

'Their book *Antarctic Oasis* . . .' Carr, Tim and Pauline, *Antarctic Oasis – Under the Spell of South Georgia*. New York, 1998 (Norton & Co.)

'like white folding screens . . .' compiled and edited by the Shirase Antarctica Expedition Supporters Association, *The Japanese South Polar Expedition 1910– 1912*, translated by Lara Dagnell and Hilary Shibata. Huntingdon, 2011 (Bluntisham)

### Chapter 4 – Antarctica at Last!

'Snow rolled on forever . . .' Byrd, Richard E., *Alone*. New York, 1938 (G. P. Putnam's Sons)

'We dubbed it . . .' Stonehouse, Bernard, 'David Geoffrey Dalgliesh – Obituary', *Polar Record*. Cambridge, 2010 (Cambridge University Press)

'Yes, an expedition . . .' Dalgiesh, D. G., *Two Years in the Antarctic*. St. Thomas's Hospital Gazette, 50: 62–5 & 111–7, 1952

'a man or properly . . .' Dorsey, N. Ernest, *Properties of Ordinary Water-Substance*. New York, 1940 (Reinhold Publishing Corporation)

### Chapter 5 – High Days and Holidays

'our sooty-faced cook . . .' Worsley, Frank, *Endurance: Shackleton's Boat Journey*. London, 1933 (Philip Allan)

'To my mind . . .' Hudson, W. H., *Idle days in Patagonia*. London, 1893 (J. M. Dent & Sons)

### Chapter 6 – The Hinge of the Continent

'There is, I feel sure . . .' Pirie, Rudmose Brown, Mossman, *The Voyage of the Scotia*. Edinburgh, 1906 (Blackwood & Sons)

'exceptionally well adapted . . .' Grant, Iain et al., 'Psychological selection of Antarctic personnel: the "SOAP" instrument', *Aviat Space Environ Med*, 78: 793–800, 2007

'other studies have found . . .' Mocellin, Jane, 'Anxiety Levels Aboard Two Expeditionary Ships' *Journal of General Psychology*, 122: 317–24, July 1995 'the language of birds . . .' White, Gilbert, *The Natural History of Selborne*, Letter XLIII. London, 1789

'In a gruelling . . .' Robin, J.-P. et al., 'Anorexie animale: existence d'un "signal d'alarme interne" anticipant la depletion des reserves énergétique', *Bulletin de Société Ecophysiologie*, 12: 25–59, 1987

'In their culture the leader . . .' and 'After the death . . .' Rink, Hinrich, *Tales and Traditions of the Eskimo*. London, 1875 (Blackwood & Sons)

'Made up in half-pound . . .' Worsley, Frank, *Endurance: Shackleton's Boat Journey*. London, 1933 (Philip Allan)

'swallowed up in the eternity . . .' Pascal, Blaise, *Pensées*. Paris, 1803 (Renouard, author's translation)

'It is like a momentary . . .' Nabokov, Vladimir, *Speak, Memory*. London, 1951 (Victor Gollancz)

## Chapter 7 – Waiting for Winter

'HORIZON *n.* an explication . . .' Hamilton Finlay, Ian, *Six Definitions*. 2001. This poem is engraved on the perimeter wall outside the Dean Gallery in Edinburgh.

'as if the world . . .' Cherry-Garrard, Apsley, *The Worst Journey in the World*. London, 1937 (Penguin) Reproduced with the permission of the Scott Polar Research Institute

'And the fear of you . . .' King James Bible, Genesis 9:2

'it is like a defiant . . .' Wilson, E. A., 'National Antarctic Expedition 1901–1904 Scientific Reports' Vol. 2, *Aves*. London, 1907 (British Museum)

'the most truly . . .' and 'the courtship behaviour . . .' Murphy, Robert Cushman, *Oceanic Birds of South America Vol. I*. New York, 1936 (Macmillan)

## Chapter 8 – Darkness and Light

'The stars are . . .' Cherry-Garrard, Apsley, *The Worst Journey in the World*. London, 1937 (Penguin) Reproduced with the permission of the Scott Polar Research Institute

'Thoughts of life and the . . .' Byrd, Richard E., *Alone*. New York, 1938 (G. P. Putnam's Sons)

'in a strain of time . . .' and 'a new witness . . .' Hopkins, Gerald Manley, *A Selection of his Poems and Prose by W. H. Gardner*, Penguin Poets Series. London, 1953 (Penguin)

'Its author, Mike Sheret . . .' Sheret, M. A., *Analysis of Auroral Observations, Halley Bay, 1959*. FIDS Scientific Reports, London, 1961

'They were gold . . .' Cherry-Garrard, Apsley, *The Worst Journey in the World*. London, 1937 (Penguin) Reproduced with the permission of the Scott Polar Research Institute

'It seems incredible . . .' Glenister, T. W., 'The Emperor Penguin *Aptenodytes forsteri* Gray. II Embryology'. FIDS scientific reports, London, 1953

'There is perhaps . . .' and '[it] is absolutely unique . . .' in Sibley, C. G. and Ahlquist, J. E.', *Phylogeny and Classification of Birds – A study in molecular evolution*. New Haven, 1991 (Yale University Press)

**Chapter 9 – Midwinter**

'And this is the tale . . .' Shackleton, Sir Ernest, 'Midwinter Night', in *Aurora Australis*. Antarctica, 1908 (British Antarctic Expedition, 1907–9)

'My project used . . .' Francis, G. et al., 'Sleep during the Antarctic winter: preliminary observations on changing the spectral composition of artificial light', *Journal of Sleep Research*, 17(3) 354–60, 2008

'as the heat . . .' Davis, John, 'The World's Hydrographical Description', London 1596. Also in *The Voyages and Works of John Davis*. Hakluyt Society Vol. 59. London, 1880

'This was the polar night . . .' Byrd, Richard E., *Alone*. New York, 1938 (G.P. Putnam's Sons)

'to-day the sun has . . .' Shackleton, Sir Ernest, *South*. London, 1919


**Chapter 10 – The Third Quarter**

'An almost monotonous . . .' Cook, Frederick A., *Through the First Antarctic Night*. New York, 1900 (Doubleday)

'*accidie*, a listless . . .' Maitland, Sara, *A Book of Silence*. London, 2008 (Granta)

'It is clearly . . .' and 'Not only are facilities . . .' Bell, J. and Garthwaite, P. H., 'The Psychological Effects of Service In British Antarctica', *British Journal of Psychiatry*, 150: 213–18, 1987

'almost all winterers go through . . .' Rivolier, J. C. G. and Bachelard, C., *Summary of the French research in medicine and psychology conducted with Expeditions Polaires Francaises and Terres Australes et Antarctiques Francaises*. Paris TAAF, 1983

'From the expression in his eyes . . .' Rivolier, Jean, *Emperor Penguins*, trans. Peter Wiles. London, 1956 (Elek Books)

'if there is a third . . .' Wood, Joanna et al., 'Is it really so bad? A Comparison of Positive and Negative Experiences in Antarctic Winter Stations', *Environment & Behaviour*, 32: 84–110, 2000

'It's called stress inoculation . . .' see Anderson, C., 'Polar Psychology: Coping with it all', *Nature*, 350:290, 1991

'already self-sufficient . . .' Taylor, A. J. W. and Shurley, J. T. 'Some Antarctic troglodytes', *International Review of Applied Psychology*, 20: 143–8, 1971

'they all know each other . . .' Gellhorn, Martha, *Travels with Myself and Another: Five Journeys from Hell*. London, 2002 (Eland)

'You can grow . . .' Greene, Graham, *Journey Without Maps*. London, 1936 (William Heinemann)

'I think he was more . . .' Seaver, George, *Edward Wilson of the Antarctic*. London, 1938 (John Murray)

'Heaven knows how I . . .' Shackleton to Wilson, 15 February 1907, in Seaver, George, *Edward Wilson of the Antarctic*. London, 1938 (John Murray)

'about 6 feet . . .' in Seaver, George, *Edward Wilson of the Antarctic*. London, 1938 (John Murray)

'I had heard about . . .' See Airey, Len, *On Antarctica*, San Ramon, 2001 (Luna Books), which describes the disaster from the perspective of the Faraday Station commander.

## Chapter 11 – The Promise of Life

'Oh, how tired I am . . .' Nansen, Fridtjof, *Farthest North*. London, 1897 (Constable & Co.)

'of almost discontinuous . . .' and 'eternities of Joy' Krutch, Joseph Wood, *The Great Chain of Life*. London, 1957 (Eyre & Spottiswoode)

'There is something extravagantly . . .' Byrd, Richard E., *Alone*. New York, 1938 (G. P. Putnam's Sons)

'This is the most . . .' in Seaver, George, *The Faith of Edward Wilson*. London 1948 (John Murray)

'Wilson and Bowers were . . .' in Seaver, George, *Edward Wilson of the Antarctic*. London, 1938 (John Murray)

'His eyes have a comfortable . . .' and 'My beloved wife . . .' in Seaver, George, *Edward Wilson of the Antarctic*. London, 1938 (John Murray)

## Chapter 12 – Gathering Light

'We seemed to bathe in . . .' Scott, R. F., *The Voyage of the Discovery Volume 1*. London, 1905 (Smith, Elder & Co.)

'beyond all power . . .' and 'This glorious sun . . .' Scott, R. F., *The Voyage of the Discovery Volume 1*. London, 1905 (Smith, Elder & Co.)

'had no urge towards . . .' in Spufford, Francis, *I May Be Some Time: Ice and the English Imagination*. London, 1996 (Faber)

'On the morning . . .' and 'Dear Sir . . .' Shackleton, Sir Ernest, *The Heart of the Antarctic*. London, 1910 (William Heinemann)

'In the first dim . . .' Scott, R. F., *Journals: Scott's Last Expedition*. London, 1913 (Smith, Elder & Co.)

'Inuit peoples have developed . . .' So, J. K., 'Human Biological Adaptations to Arctic and Subarctic Zones', *Annual Review of Anthropology*, 9: 63–82, 1980

'I am all face.' Hudson, W. H., *Idle Days in Patagonia*. London, 1893 (J. M. Dent & Sons)

'arranged to track . . .' Ancel, A. and Kooyman, G. L. et al., 'Foraging behaviour of emperor penguins as a resource detector in winter and summer', *Nature*, 360: 336–9, 1992

'used them to argue . . .' Peale T. R., 'U.S. Exploring Expedition during the years 1838–1842', *Phila.*, 8, *Mammalia & Ornithology*, 5–299, 1848

'Some emperors have been found . . .' Splettstoesser and Todd, 'Stomach Stones from Emperor Penguin *Aptenodytes forsteri* colonies in the Weddell Sea', *Marine Ornithology*, 27: 97–100, 1999

'*Los muertos* . . .' and 'twin domes like bubbles . . .' MacDiarmid, Hugh, 'Perfect', *Collected Poems*. New York, 1962 (Macmillan)

'synoptic pan-Antarctic . . .' and 'the first satellite-based . . .' Fretwell, P. and Trathan P., 'Penguins from Space: faecal stains reveal the location of emperor penguin colonies', *Global Ecology and Biogeography*, 18: 543–52, 2009

'In another paper . . .' Trathan, P., Fretwell, P., and Stonehouse, B., 'First Recorded Loss of an Emperor Penguin Colony in the Recent Period of Antarctic Regional Warming: Implications for other Colonies'. *PLoS ONE*, 6(2): e14738, 2011

Spencer Champman, F., *Northern Lights*. London, 1932 (Chatto & Windus)
'an everlasting anchorage' Byrd, Richard E., *Alone*. New York, 1938 (G. P. Putnam's Sons)
'should anyone possess . . .' Cook, James, *A Voyage Towards the South Pole and Round the World: Performed in His Majesty's Ships the Resolution and Adventure, in the years 1772, 1773, 1774 and 1775*. London, 1777.
'broad-ranging anthology . . .' *From the Ends of the Earth*, ed. Augustine Courtauld. London, 1958 (Oxford University Press)

### Chapter 13 – Freedom of the Ice
'At times I'm enormously . . .' Greig, Andrew, *Summit Fever*. Edinburgh, 1997 (Canongate)
'Paying attention to birds . . .' and 'encourage a state . . .' Gibson, Graeme, *Bedside Book of Birds: An Avian Miscellany*. London, 2005 (Bloomsbury)
'Standing on bare ground . . .' Emerson, Ralph Waldo, 'On Nature', in *Selected Essays*. New York, 1982 (Penguin)
'incorrigibly plural' MacNeice, Louis, 'Snow' in *Collected Poems*. New York, 1966 (Oxford University Press)
'Discoveries of the Kent . . .' Kent, Rockwell, *Salamina*. London, 1936 (Faber)
'suddenly the light went out . . .' Woolf, Virginia, diary entry for 30 June 1927, *The Diary of Virginia Woolf Vol. III*. London, 1980 (Hogarth)

### Chapter 14 – Of Endings and Beginnings
'Devotions over . . .' Jamie, Kathleen, *The Autonomous Region*. Newcastle upon Tyne, 1993 (Bloodaxe)
'Geologists brought out here . . .' Leat, Philip et al., 'Sills of the Theron Mountains, Antarctica: evidence for long distance transport of mafic magmas during Gondwana break-up', in Hanski, E. et al. (eds.), *Dyke swarms: time markers of crustal evolution*. London, 2006 (Taylor and Francis)
'cognitive slowing . . .' Popkin et al. 'Generalised response to protracted stress', *Military Medicine*, 143: 479–80, 1978

### Afterword – The Memory of Antarctica
'These days are with . . .' in Seaver, George, *Edward Wilson of the Antarctic*. London, 1938 (John Murray)